The Future of the Catholic Priesthood in Igboland:

The Dangers and Challenges Ahead

Cornelius Uche Okeke

ISBN-13: 978-978-53198-8-0

DEDICATION

This book is dedicated to
His Grace, Most Rev. A.K. Obiefuna,
the late Archbishop Emeritus of Onitsha Archdiocese, and the
first bishop of Awka diocese, for his pioneering efforts in giving a
significant place to the formation of priests

Foreword

In the past few years, the Catholic priesthood has been the object of relentless focus of attention by the media. For some reasons that is, perhaps known only to God, the secular media has directed its searchlight on the priesthood: the doings of priests have been dissected and closely scrutinized under its microscope. Especially in the Euro-American world the media has called attention to the declining number of priests and the paucity of new vocations. Priests have even been referred to as "an endangered species". When it discusses the exploding vocations to the priesthood in the "majority world", the media is quick to dismiss such increases in vocations as an outcome of poverty. The candidates are not seen as people who are genuinely responding to God's call, but as using the priesthood merely as an avenue to a better life.

On the other hand, the media has had a field day chewing and regurgitating the recent clergy sex abuse scandals. The disproportionate exposure of these events by the media perhaps is meant to shock and titillate the public. It has had the unfortunate side effect of distorting public perception of the priesthood and priests.

The media is usually quick to blame the failings of priests on their "compulsory celibacy" or inadequate formation of priests or both. Regardless of what one may think of the media onslaught, the revelations of the sins of catholic priests should challenge the Church to reexamine and retool its methods of formation of future priests. In fact, such reevaluation and restructuring of priestly formation has been underway all over the Catholic world since Vatican II. It received a fresh impetus from the publication of the landmark apostolic exhortation on priestly formation, *Pastores dabo vobis* by Pope John Paul II in 1992.

Be that as it may, those of us in the majority world where vocations seem to be flourishing should see what is happening to the priesthood in Europe and America, not as a disgrace but a clarion call to engage in the work of the formation of our large candidates for the priesthood with all the seriousness it deserves. We should not wait until the sad events of Europe and America begin to happen here before we take action. Prevention, they say, is better than cure. Indeed, the problems of priests in the developed world are already at our doorsteps, whether we like it or not. That is why the work, *The Future of the Catholic Priesthood in Igboland: The Dangers and Challenges Ahead*, by Father Cornelius Uchenna Okeke, is both timely and needed. In fact, it is the first of its kind in our local Church. As far as I know, it is the best empirically based study of Igbo seminarians that provides concrete data that is immediately relevant to formation of future Igbo priests. As Father Okeke noted in his introduction, "various aspects of the crisis in the priesthood today can be traced to formation: selection, discernment and actual training of priests".

In the work, Father Okeke examines the present status of the Catholic priesthood in Igboland with all its hopes and problems. Using empirical data he gathered from the seminarians regarding their expectations of the priesthood, he finds that there exists "a dialectical tension in seminarians between the values of the priesthood and Igbo cultural ideals". Father Okeke further evaluates the current formation methods in place in the seminaries in Igboland and finds them wanting. He then proposes a formation model that is capable of addressing the issues raised by his findings.

Father Cornelius Okeke is uniquely qualified to write this book. A graduate of the Institute of Psychology of the famous Gregorian University, Rome, he has also been a formator for several years. He surely knows what he is talking about.

Although not without methodological shortcomings, this work is an important service to the local Churches of Igboland, and, indeed, the whole Catholic world. While the context may be different, the problems faced by Igbo priests and seminarians are not far different from the problems faced by Catholic priests and seminarians all over the world. This book should be in the hands of all those who care for vocations: bishops, seminary rectors, formators, vocation directors, priests, seminarians, and indeed all those who are concerned about the future of the Catholic priesthood. I highly recommend it.

Fr. Anthony E. Eze
Bigard Memorial Seminary Enugu.

The Reason Why

The Future of the Catholic Priesthood in Igboland: Dangers and Challenges Ahead, by Fr. Cornelius Uchenna Okeke, is an especially timely and valuable contribution to the evaluation of the Catholic Priesthood and of the seminarians as regards how far the gap between the expected and the observed is filled. The book is constructively critical, comprehensively educative, and informative in its presentation of facts as regards Igbo Catholic priesthood in the eyes of fellow Catholic priests, and the general lay public. It is a book of daring boldness that has broken the ice to engage in selfless self-criticism of Igbo Catholic priesthood to which he belongs. The ideas expressed in the book are unbiased, fair and empirical, thus removing all shred of bias and selfishness.

According to the author, "this book is born out of the desire I have to see that we, as the Church in Igboland, utilize well this springtime of the many vocations to the priesthood". The book gives a grassroots approach to the issue of Igbo Catholic priesthood by starting with the seminarians at the formative period in the seminaries and how the 'garbage in' in the seminary will produce the 'garbage out' that determines the quality of our priests.

The book is not a jaw-jaw write-up, but a strictly empirical piece that supports theories with robust empirical findings. It is God-sent radical book that will help the Church make a seasoned stock-taking exercise as regards Igbo Catholic priesthood. Everyone concerned about the future well-being of the Catholic Church in Igboland in particular, and in Nigeria in general, will find the book invaluable.

The book is not oblivious of Christ's concern when He asked: "Do you think when the Son of Man comes again He will find any faith?" Priests and knowledgeable members of the laity will find this book a source of inspiration, reformation, and readjustment in a world that is going hair-wire vis-à-vis moral and religious practice that make the Catholic Church stand out head and shoulders above other religious interests. To this book I wish *lux fiat* and may it effect the desired changes.

Professor Norbert N. Okoye, (KSM; PhD, fipa, MNPS, MIAAP)
Prof. Emeritus of Psychology, Nnamdi Azikiwe University, Awka.

Acknowledgement

This work would not have seen the light of the day without the help of many people. First of all, I thank my bishop, Most. Rev. S.A. Okafor for giving me the opportunity to make this study. I wish to thank Fr. Barth Kiely, S.J. for his encouragements and professional guidance during the research. Fr. Ifunanya Aneke is a bosom friend with whom I had series of discussion on the content of this work. I thank him for his friendship and for his frankness in our discussions. I also thank Sr. Mary Jane Aririguzo who helped me in collecting some relevant data. Fr. Anthony Eze took his time to read through this work and write the foreword. I remain deeply grateful for his critical assessment of the work which improved the writing, division of the work and documentation,. I'm indebted to his kindness and professional suggestions. Professor Norbert Okoye showed great interest in this book. He read it critically and wrote a concise comment about it. I am grateful to him. Sr. Theresa Eke is a dear friend who is always there for me. I thank her for her encouragement and for proofreading the work and offering her invaluable remarks. I am indebted to Wanda Edie for providing me with some books and also for supporting me financially in the publication of this work. I thank Matt and Carol Fetts who helped me in the purchase of some important books. In the same manner I thank Bill and Jan Roland for always supporting me financially. I remain grateful to the Rector of Pope John Paul II Major Seminary, Fr. Augustine Oburota for his encouragements and for making out time to go through the work and offering his constructive criticism and comments. I thank Fr. Lawrence Nwankwo, a dear friend, for his continuous support and critical discussions with me. Michael Lavigne offered to design the cover of this book without charge. I remain ever grateful to him and his family for their generosity. Martina Ebere Okeke assisted in running some errands in the course of the publication. I appreciate it a lot. To all the seminarians and priests who participated in this study, I remain grateful for their cooperation. And to all others who have desired and prayed for this work to come out finally as a published material, I appreciate your good wishes and prayers.
1st November, 2006 Feast of All Saints.

Table of Content

Pages

Dedication iii
Foreword v
The reason why vii
Acknowledgement viii
Table of content ix
Introduction xi

Part I: Igbo Catholic Priests: the Good, the Bad, the Ugly

I: Lights and shadow of Igbo Catholic priests....................1
  The signs of the times..1
  The light of Igbo priests.....................................4
  Increase in vocation: An ambiguous situation.........8
  The shadows of the Igbo Priests.............................17

II: **Understanding the shadows of Igbo priests: review of literature**..33
  First hypothesis: Influence of culture and society...................34
  Educated Laity: Threat to the power of priests.....................48
  Second hypothesis: Stress and lack of satisfaction
  in the ministry...55
  Third hypothesis: Problems in formation...............67
  Diocesan and religious priests in Igboland.............74

Summary...79

III: **What are Igbo seminarians looking for in the priesthood?...80**
  Life, expectations, and the priesthood.....................80
  Future expectations affect the present....................81
  Lived life and future expectations.........................85
  Research method and results.................................88
  The research design...93
  The results...97
  Trust hypothesis...104
  Second hypothesis..104

Part II: Implications of Empirical Data

IV: Igbo priests and their struggles: The cultural factor............110
Psychology of the Igbo people in brief....................................111
Igbo cultural values in the stories of Igbo seminarians........121
The basic struggle of the Igbo priest: to belong.....................131
Psychological insight into the struggles.................................143

V: The meaning of vocation boom in Igboland...........................154
What does the vocation boom suggest?..................................154
Weak spiritual motives for the priesthood.............................155

Summary..165

Part III: Formation and the Future of Catholic Priesthood in Igboland

VI: The current methods of forming Igbo priests.......................168
The conformity/institutional model of formation................169
The progressive model..171
What difference does it make?..173
Why the situation has remained unchanged.........................175

VII: Theoretical and practical orientation for the formation of Igbo priests..178
Theoretical starting point...178
An integrated systematic approach to personal formation..190
Practical issues that need attention...198
Final remarks..206
Limitation of studies..208

Notes..209

Bibliography..248

Introduction

The growth of the Catholic Church in Africa has been described as prodigious, seen in the increase in the population of Catholics, priests and religious within a short period[1] following the third phase of its evangelization in the nineteenth century[2]. The number of Catholics baptized in one year in Africa, for instance, has risen by over one hundred percent in few decades. Priests and seminarians are also increasing in number. For instance, between 1978 and 2000, there was an increase of 208.01% in the number of diocesan priests. The number of seminarians also rose from 5,636 in 1978 to 20,383 in 2000, a variation of 261.66% between 1978 and 2000[3].

These data testify to the vitality of the Church in Africa and the hope that the Catholic world places in this young Church. The late Pope John Paul II saw this development as a grace of God to the Church; having been evangelized by European missionaries, it is the time for this Church also to send its missionaries to those countries[4].

The Church in Igboland is a significant aspect of this vitality of the African Church: it is a vital source of the vocations to the priesthood seen in Africa, and is already a missionary church that sends its priests and religious to work within and outside Africa. At this springtime of the Church in Africa and in Igboland particularly, it is important to realize how the vibrancy of this church is connected to the quality of the formation of its agents of evangelization, especially its priests and religious[5]. In this regard, the large number of vocations to the priesthood and to the religious life is both a *grace* and a *challenge*: it is a grace because every vocation is a gift of God and sustained by God; it is a challenge because it calls for adequate preparation of the candidates so that they will be able to give a *personal response* to God who has called them and *serve* that portion of God's people to which they are sent with the joy of the gospel. This is made possible by growing in the *consciousness of being called by God* and in *being faithful to one's relationship to God*[6]. These two dispositions are reflected in the personal conviction of the priest which enables him to bear *effective witness* to the values of the Gospel in his life[7].

This study on the future of the Catholic priesthood in Igboland is an effort to understand the problems that are observable in Igbo priests and the impact they have on the Church in Igboland. Secondly, this study is intended to emphasize the importance of giving serious attention to the formation of Igbo seminarians of today. Without good formation of its principal agents of evangelization, the Church in Igboland courts many risks in the future, especially the risk of admitting to the priesthood persons who could bring trouble to themselves and to the Church.

There are various aspects of the crisis in the priesthood today in different parts of the world. But most of these problems could be traced to formation: the selection, discernment, and actual training of priests. As a young church with many vocations, the stories of the problems of priests in other parts of the world should send a cautious note to us to take formation of our future priests seriously. In his meeting with the bishops of Ghana on April 24, 2006, Pope Benedict XVI called the attention of the bishops to the central issue of formation, exhorting them "to ensure the suitability of candidates for the priesthood and to guarantee proper priestly formation for those who are studying for the sacred ministry"[8]. The formation of Igbo priests has to take into consideration the dialectical tension between the values of the priesthood and the Igbo cultural ideals expressed in the struggles of Igbo priests in general, and in their individual personalities. The future of the Catholic priesthood in Igboland depends on how far we are able to understand and address this tension and create a formation program that will enable Igbo seminarians become good and happy priests who are willing to serve God's people in the future, and not serve themselves or use the priesthood to pursue their personal ambitions.

It is the underlying assumption of this work that the increasing number of vocations to the priesthood in Igboland today could pose serious danger in the future, if serious and careful attention is not given to the selection, discernment and formation of these persons. This is why this work is titled, *The Future of Catholic priesthood in Igboland: The Dangers and Challenges Ahead*. The danger could come as the cumulative result of carelessness or inattention or even inaction in the face of superficialities and incongruous lifestyles among Igbo priests and seminarians; the challenge is to face the onerous task of discerning properly these vocations.

The study has three parts which span through seven chapters. The first part has three chapters. Chapter one presents the current status of the Catholic priesthood in Igboland, the lights and shadows, hopes and problems. In chapter two I shall focus on the views of other people in trying to understand the shadows of the Igbo priests. This chapter shall review the available literature on the subject matter. It is my conviction that many of the problems many Igbo priests face today could be traced to the formation system they went through, which, in my opinion, could not relate effectively to the basic formational needs in some of them. Chapter three explores empirically, the expectations seminarians have of the priesthood. This chapter contains the assumptions of the empirical research, the method, the hypotheses, and the findings.

The second part has two chapters, and basically deals with the implications of the findings. The fourth chapter exposes the struggles of Igbo priests from the cultural and psychological perspectives in the light of the empirical findings. Chapter five assesses the current status of vocations in Igboland, trying to find out the meaning of our vocation boom. The third part has two chapters, and it deals with the future of Catholic priesthood in Igboland, considering the implications of the data of this research. Chapter six is an evaluation of the formation methods in our various seminaries. Chapter seven draws out the formational challenges that face the Igbo Church and proposes a kind of formation model that takes into consideration the culture of Igbo seminarians and their persons.

Part I

Igbo Catholic Priests:
the Good, the Bad, the Ugly

I

Lights and Shadows of Igbo Catholic Priests

The Signs of the Times

At different moments in history, individuals, groups and societies, read the signs of the times in which they live. The fathers of the Second Vatican Council in the Pastoral Constitution on the Church in the Modern World, *Gaudium et Spes*, acknowledge the responsibility of the Church to read the signs of the times and interpret them in the light of the Gospel[1]. It is not only the Church that feels this responsibility; nations and organizations know that they have to read the signs of the times always, understand them, and develop appropriate strategies that address these signs[2]. It is also possible to ignore, neglect, or misinterpret them. When they are neglected, the group in question may be overtaken by change, and this can be disastrous to its existence. Furthermore, the group concerned may misread the signs, and take for granted that they are clear and so develop responses that are directed to every other thing except the signs in question. Such neglect or oversight of the signs that call for attention can have serious consequences[3]. This shows the importance of reading correctly the signs of the times. It is necessary because humans and their society are open systems. This means they are stable but always changing. Therefore, they must give appropriate response to the changes that constantly occur.

The face of the Catholic Church is changing in Igboland of South-eastern Nigeria. One important area in which these changes are strongly felt is in the vocations to the priesthood. For this reason, the bishops of the Onitsha and Owerri ecclesiastical provinces, representing the Catholic Church in Igboland, gathered at Onitsha in 1999 to identify and discern these signs of the times, especially to prepare the Igbo Church for the new millennium in which we live now. The result of their meeting is contained in the document, *The Igbo Catholic Priest at the Threshold of the Third Millennium*[4]. The main purpose of their meeting was to listen, understand, and apply what the Lord was telling them through the signs[5]. This basic objective is divided into two: "To undertake *an honest self-appraisal and a collective stock-taking*, and *to challenge ourselves to greater fidelity to our vocation and mission in Christ*"[6]. After some years of its publication, the purpose and the insights of the document remain valid, and call for careful study and understanding. If the document were to be written today, perhaps, the bishops would repeat the same things and even become stronger in their wordings. This document provides a clear analysis of the present situation and we shall follow the outline contained in it.

The document has sixty-eight paragraphs that are divided into six chapters. Chapter 1, the introduction, has eight paragraphs. In it, the bishops lay the historical foundation for the content of other chapters. Drawing from *Ecclesia in Africa*,[7] the document makes a very brief presentation of the three phases of evangelisation of the African continent and situates the growth and vibrancy of the Church in Africa in the third phase, which began in the nineteenth century[8]. It then affirms that "this splendid growth is most noticeable among the Igbos of Southern Nigeria"[9]. They attribute the growth of the Church among the Igbo people to "God's answer to the prayers, and his acceptance of the sacrifice of our early missionaries …"[10]. For this reason, there is no cause for "worldly triumphalism; instead what is called for is an attitude of humility, thanksgiving to God, constant self-examination, evaluation and renewal, so that we can respond to God's gratuitous initiative with greater generosity and more effectiveness"[11]. It is against this background that the document spells out its purpose of discerning the signs of the times.

Chapter 2, which comprises ten paragraphs, restates the identity and mission of the priest as the background against which the evaluation of life and ministry of Igbo priests is to take place. To understand better the signs of the times in relation to the life and ministry of Igbo priests, the document goes on to analyse their socio-cultural context in Chapter 3. This approach is important because "the socio-cultural context from which the priest originates and in which he works influences him,…"[12]. The chapter, which comprises ten paragraphs, juxtaposes the socio-cultural reality of the Igbo priest with the ecclesiastical context, that is, the pastoral condition in which he struggles to live and to minister.

Chapter 4 spans sixteen paragraphs and is titled "Lights and Shadows". This title is taken directly as it is from *Ecclesia in Africa*[13]. As the title indicates, the chapter presents the struggles of the priests, their ups and downs, as they live out the dialectical tension between "the universal ideals" of Catholic priesthood and the concrete "socio-ecclesial and cultural situations of the Igbo people"[14]. After exposing the "shadows" that blur the brilliance of the light of witnessing to the Gospel in the life of the priests, the document proposes some pastoral solutions in Chapter 5. This is the longest chapter, containing twenty-five paragraphs which are subdivided into two sections. The first section delineates some basic pastoral helps to redress the situation. This section is further divided into five subsections involving improvement in the formation of priests[15], deepening of life of prayer[16], the importance of ongoing formation[17], adequate maintenance of priests[18], and the necessity for solidarity among priests[19]. The second subdivision is concerned with some disciplinary measures to check some inconsistent behaviours. It is titled "Additional Help"[20]. The disciplinary measures are drawn from the wisdom of the Igbo people and of the Church. This section is again subdivided into two, dealing with policies and regulations[21], and methods of carrying them out[22]. In the conclusion, which is Chapter 6, the bishops restate their central objective and make a passionate call for renewal, individually and collectively, among Igbo priests.

I shall now describe these signs of the times that express the lights and shadows of Igbo Catholic priests.

The Lights of Igbo Priests

Hard-work and Dedication

It may not appear anything exceptional to say that Igbo priests are hardworking and dedicated in their life and ministry. The specific circumstances of the socio-cultural and ecclesiastical contexts in which they exercise their ministry seem to have motivated the bishops to acknowledge and appreciate their priests' attitude to work.

> They give themselves, their time and energy, to serving their people, in circumstances where expectations are high but resources are far from adequate. They have to carry out their prophetic, cultic and pastoral ministry in a socio-cultural setting that is rich in potential for good but at the same time replete with contradiction. Most priests manage to remain sound and live above board in the face of these challenges[23].

The contemporary Igbo priests have to build structures and catechise the people, celebrate about three Masses every Sunday; they are faced with an incredible number of penitents every week, and are challenged daily to update their knowledge and skills to meet the changing culture. They do all these in the midst of insufficient facilities for good parish administration. In his address to the priests and seminarians at the Bigard Memorial Seminary Enugu, during his visit to Nigeria in February 1982, Pope John Paul II recognized as a sign of hope the dedication of these priests in the difficult circumstances in which they discharge their priestly assignments.

> I understand well that most of you are grossly overworked. Some of you parish priests have ten thousand Catholics to serve; some of you may have even many more. There may even be fifteen outstations to a single priest. Most of you celebrate two or three Masses every Sunday in distant places, teach Christian doctrine, and give Eucharistic Benediction. Your people flock to the Sacrament of Reconciliation. You patiently and lovingly discharge this

ministry. I understand that in some places all the priests in neighbouring parishes join in a cooperative effort to make this sacrament available[24].

The vibrant growth of the Catholic Church in Igboland is largely due to the dedication and single-minded commitment of many Igbo priests, right from the time the missionaries left the land[25]. A typical example can be cited: Awka diocese was created on 10th November 1977 with only 18 parishes and forty priests. But at the close of 2005, this diocese had 137 parishes and 436 priests[26].

This light of dedication does not shine only in the administration of the sacraments to the people of God; the priests are involved in the social, cultural and political arena of Nigerian society, bringing their Gospel-infused values and their education to bear on the cultural tendencies and prevailing political and social philosophies that oppress rather than liberate the people. They do this mostly through their writings, the organization of seminars and workshops, and prophetic utterances that are directed at changing oppressive and repressive government policies and the conscientization of the people to their rights and dignity as children of God. F.U. Okafor, for example, appreciates the impact of certain works written by the priests on "the prescription and proscription of certain political ideals and ills"[27] in Nigerian society. The writings of Fr. John Odey of Abakaliki diocese are fearless assessment and denunciation of the dehumanizing policies and leaderships that have been in place since the foundation of Nigeria[28]. Further, J. Ezeilo welcomes and recognises the significant role the priests are playing in the promotion and protection of the rights of women[29].

The dedication of Igbo priests to the transformation of the social polity, is also felt in their prophetic denunciation of corrupt and oppressive governments at both the federal and state levels. A good number of priests speak out against the political and economic situation of the populace, reminding the political class of their duty to the nation.

In all collectivist-communitarian cultures, the group impact is so strong that the individual is sometimes considered secondary[30]. It is such that in Igboland, where the extended family system is powerful, the priest constantly struggles between attention to the unending demands of his many relatives and the claims of his universal family, the Church. It is not an easy struggle. Yet, many Igbo priests weather the storms and maintain a sound balance that is founded on a lively faith in Jesus Christ and in the family of the Church. Such an undaunted commitment encourages the growth of the Christian faith among the Igbo people and raises the trust people have in their ministers. The lay people are aware of this struggle and, as a result, in 1998 the entertainment industry produced a movie titled *My Cross*, in which the protagonist, a Catholic priest called Francis, had to withstand the many suggestions of his family members that he compromise his Christian and priestly commitments[31]. In his commentary on the movie, R. Anasiudu emphasises that "in Fr. Francis, as portrayed in *My Cross*, is seen a person who is every inch what a Catholic priest should be"[32]. This commentary can be read in two ways: first, it can mean that the film producers desire that the Catholic priests live the way Fr. Francis lives in the film, in which case it represents solely the ideal, the way things should be. Secondly, it can be read as appreciation and encouragement of the actual status of Catholic priests who live that way. These two ways of looking at it are not contradictory and could be said to be present in the film.

In their dedication to the priestly life and ministry, the Igbo priests stand before the people of God as beacons of hope and shining lights that show the way to authentic Christian and human living. They bring the consolation of God to the people and challenge civil society to respect the dignity of the people and improve their living condition[33].

Growing Number of Vocations to the Priesthood

The growing number of vocations to the priesthood in Igboland is an important sign of hope for both the Church in Igboland and light for the universal Church. The bishops say in the document that a "significant number of priests and laity in Nigeria are Igbo, and their impact can be felt in all the dioceses"[34]. The following statistical data demonstrate the extent of this increase.

Table 1
Growth in Vocations to the Catholic Priesthood among the Igbo of Nigeria from 1985 -2006

Diocese	1985[35]	1992[36]	1999[37]	2006
	No. of Priests	No. of Priests	No. of Priests	No. of Priests
Aba	-	36	48	90[38]
Abakaliki	22	30	54	79[39]
Ahiara	-	61	100	183[40]
Awka	85	128	186	436[41]
Awgu	-	-	-	40[42]
Enugu	102	134	147	210[43]
Nnewi	-	-	-	168[44]
Nsukka	-	30	91	135[45]
Okigwe	60	98	121	255[46]
Onitsha	112	119	234	348[47]
Orlu	58	95	150	262[48]
Owerri	101	61	140	248[49]
Umuahia	62	32	54	90[50]
Total	**602**	**824**	**1325**	**2544**

Table 2
Variation in Vocations to the Catholic Priesthood among the Igbo within the Period

Years	Priests
1985 – 1992	+27%
1992 – 1999	+38%
1999 – 2006	+48%
1985 – 2006	+76%

From Table 2 it can be seen that between 1985 and 1992, there is a 27% increase in the number of Igbo priests. From 1992 to 1999, the number of priests in Igbo dioceses had increased by 38%. From 1999 to the close of 2006, the number of priests had grown by 48%. Within the period of twenty-one years, from 1985 to 2006, there is a 76% increase in the number of diocesan priests in Igboland. These figures strongly substantiate the claim of the bishops that vocations to the priesthood are on the increase in Igboland.

Missionaries to the Universal Church

The Catholic Church in Igboland had its centenary celebration in 1985. Though it may be considered an infant church in some sense[51], it is rapidly growing and responding to the missionary challenges of the Church. It is already sharing its personnel with other churches around the world in accordance with the teaching of the Second Vatican Council[52] and the desires of the Special Assembly for Africa[53]. The missionary activity of the Igbo priests, both diocesan and religious, is directed both within and outside Nigeria. Inside Nigeria, Igbo diocesan priests are on mission in the Archdiocese of Lagos, Dioceses like Kano, Ogoja, Calabar, Ijebu Ode. In Africa, Igbo diocesan priests are on mission in Chad, Niger Republic, Cameroon, and South Africa. In Europe, they are ministering in Germany, Austria, France, and Switzerland; in America, they are present in the United States, Canada, and in the Caribbean (West Indies). They are also present in Australia[54]. Take the example of Awka diocese as at the close of 2005: about 47 of its priests are on mission in different parts of the world[55]. Ahiara diocese has 25 of its priests on mission[56]. The dioceses that send them also support them financially[57].

Increase in Vocations: an Ambiguous Situation

The hypotheses that have been adduced to explain the influx into the Catholic priesthood, especially in the developing world range from the sociological to the psychological and theological.

The first hypothesis holds that there is a positive link between

8

material and social poverty and increase in vocations to the priesthood. Donald Cozzens argues in support of this hypothesis from the historical context of the United States of America. He holds that there were many vocations to the priesthood when the United States were "mostly immigrant and ethnic" so that the Catholic substructure "provided security and assistance to first generation families striving for a foothold in a new world that was both suspicious and often hostile to Catholic newcomers"[58]. In other words, this social security provided by the Church served as incentive to young boys and their families to opt for the priesthood. A significant dimension of this social security according to Cozzens is the education, considerable status and influence which the priest enjoyed among his siblings and friends, and which gave him an edge over them. Comparing what happened in those days with what is happening today in Africa and Asia, he concludes:

> In the Catholic world of the early and middle twentieth century, the priest, without owning even an acre of land, belonged to the Catholic equivalent of a "landed-gentry." Where else could working class sons, after six or eight years of seminary, come to enjoy the benefits of household servants? Some of these factors appear to be at play in the burgeoning number of vocations coming from countries in Africa and Asia[59].

J. Aniagwu, the former rector of Saints Peter and Paul Seminary, Ibadan, Nigeria, agrees with Cozzens. He refers to his experience of Ireland and argues that there was little problem in priestly vocations when Ireland had not yet joined the European Union. "In 1981 much of that country was rather rural, slow paced, sedate. Churches were packed full, even though there was little lay participation in the liturgy"[60]. By the time he visited again in 1994, Ireland had joined the European Union and "there was affluence everywhere"[61]. He concludes:

If Nigeria suddenly strikes gold, and there is affluence everywhere, if there is no longer so much shocking poverty around, if people's basic needs begin to be adequately met, will our churches continue to be filled on Sundays? "Poverty is good for religion" may be a wicked cliché. But it is sadly true. It has been verified again and again since the days of decadent Rome[62].

B.S. Aniko agrees with him when he notes that "priests are not among the poorest ..., some young men may be attracted to seminaries because of economic advantage that goes with that status, including the avoidance of the high rate of unemployment"[63].

Ikenga Ozigbo supports this hypothesis and specifically directs it toward the Igbos. He attributes the growth in the vocation to the priesthood and to the religious life among the Igbos to the fact "that Igbo priests and sisters assumed highly visible profile since the 1970s"[64], immediately after the expulsion of the expatriate priests and nuns and the taking over of the local church by the local clergy and religious. This "highly visible profile" was also boosted by the lavish ordination and profession ceremonies which "leave deep impressions on the young" so that "despite the prohibitive demands of celibacy and personal poverty, the priesthood and the religious life have been generally perceived by the Igbo as sure avenues of social mobility"[65]. From this, Ikenga Ozigbo strongly asserts that "it is a fact that the majority of the candidates for the priesthood or the religious life come from non-affluent homes. The poor seminarian or novice graduates into the privileged class of the clergy by virtue of his ordination or her profession"[66]. While it cannot be disputed that there may be some truth in this argument, it does not seem to explain, by itself, the increase in vocation among the Igbos, especially because his claim does not have any significant empirical data to support it.

Though J. Aniagwu holds to the hypothesis that there is a link between increase in vocations and poverty and therefore also between affluence and decline in priestly vocations, he admits the existence of other factors in the decline of vocations in Ireland. He mentions the self-doubt of some members of the clergy and their lack of trust in the institutions they represent. "Their role had become largely that of sacramental agents"[67]. On the contrary, Cozzen's argument appears overly confident. He was trying to shed some light on the shortage of priests in the United States. The question he did not answer was whether the present generation of priests in the United States no longer enjoys those material and social benefits or that the benefits are there, but are not only the privilege of the priests. This question is important because the single factor of poverty may not explain fully this phenomenon.

In their research on men's vocations to the priesthood and the religious life in the United States, Dean Hoge, Raymond Potvin and Kathleen Ferry, identified some factors that probably have contributed to the decline in priestly vocations. They include: upward mobility, assimilation, the sexual revolution, and suburbanisation; the gradual disappearance of Irish communities from which vocations largely came; the emergence of a youth culture; institutional crises in the Catholic Church in America; the problem of celibacy; the confusion in theological circles about priestly identity[68]. By implication, vocations would have been on the increase if these factors were not there. Therefore, one would not explain the increase in vocations in the developing world solely on the basis of the search for social and material security.

If this were the only factor, the increase in vocations would not be limited to certain areas of the developing world. For example, it would have been equally distributed throughout all Catholic areas in Nigeria. But this is not so. It points to the need for some other explanations. Secondly, there is a good economic condition of priestly ministry in the industrialised countries of Europe and

North America. J.S. Okwor argues that in Germany, for instance, "priests receive fat salaries and enjoy high standard of living but this high position has not improved the number of vocations to the priesthood"[69]. The condition is not able to attract many young men to the priestly vocation. André Godin has suggested that the decline in vocations could be linked to the fall in the number of practising Christian families. Taking the example of France, he asserts that about 90% of seminarians used to come from active Catholic families: "the proportion of priestly vocations in those families is virtually constant"[70]. Between 1959 and 1969, the number of Catholics who attended Mass weekly had dropped by 11%, according to the Gallup polls.

Francis Cardinal Arinze would support the position of Godin. He observes that vocations to the priesthood and to the religious life are mostly favoured "by a climate of healthy family life where children are gladly and thankfully welcomed, by Christian practice in the home and the neighbourhood, by a spirit of sacrifice and readiness to share as is often best seen in families with many children, and in a Christian approach to marriage and the family"[71]. He does not deny the impact of the poverty-richness factor in the increase and decline of vocations to the priesthood. He rather proposes a different way of looking at it: "It would not be correct to say that the poorer parts of the world have more vocations than the richer areas. Nevertheless, it is noticeable that vocations become a greater and more difficult challenge where material well-being is prevalent"[72]. This argument matches the contention of John Paul II that material well-being is one of the standing obstacles to the vocations to the priesthood, especially in wealthy countries:

> Material "well-being", which is so intensely sought after, becomes the one ideal to be striven for in life, a well-being which is to be attained in any way and at any price. There is a refusal of anything that speaks of sacrifice and a rejection

of any effort to look for and to practise spiritual and religious values[73].

The hypothesis of poverty, therefore, though it may not be totally untrue, does not seem to be able by itself to explain the phenomenon. It appears to be a significant factor in the increase of vocations to the priesthood in the poor countries, just at this time that the number of vocations is declining in the affluent, industrialized parts of the world.

The second hypothesis put forward is that the increase in vocations to the priesthood is due to the social status and prestige it confers on the priests, related to the power of education and control which the priest exercises over the illiterate masses. This hypothesis holds that whenever the seminary is the most accessible place for higher learning, and priests are largely the only ones with higher education, the priesthood will become attractive to young men.

This hypothesis is invoked in explaining the growth in the vocations to the Catholic priesthood in Nigeria and among the Igbos. Ekwunife maintains that the missionaries presented and left to Nigerians an image of the priest as one with "unlimited power" before the 1970s[74], the exercise of which touched all facets of the people's life. Politically, it expressed itself through the "marriage of convenience"[75] between the missionaries and the European colonial authorities in which "the missionaries depended on the Europeans for help in keeping the rebellious African Chiefs in their place while the European authorities hoped to conquer by religious persuasion what they failed to achieve by force of arms"[76]. Religiously, it expressed itself through the condemnation and demonization of all religious symbols of the Nigerian people and establishing in its stead Christianity as the powerful religion[77]. Economically, the image of the priest as one with unlimited power was projected and enhanced by the positions they held in society.

> Being principals and managers of the various schools in their care, they controlled the economy of the elite of the people and indirectly controlled the people. Thus, they were able to enforce discipline among teachers and students. He who can dismiss, transfer, promote teachers, pay them and withhold payments, certainly enjoys great power among the people[78].

The priest then had much power at his disposal and he used it at will and "no one dares question this unlimited power"[79].

Ikenga Ozigbo argues in support of this hypothesis from what he calls the "psychology of the Igbo man", which would not permit him to go for anything that is less than prestigious. As a historian, he links the lack of success of the Little Brothers of Jesus and of the Sisters of the Poor among the Igbos since 1975, to the fact that these two congregations promoted the kind of values that were alien to the Igbo mentality and ethical thought. The values of the two congregations include "exaggerated humility, reticence and self-abnegation..."[80]. For this reason, he concludes, "an Igbo boy would first try his hand at the priesthood rather than the brotherhood"[81]. The fascination of western education generally available in the seminaries is also an added incentive[82].

Working with the same hypothesis of prestige, Cardinal Arinze suspected that the vocations to the priesthood and to the religious life became more attractive immediately after the Nigerian Civil war ended in 1970 when parents began to see that if their sons or daughters succeeded in these vocations, it would be an honour to them[83] and would raise the prestige of the family. A.K. Obiefuna agrees with him that the status the priesthood gives to the family still remains a strong force in motivating seminarians to enter and persevere in priestly vocation[84]. The motivation of prestige, this time, does not come from the young man alone but also from the parents; the young man would receive maximum support from the parents and relatives.

In the United States of America, research demonstrates that since the possibility of attending schools of higher learning increased and more and more members of the lay faithful became highly educated, the prestige of priests began to decline. Educated Catholics were more inclined to be critical of priests[85]. Loss of the prestige of priests also became a factor in the shortage of vocations to the priesthood. A further factor was the ecclesiology of the Second Vatican Council that awakened the laity to its authentic position and duty in the Church. This hypothesis implies that as long as priests occupy a privileged position in society, there would be many vocations to the priesthood.

There is no doubt that the Catholic priesthood could be perceived as a prestigious symbol of power, and that this could be a powerful incentive to young men who had ambitions to achieve and exercise control over others[86]. It would square well with Igbo mentality and desires. But though it is possible that prestige might be a factor in the explosion of vocations in the developing world, and therefore in Igboland, it is difficult to reconcile this argument with the fact that many of these priests live and work in extremely hard situations. Some are sent on mission to very difficult places outside their own native places and countries where there is little or no opportunity to display power or to live a privileged lifestyle. Instead, these priests have to insert themselves in the poor condition of the people and have to struggle to live like the people they came to serve. This means that there could be other reasons that transcend the search for prestige and honour, at least in some of the priests.

Some important historical factors should also be considered in understanding the number of vocations in Igboland. Some authors see this "vocation boom" as linked to the impact of minor seminaries and countless schools established by the missionaries[87]. Missionary schools have dwindled since the expatriation of missionaries shortly after the war, but the minor seminaries are still valid sources of priests in Igboland. One might object that there are minor seminaries in almost all parts of Nigeria. Yet they do not produce as many priests as the minor seminaries in Igboland. To this argument therefore should be added the factor of a large Catholic population in Igboland in comparison to other parts of Nigeria. As C.A. Obi rightly argues quoting the Igbo proverb: *"Anụ isi ya ka, ka agba ya na aka.* (That animal which has a bigger head will naturally have a bigger jaw-bone than another with a small head)"[88].

While these two hypotheses, and others that may be proposed, do not alone explain the growth in vocations to the priesthood in Igboland, they accomplish one thing: they show the urgency of better discernment of vocations in order to nurture them well[89]. There are always ambiguities in the human condition. Many factors interact within a particular social condition and climate. Before the Second Vatican Council, diocesan priests in many parts of Europe were well off and well respected. The Jesuits had the reputation of being academics with corresponding prestige. It could well be a booster to one's ego to become a Jesuit then[90]. But now in the present circumstances, the same ambiguities are still found. In the United States now, to become a priest is perhaps to risk suspicion of being a homosexual or even a paedophile. What is important is to reduce, as much as possible, the ambiguities that surround the vocations to the priesthood. This is good for the individual and for society. To the individual, it gives him greater focus and meaning in his vocation, and to society, it calls forth greater trust and faith in the priests and in the Church.

This ambiguity that can be found in vocations to the priesthood becomes even more relevant when we consider the shadows which Igbo priests cast on the horizon of the Church in Igboland today. These shadows create difficulties for the Church and even heighten the suspicion that these vocations may not be authentic. No one ever expects that all the persons who seek to be priests are totally authentic; that is not possible in any human situation. Rather, growth demands that the number of inauthentic vocations be reduced. The danger that lies ahead is that we may be careless enough to allow a good number of persons with inauthentic vocation to pass over to the priesthood, and so create serious problems in the future. We are already living with some of the unsavoury attitudes of priests. We shall now present and examine the shadows of Igbo priests with the observatory attitude of scientists so that these vocations could be discerned, understood and harnessed better.

The Shadows of the Igbo Priests

The bishops of the Onitsha and Owerri ecclesiastical provinces did not stop at recognizing the aspects of the life of the Igbo priests that reflect their self-gift to God and to the world; they also noted their shadow side, which is evident in the incongruous lives of some Igbo priests.

In Chapter 4 of *The Igbo Catholic Priest at the Threshold of the Third Millennium,* the bishops highlighted the "shadows" of priestly life and ministry against the background of both the universal ideals of the Catholic priesthood and the socio-ecclesial and cultural conditions of the Igbo people[91]. They also looked at some contradictory attitudes of the priests from the understanding of priesthood in African-Igbo religious tradition. This method has some advantages: first, it implies that the Catholic priesthood is not totally contradicted by the African-Igbo view of the priesthood. Instead, understanding the way priests should live in relation to the African-Igbo traditional religion should be appreciated and incorporated into the Catholic priesthood when it does not distort the Christian message. In this way, African-Igbo and Christian cultures enrich each other. The second advantage flows from the first: it shows where the life of the African-Igbo Catholic priest diverges from that of the priest in African-Igbo traditional religion.

The incongruity between lifestyle and ministry delineated in the document appears in four general areas: attitude to temporal goods, relationship with women, exercise of authority, and pastoral ministry. Though this grouping is not in the text, it is not arbitrary. The bishops seemed to have followed the outline of the priestly values of poverty/simplicity, celibacy, "authority" and pastoral charity, in carrying out the evaluation of the current lifestyle of Igbo priests. It is striking that instead of assessing the life of priests under obedience, the bishops chose to speak of the "exercise of authority" among the clergy[92]. This shift in emphasis seems to imply that they were aware that they themselves belong to the "Igbo clergy"; so they were concerned with how all the members of the Igbo clergy, including themselves, exercise priestly authority, rather than with how the priests or deacons relate to the bishops. The language is inclusive and shows some pastoral genuineness in this exercise of self-examination[93]. The shift in emphasis suggests that the exercise of authority is more urgent, probably because it directly pertains to the relationship between the priests and the people entrusted to them. We shall now examine these areas one by one.

Attitude to Temporal Goods – Materialism

An unhealthy attitude to temporal goods dominates the scene both in the document of the Igbo bishops and in some other related writings. Though only a single paragraph[94] is clearly dedicated to it, there are references to it in other paragraphs[95]. There are two ways in which the unhealthy attitude of Igbo priests to temporal goods can be understood: the first concerns the acquisitive tendency, the sheer desire to acquire money, things and titles; the second has to do with the use of money or the things acquired, that is, the display of wealth or affluence.

In the first way, the bishops noted that the desire to acquire money and other material things is increasing among Igbo priests to a disturbing degree. In order to acquire money, some unduly prolong their studies overseas and then refuse to return. Some embark on personal projects with the help of the connections they made during their studies overseas, and with no permission from their bishops. As far back as 1993, the then bishop of Awka diocese, Most Rev. A.K. Obiefuna, regretted that "a good number of priests who study outside the country and even some who were given benefactors through me continue to get financial help strictly marked 'for pastoral work' and often sent through me consider such gifts as personal. This is totally wrong"[96]. Other priests imprudently run after rich people and "even extort money through various abuses, such as enslaving the Gospel or bringing the priesthood to disrepute"[97].

This observation concerning the Igbo priests seems to be a serious problem among the Nigerian clergy as a whole. For example, Theophilus Anyanwu notes that some Nigerian priests are "involved in personal fortune-making ventures and spend unlimited time on them instead of on their own souls"[98]. In the Third Missiological Symposium held at the Spiritan International School of Theology Enugu in 1992, D.D. Dodo, then chairman of the National Laity Council of Nigeria, said that in the Nigerian Church, lay people observed that "some priests who are in rich parishes do not willingly accept transfer to other parishes that are poor or not as rich as the parishes from where they are being transferred in spite of their vow of obedience to their own ordinary..."[99]. In her own paper, G. Ujomu noted also that sometimes more time is spent in preaching money than in preaching the word of God[100]. In their reaction to the Memorandum addressed to the Leaders of the Nigerian Church by George Ehusani of the Catholic Secretariat of Nigeria, priests, religious and lay people voiced the same disenchantment with this craze for money among the clergy: Matthew Kuka admitted that "materialism on the part of many priests and religious has become the greatest threat to our mission"[101]. A. Njoku regrets that materialism among priests is "a major distraction from the Church's commitment to the prophetic message of Christ"[102]; "it is perhaps the number one headache of the Nigerian Church today"[103]. Because of all these, the Catholic Bishops Conference of Nigeria in the document it issued in 1987 regarding the conduct of priests emphasized that "priests and bishops ought to live a life-style that does not pander to the materialism of modern life"[104]. As things stand today, materialism is steadily on the increase among priests and religious men and women.

The same quest for temporal goods is also present even in the ministry of prayer. The bishops express worry over some aberrations and exaggerations in attending to people's plea for miracles. These include such things as "burying of crucifix and head of a goat in invented rites of exorcisms,…"[105]. Priests engage in various forms of prayer-meetings in which the manner of praying, practices, and gestures are often closer to magic than to Christian faith. The bishops suspect that behind these aberrations and exaggerations might be the "thirst for money, power, control, and popularity …"[106].

An aspect of this acquisitiveness that is disquieting is the irresponsibility often demonstrated in the management of church property. It is observed that "clear separation is no longer maintained between Church money or property, and personal one"[107]. A.O.C. Anigbo extended this problem of management of church money to include "accountability; the methods of raising money; the money raised and where and how they are spent. In other words, can we say that the entire money raised in the course of the apostolate is spent in its promotion?"[108]

The two lay persons present at the Symposium held at Spiritan International School of Theology demanded accountability as a quality that priests should demonstrate to the people, a quality often lacking. G. Ujomu reminded the audience made up of priests and seminarians that "since we all agree that it is no longer 'Father's Church' alone, a priest is expected to be open in his accounting system"[109]. D.D. Dodo observed that:

> Some priests still administer the finances of the Church according to the pre-Vatican II system in which the priest is all in all and administers the finances as if it were his personal money in spite of the provisions in No. 16 of Ad Gentes Divinitus – Vatican II and canons 492-494 and 537 which direct that finance committees should be set up at diocesan and parish levels[110].

The problem of acquisitiveness goes beyond the craze for money. There is also a notable insatiability in acquiring secular titles and academic degrees[111]. Some strongly desire that a string of degrees and titles be attached to their names. For this reason, "some priests plan for further studies on their own without their bishop's approval; or if they are sent officially, they would pursue some other areas of study in addition to, or other than what they are sent to study"[112]. A. Ekwunife observes that the titles and degrees which the clergy of today seek could be secular and traditional. Since the requisite for reaching positions of power in Nigeria is the possession of paper qualifications in the form of secular degrees, "most Nigerian priests silently and openly aspire to it. No-one is content with mere ecclesiastical degree even at its highest level, since most of the time it is not marketable in the Nigerian society"[113]. When these degrees are eventually obtained they must be appended to the name of the priest as recognition of his achievement. "Hence, instead of Rev. Fr. so and so, what is more acceptable is Rev. Dr. so and so. Fr. is a humiliating image while Rev. Dr. is an acceptable image"[114]. Ekwunife may be exaggerating in saying that the title of Rev. Fr. is humiliating; but that it does not seem to be sufficient for the kind of image some priests want to create in society.

Sometimes even these secular degrees are not enough; traditional titles should also be added. When secular degrees are not easy to come by, one becomes content with traditional titles. It is not a surprise then to see that in Igboland today, some priests are "addressed with the following titles Rev. Dr. so and so, Ichie Okaomee I or Ichie Ekwueme I of say Awka or Ehime"[115]. This practice begins from the seminary where some of the members of the Society of African Thought and Culture receive titles in a once-a-year ceremony of title-taking. The central objective of the association is to promote African Culture, and this is a good intention. Some parishes honour their priests with different traditional titles in appreciation of the work done for them in the parish. This is in consonance with the African practice of honouring distinguished sons and daughters with some traditional titles in appreciation of their moral rectitude and selfless service to the community[116]. But since human desires can be ambiguous, this good intention is sometimes misunderstood and taken to be self-exaltation. This is probably what happens when some priests get annoyed if addressed only by the title of Rev. Fr. without adding the traditional title either ceremonially given in the seminary or chosen by themselves.

The second way in which this unhealthy attitude of priests to temporal goods manifests itself is in their use. There is often a flagrant display of wealth among the clergy to the displeasure of the masses[117]. Even if the money belongs to the priest, the use of it is often not "guided by the spirit of poverty and charity as demanded by priestly way of life"[118]. It is now becoming the fashion that once a diocesan priest is ordained, the townspeople remark that the family of the priest has been promoted to the upper class because of the changes that might soon be noticed in the family. For this reason, some people now believe that priests are part of the bourgeois class.

Some priests are not content with just having a car for ministry; they go for highly expensive ones[119]. There are those who have not just one of these expensive cars but two or three of them. In some cases the newly ordained priest, filled with the spirit of narcissistic entitlement, bluntly curses the people of God because the car given him belittles him. In 1992, the *Vanguard* newspaper carried the news of a newly ordained priest who was angry at the poor reception given to him by the townspeople. He was reported as saying:

> The poor reception and the cheap VW car you gave me at my reception after my priestly ordination shows that you can't appreciate the sacrifice I have made to become a priest. Even a little piece of meat from the cow slaughtered for my reception was denied me. You will pay for all these in hell[120].

Another story was told of a deplorable attitude of a priest at a time when fuel was scarce. The priest told his parishioners that he was not going to celebrate any mass for them if they could not buy him the fuel he needed to run the generator in the father's house. In actual fact, he needed the power to watch his cable television and movies. The *Daily Sun* of Wednesday, March 29, 2006, carried the news of the revolt of the parishioners of a parish against their priest. Among the people's grievances was "the introduction of flag to any burial ceremony in the Catholic denomination and collection of N1500 after normal clearance that is being done in Catholic Church". In another incident a priest refused to go to an out-station for Mass when it rained because he felt the road would not do his beautiful car good! These are examples of that irresponsibility spoken of by E. Uzukwu, which reveals itself in a scandalous insensitivity to the social realities around[121]. In a nation that often suffers from abject poverty, such narcissistic insensitivity, greediness, and arrogant flaunting of wealth among us, the leaders of the Church, is not just a scandal but also a kind of violence to the poor. It is for these reasons that A.K. Obiefuna asked the priests of his diocese in 1993: "Are we here [in the priesthood] to look after ourselves or to look after the flock committed to our care? What does the scripture say about the shepherds that feed themselves and not the flock?"[122] But the people do not keep quiet all the time; sometimes they react[123]. As Most Rev. S. A. Okafor, the bishop of Awka diocese, rightly noted to his priests in 2004, "if we begin to do the things contrary to our priestly life, … people are ready to oppose us to any degree. They may begin to criticise, condemn and make cases. And no matter how we pretend, once we are at fault, we are at fault"[124]. The situation has been summarized in the *Lineamenta* prepared for the First National Pastoral Congress:

> Voices are being raised nowadays against the excessive materialism pervading the ordained, regarding the number and choice of cars, the building and furnishing of presbyteries, etc. Some priests want more money than they actually need to sustain a lifestyle they have set for themselves, maintain their bevy of friends, pleasure, recreations, etc.[125]

Many of us priests are guilty of this thirst for money, other material things, and the titles of honour. We are not expected to live in squalor, or abject want, but prudence enables us to differentiate between what is a need from what is mere luxury. It is this luxury that the people frown at.

Relationship with Women

In this area of relationships with women, the document, *The Igbo Catholic Priests at the Threshold of Third Millennium*, loses the

24

directness with which it treats the problem of materialism. It gives many examples of the errors of priests in the quest for and management of temporal goods. But in this case, it assumes a rather cautious posture. The only issue it occupies itself with is that of female relatives who stay in the presbyteries, so that people question the authenticity of priestly celibacy[126]. The bishops call for modesty and caution that "discipline and prudence are to be exercised in all affairs relating to women" because "in the eyes of people and whether we like it or not, celibacy is the test of integrity for the Catholic Priesthood"[127].

The message of the bishops is that society is scandalized at the imprudence of some priests in dealing with women. What this imprudence consists in is not explicitly stated. Indirect reference to it is made in dealing with the manner in which female relatives live in the presbyteries. The document simply shies away from being specific and giving other possible examples.

In other writings concerning this issue on the national level, the tendency to shy away from the specifics and take a cautious stand is also noticed. The *Lineamenta* prepared for the First National Pastoral Congress followed the line of the bishops in *The Igbo Catholic Priests at the Threshold of the Third Millennium* in cautioning against imprudence in keeping female relatives in the presbytery. Again it ends this caution by exhorting the priests that "the more depraved the society, the more it demands a heroic example to convert it. The society has a right to expect such examples from Church Ministers"[128]. G. Ujomu also follows this cautious modality and agrees with the position of the document when she remarks that "many other shortcomings of a priest are not as destructive as this one and my advice is that a priest must pass this acid test by all means. It is not negotiable"[129]. She notes that because of the sexual misbehaviour of priests in some parishes, some of the parishioners refuse to go for the sacrament of reconciliation in their own parishes and prefer to travel to distant places to receive it[130]. For the same reason, the imprudence of some priests in dealing with women, "there are many women who cannot release their daughters for youth activities in our churches for sex reason"[131]. She does not give concrete examples. P.N. Chinyelu observes also that lay people now see their priests as "wolves in the cloak of shepherds. Many of the faithful are even afraid to meet their pastors for one problem or the other. For them, their pastors should be seen more as masquerades than the shepherds of their souls"[132].

It was D.D. Dodo who raised a more fundamental problem behind the sexual misbehaviour of some priests. He agrees with the bishops that a priest's dealing with women is the sure test of his trustworthiness. If he cannot be trusted on this issue, his image is tarnished and no matter how hard he works and how well he does things, he may not be able to redeem himself. "He might earn the name 'Pumemen' which is the sound that the he-goat makes when it wants to have sex with the she-goat"[133]. Some Catholics and non-Catholics have accused the priests of imprudence in dealing with women to the extent that "we are tempted to ask for a redefinition of priestly celibacy as what we see do not tally with our own understanding of the meaning of priestly celibacy especially when we are being told and sometimes shown some children who are said to be fathered by priests"[134]. But that is not his main point; he is concerned with the confusion about the true meaning of celibacy.

This confusion is illustrated by an incident during which a woman confronted a priest for having an improper relationship with another woman. The priest told the woman that priestly celibacy meant "that a priest should not marry but it does not stop him from having sex"[135]. D.D. Dodo therefore called on the audience who were mainly priests and seminarians to re-educate the laity if their understanding of priestly celibacy was wrong.

This issue is fundamental. It suggests that underlying some sexual abuses, there is an erroneous view of priestly celibacy: that celibacy does not include chastity[136]. Ikenga Ozigbo acknowledges the presence of this kind of logic and sees it as a fundamental aberration in traditional forms of religious life in Igbo Catholicism[137]. This logic outrages D.D. Dodo and other lay members of Christ's faithful because "our understanding of priestly celibacy is that a priest should abstain from sexual intercourse as such act is a violation of the commandment of God and therefore a sin"[138].

What we are dealing with here is not simply human weakness but bad will which attacks the root of the value of celibacy. In this kind of situation, the Igbo people say that "*Mmiri siri n'isi wee gbaruọ*" meaning that "the stream has been fouled from its source". This is different from actions resulting from mere human weakness, because a stand is consciously taken against the totality of the value itself. This is the critique levelled against the Catholic priests in the movie *Beyond the Vows*. The film was produced in 1997 by Gab Onyi Okoye of Gabsky and Chezkay Films. Fr. Francis, the chief protagonist, is depicted as operating under this logic of "celibacy without chastity" in his romantic relationship with Sr. Maria to the point of claiming that the love they have for each other accords with God's law of love and, therefore, cannot be impeded by the law of celibacy. This involves a radical separation between celibacy and chastity. R. Anasiudu believes that the way this point is strongly emphasized in the film "suggests that it is the producer's viewpoint that is put in the mouths of characters"[139]. But it may not be totally the conjecture of the producer. The film was produced in 1997 but D.D. Dodo presented this living experience in the paper he delivered to priests and seminarians at the symposium held in 1992. This is to say that there is some truth in what the film set out to criticise. The good thing about it, however, is that at the end, Fr. Francis and Sr.

Maria were unfrocked by their superiors thereby reinstating the true value of the priestly and religious life. The call for the reform of the system appears then to be the ultimate objective of the film. It might be an unintended objective of the producers; however, the message was clear.

I am sure that many of our lay brothers and sisters no longer believe that we priests live our celibate commitments. Most people would agree with this statement of a seminarian: "I am unwantedly faced with the problem of my sexuality that I tried to question whether celibacy is true. Secondly, the attitude of 99.9% [of the] seminarians and more especially priests at violating this is sorrily alarming. It may be true that every priest and seminarian violates it (often), except – probably if any – about 0.01%"[140]. Whatever the exaggeration of this seminarian, the wave of sexual abuse by priests that is sweeping through the United States of America and Europe is a lesson for every church in the world to take the sexual life of priests seriously. I am sure that the American situation is not an isolated case; it is just that there is more media involvement.

In order to forestall problems emanating from sexual misconducts and abuses among priests, the Catholic Bishops' Conference of Nigeria published the document titled *Called to Love: Ethical Standards for Clergy and Seminarians in Nigeria* in March 2006. The document serves as a caveat for priests and seminarians to check their sexual attitudes and behaviours. The high point of that document is the "Indemnity" Form to be filled by priests of every diocese stating that the diocese or archdiocese is not to be held responsible for "any damages or claims of compensation or settlement arising from any cases of sexual abuse attributed to me"[141]. The word 'attribution' is very vague in the formulation. Not all attributed sexual abuse may be verified to be true. Secondly, the tone of the Form seems to be heavily legal rather than pastoral. In this sense, it follows strictly the Zero-

Tolerance policy of the United States Conference of Bishops. This notwithstanding, the central objective of the document is to enable priests and seminarians to take their vowed celibate life seriously.

Highhandedness in Exercising Authority

The question of the exercise of authority is treated in paragraphs 41 and 42 of *The Igbo Catholic Priest at the Threshold of the Third Millennium*. In paragraph 41, the priests are reminded of the "love, recognition and respect"[142] the Igbo people accord them and the great sacrifices they make in the training of priests, at their ordinations, in building the presbyteries, and for the general success of priestly ministries. The priests are then invited to reciprocate this love of the people "through a leadership service"[143]; an exercise of authority carried out "in the spirit of service, as *amoris officium*"[144].

The document proceeds to exhort that "the pastors working in Igboland should as much as possible live the spirit of dialogue in exercising pastoral authority"[145]. This exhortation is necessary because "there are cases of arrogance and high-handedness, even dictatorship, in the way some priests exercise their responsibilities"[146]. No instances are given, in contrast to the method used in dealing with the question of temporal goods.

The *Lineamenta* prepared for the National Pastoral Congress tries to describe this attitude of authoritarianism in concrete terms. It consists in "issuing orders and decrees and demanding unconditional obedience, with very little consideration of the people's conscience or reasons"[147]. Sometimes priests give orders to the lay faithful and do not tolerate any objection. At other times they take unilateral decisions without considering the feelings or condition of the people. For example, there are cases in which a priest changes the time for the daily and Sunday masses without considering the social condition of the people like market days or the season of the year. When the faithful approach him for dialogue he gets angry and tells them that he is the one in charge of the parish, as if the people had no right to be considered. The problem is found also among the bishops in their relationship with priests and with seminarians. A bishop was reported to have addressed his seminarians in these words: "We are the church, you are not the church; the church speaks, you listen; we talk, you do the listening; we give directives, you obey; you are there, we are here; we send you, you go!"[148]

The experience of authoritarian leadership on the part of the clergy made Bridget Itsueli to ask the question: "Are priests trained to recognize that parishes do not need Mussolinis who will rule and regiment vast numbers of diverse people according to their own limited views and resources?"[149] It is on this concrete basis that the *Lineamenta* distinguishes the reactions of the lay faithful to dictatorship by priests from anticlericalism: "... a people may reject a particular priest and accept another, their attitude cannot be described as anticlerical, which by definition is an *apriori* rejection of priestly leadership"[150]. But sometimes the reaction against authoritarianism could shade into anticlericalism so that it becomes difficult to differentiate them. In many of these cases, the people of God rise against the priest and demand his removal from the parish. I am sure that these are among the nagging cases on the desks of the bishops. Sometimes these complaints of the people are left to linger until they get out of control.

Highhandedness in the exercise of authority seems to be pervasive. To the people, bishops and priests are like "sacred cows". Being fundamentally sensitive towards the sacred, the Igbo people revere their priests and in most cases are even afraid of them. Some even believe that talking about the priest or challenging him might incur the wrath of God to whom the priest is consecrated. This psychological disposition of the people makes it possible for some priests to exercise their authority in an absolute way; and many are guilty of it. The situation discourages a good number of the educated members of the laity who demand to be understood and persuaded.

Lack of Enthusiasm in Pastoral Ministry

Though many Igbo priests are hard-working and carry out their pastoral ministry with dedication, there are also signs of diminished enthusiasm among some of them; this generally implies the reduction of motivational energy, resulting in a "lack of zeal and enthusiasm in attending to pastoral duties"[151]. For these priests, pastoral ministry becomes drudgery, with an increased tendency to passivity as a way of safeguarding their meagre psychic resources. The demands of pastoral activities become stressful to the point that in place of the compassion and availability of the pastor, one meets cynicism and resentment[152].

This psychological state has a negative impact on the people of God, especially on the young ones, hindering them from identifying with the Church[153]. The priest appears distant from the people and less approachable. He may withdraw into the comfort of the presbytery and live his life as he wants it, removed from the realities around him. People tend to interpret such a withdrawal to mean that he is "enjoying life despite the prevalent misery and hardship: fiddling while the house burns"[154]. It might appear he is enjoying life, but the underlying reason for taking refuge in the comfortable life he displays could be his diminished enthusiasm. In some cases, the priest fails to respect proper boundaries in relationships with the parishioners[155].

The bishops also suspect that "loss of faith in the Word of God and the sacraments is possible among the ordained ministers"[156]. They see it as the reason "for some excesses, misplaced emphases, syncretism, and total aberration, noticeable in contemporary times in the proclamation of the Word, the celebration of the sacraments and sacramentals"[157]. But a loss of enthusiasm may contribute also, because it feels like loss of meaning and loss of interest in what one does. This is not a pleasant feeling, and so one desires to get rid of it. Some could seek to deal with it through different forms of excitement like eccentric behaviours or aberrations or through restless activism, others through alcohol or even through sexual acting out.

The restless activism connected with lack of enthusiasm is again to be seen in the disorderliness and confusion that are present in the life of a good number of priests. Some wake up in the morning and, like a machine that is switched on, they keep running until they are exhausted in the evening. T.O. Anyanwu notes that in such a situation, "a lot of things are done at random according to the mood of the moment, such that they interfere with one another. Many a time too, things are neglected, or entirely omitted, or at best done mechanically"[158]. It shows in an improper distribution of time and difficulty in organizing one's life.

Igbo people are in general a hardworking people who are not easily discouraged, and the number of Igbo priests who suffer this lack of enthusiasm in a more visible way would be small. Again, the collectivistic nature of the culture would tend to cover it up because the priest in those moments of meaninglessness and loss of enthusiasm could find peace and solace from his family members and relatives. Furthermore, because of the increasing number of priests, a tired priest could easily find another priest to supply for him. These social factors may protect Igbo priests from a serious loss of enthusiasm, more than might occur in a situation of individualism or acute shortage of priests.

II

Understanding the Shadows of Igbo Priests: Review of Literature

Having described the situation, the lights and shadows in the lives of the Igbo Catholic priests in the last chapter, the next step is to understand them. At present, the number of vocations to the priesthood is increasing rapidly but there is also such a decrease in priestly standards that the respect given to priests is fast declining and "people have begun to beat up or threaten to beat up priests"[1]. Two important questions emerge: first, what is the meaning of these signs? Secondly, what are these signs saying to the Catholic Church in Igboland? Both questions call for a deeper study of the signs themselves.

To understand these signs, it is important to recognise that these priests live in the socio-cultural and religious tradition of the Igbo people. Now and again in *The Igbo Priest at the Threshold of the Third Millennium*, the bishops reiterate that the Igbo priest is constantly in dialogue with his socio-cultural milieu[2] which "influences him, giving him a human character"[3]. In other words, the Igbo priest, who is an Igbo man with an Igbo worldview, a Christian and a Catholic priest, constantly lives out in his being and ministry the dialectical tension between Igbo culture and the Christian message. Such is also the experience and the life of the Igbo lay Christians. In this dialectical tension, it is possible that, for instance, "pressured by expectations of supplicants and prevailed upon by a false notion of prayers, pastors may be tempted to satisfy every request for 'miracle'"[4]. The acts of burying crucifixes and heads of goats in different types of exorcism rites[5] are examples of this. The wine of the Christian message is not always well preserved in the wineskins of Igbo socio-cultural worldview. If "the religious climate tends to syncretism and 'neo-paganism'"[6], it means that tension still exists between the Christian message and the Igbo culture; and this is profoundly experienced and lived out by every Igbo Christian, priests and lay alike. This tension will never go away, but it should be understood in its different aspects.

In this chapter, we shall try to present, in a more systematic way, the three hypotheses proposed by some authors as explanation for these shadows in the lives of Igbo priests, and review the studies that have been done to prove them. The first hypothesis states that Igbo culture and the social changes in Nigerian society affect the priests to live in a way that is not wholly in agreement with the priestly vocation; the second holds that the problems of Igbo priests are due to stress and lack of satisfaction in the pastoral ministry; and, the third hypothesis holds that the priests are living the way they do because they received inadequate formation in the seminary.

First Hypothesis: Influence of Culture and Society

The first hypothesis holds that certain ideals rooted in the Igbo culture and the changes that have occurred in Nigerian society affect the priests so that some of them live in a way that is not in agreement with the priestly vocation. In other words, Igbo priests are influenced by the socio-cultural milieu in which they live. These influences basically come from three areas: first, the clash between the Igbo worldview and the Christian worldview; secondly, social changes like the secularisation of Nigerian society; and thirdly, the growing population of educated laity. These three areas have been chosen for closer examination based on the theme of our study, that is, as they affect Igbo Catholic priests and seminarians.

Conflict between the Igbo and Christian Frames of Reference

The phrase "frame of reference" simply means "the overall context within which a particular event takes place and, hence, is interpreted or judged"[7]. Two elements are present in this definition: first, the *overall context* made up of certain principles that differentiate the context from other contexts; secondly, events that happen within this context are *interpreted* or *judged* using the same principles that define the context. The "overall" attached to the context suggests the extensiveness of the context. It thus can refer to the interpretative scheme usually used by an individual (psychology)[8] or a group of persons (sociology/cultural anthropology)[9] in their relationship with the world of reality. A worldview serves as a frame of reference, and "includes the perception and interpretation of the underlying order in the whole cosmos, the categories of beings in it, the permanent values and ethos which are concomitant ingredients of the perception and interpretation of the whole reality of life"[10]. The extensiveness of worldview as an interpretative scheme is seen in the fact that it "spans the whole of the cognitive, affective and psychomotor domains of any people"[11].

The development of individuals takes place in different cultures by means of socialisation. These cultures have their specific worldviews as frames of reference for understanding and interpreting reality[12]. They define the ethos guiding men and women, their immediate and ultimate aspirations, their understanding of life situations, problems and their solutions. These elements constituting the worldview are objectified in the *nomos* of the particular society and culture and subjectified in the psychological world of the individual during the process of socialisation[13]. The *nomos* of a particular society or culture, having been internalised by the individual in this process, does not change easily. It endures because it is the source of the identity of the individual and, therefore, the basis of his stability in the world. Thus, the young Igbo Christian and also the Catholic priest carry in themselves the length and the breath of their cultural heritage and worldview.

It follows that Igbo Catholic priests are influenced by the socio-cultural milieu in which they grew up and are working. The influence can generate conflicts between the cultural values and the Christian ones. The bishops of the Onitsha and Owerri ecclesiastical provinces in the document, *The Igbo Catholic Priest at the Threshold of Third Millennium*, acknowledge this influence only in a general manner[14]. No particular paragraph is dedicated to this theme of conflict. It can only be inferred from points made here and there in the text. However, paragraph 22 gives a brief enumeration of the cultural values that the Igbo people hold, and describes the basic characteristics of a typical Igbo man, his attitudes, basic expectations from life, and his aspirations, immediate and ultimate. These include the family, unity and solidarity, deep-rooted devotion to one's kin, loyalty to the community and respect for elders, a strong desire to achieve and corresponding sense of industry, success-oriented and acquisitive traits, a high premium placed on social status and social recognition. In general, Igbo culture, like all African cultures, is communitarian, but specifically it is an ambitious culture; or as L.N. Mbefo describes it, "a culture of excellence" in which "each individual defines and finds a niche for himself in Igbo society through personal achievement socially recognised as such"[15].

When these cultural values are confronted with the values of the Catholic priesthood, it becomes apparent that there will be some conflicts. While the values of the priesthood emphasise the selfless giving of oneself to God in the service of other human beings, Igbo cultural values especially in their modern forms, emphasise the active pursuit of personal/family achievement, social status and social recognition[16]. It is possible that the wine of the Christian message will not adapt easily to the wineskins of the Igbo cultural value system. There seem to be two areas in which this conflict manifests in the life of Igbo priests: their style of life and the pastoral ministry.

In their style of life, this conflict shows itself in excessive material acquisitions and in imprudent display of wealth; in the unending financial assistance rendered to brothers and sisters of both nuclear and extended family; in the fact that they can be imprudent in keeping female relatives in the presbytery. Their industry is connected to their strong desire to achieve and win social recognition through gaining titles, academic and traditional.

In the area of pastoral ministry, the Igbo priest may be driven to acquire and make his mark in the society. He is generally inclined to evaluate his achievement in quantitative terms by the number of visible structures or things he has achieved[17]. For this reason, he tends to lay too much emphasis on work and ends up cultivating attitudes of activism or functionalism that can easily take away his inner peace[18]. As he shares the same worldview with the rest of the Igbo Christians, in moments of difficulty, and when confronted by phenomena such as witchcraft or belief in dreams that are unexplainable by the "scientific method", it is very likely that he will draw on his cultural stock and pull out a culturally determined interpretative key. This is what seems to underlie the different forms of aberration or exaggeration that happen especially in the healing ministries. L.N. Mbefo explains the matter well:

> Now that the continued existence of the church has been entrusted to indigenous clergy, questions which were not posed and which perhaps were posed and not answered have again come to the fore. There has been disenchantment and many have fallen back to the traditional answers: the old is better. If there are defections

from the Christian church today – and there are such defections in favour of traditional religions – then it goes to show that Christianity has not proved itself beyond all, reasonable doubt to be superior to African traditional religion[19].

It seems unnecessary to think in terms of superiority, inferiority and competition; this does not really resolve the issue at stake. The basic problem is that of deepening the Christian faith which must happen through a continuous "conversation" between the wine of Christian message and the wineskins of the Igbo tradition. C.J. Uzor tells the story of a seminarian who, despite the Christian formation received in the seminary, resorts to this cultural explanatory model in interpreting the sickness of his brothers and sisters as the effect of the witchcraft of his aunt[20]. V. Ekezuike sees this phenomenon as a kind of double living in which the Igbo or Nigerian Christian "inwardly believes in 'osu', 'ọgwụ', 'ọgbanje', 'witchcraft', 'charm', and so forth. They do not prevent him at the same time from believing in the Blessed Trinity, the Bible and the Dogmas of the Church"[21]. C.B. Okolo reads this attitude as a sign of "shallowness of faith"[22]. While these assessments have elements of truth in them, C.J. Uzor sees the problem as deeply rooted in the high level of tension between the Igbo mindset and the Christian message[23]. Ikenga Ozigbo would agree fully that this "ambivalent spirituality"[24] present among the Igbo Christians is largely a consequence of the fact that Christ has not breathed the Igbo air; he has not lived the Igbo life nor has he spoken the Igbo tongue[25]. Thus, the resilience of cultural and religious worldviews makes A. Ekwunife to believe that "aberrations in religious understanding and interpretations and practices are bound to exist"[26].

The Research of C.J. Uzor

Uzor carried out empirical research to verify this hypothesis of the conflict between Igbo frame of reference and the European-

Christian frame of reference as it is played out in the life of Igbo seminarians. The research was his doctoral dissertation at the Institute for Practical/Pastoral Theology of the University of Innsbruck, Austria, in 1999, and was published in 2003. I will make use of both the published and the unpublished editions of his work.

His basic assumption was that "the frame of reference of the seminary differs in many fundamental respects from the cognitive world of the Igbo society from where the seminarian hails and to which he returns at every holiday, and finally at the end of his training"[27]. The differences were supposed to generate some tensions in the cognitive world of the seminarians which, naturally, should be reflected in the inconsistencies in their concrete behaviour. He, therefore, had four propositions to prove:

i. That any dissonance between the Present Behaviour (PB) of the seminarian and his Personal Ideal (PI), the Societal Ideal of the Igbo society (SI) and the Institutional Ideal of the seminary (II) was bound to generate intrapersonal tensions in the seminarian.

ii. That the existence of such intrapersonal inconsistencies would indicate that the internalisation process was abortive and that it would generate greater anxiety in the seminarian the more he is aware of them.

iii. That the personal ideals of the seminarian (PI) would often be in opposition to the institutional ideals of the seminary (II) and also to the societal ideals (SI) of the Igbo society. The relevant relationships are PI-II and PI-SI[28].

iv. That the course of years of seminary formation would have modified the cognitive world of the seminarian so that he would be closer to the institutional ideals and farther away from the societal ideals of the Igbo society. Therefore, "the higher the degree of identification with and internalisation of the institutional ideals, the higher the level of acculturation from the Igbo cultural society"[29].

The constructs used, the present behaviour (PB) of an Igbo seminarian, the societal ideals of the Igbo society (SI), and the institutional ideals of the seminary were taken from the work of L.M. Rulla – J. Ridick – F. Imoda, *Psychological Structure and Vocation*. Uzor developed a questionnaire of 120 items. For each item, participants were expected first, to answer whether it was *consistent with, inconsistent with* or *irrelevant to* his personal ideals, institutional ideals, or ideals of Igbo society; secondly, they were expected to answer whether each of the items was *true* or *false* as a description of their present behaviour at that particular time in their lives[30]. Some of the items were taken from the work of L.M. Rulla and his colleagues but modified as the occasion demanded to reflect the Igbo societal ideals, while some were developed by the author himself. From these items, 10 scales were developed: (1) Respect for elders/authority, (2) Family ties, (3) Success in life, (4) Diligence and responsibility at studies/work, (5) Traditional religious belief, (6) Observance of seminary rules and regulations, (7) Obedience/hierarchy, (8) Chastity/celibacy, (9) Mortification, and (10) Piety. If the statement of any of the items is true of the present behaviour of the seminarian, but inconsistent with his personal ideals (PI), or the Societal Ideal (SI), or the Institutional Ideal (II), there is the likelihood that there will be a high discrepancy in his experience of the situation. The subjects came from two diocesan major seminaries in Igboland: Bigard Memorial Seminary, Enugu (BMS) and Seat of Wisdom Seminary, Owerri (SWS). The actual analysis and interpretation were performed on the second-year students of philosophy and fourth-year students of theology of both seminaries. For the students of philosophy: BMS = 40, SWS = 35; for the students of theology: BMS = 40, SWS = 35. No reason was given for this choice; presumably it is meant to take those who had just begun studies in the major seminary (the 2nd year students of philosophy) and those who were about to finish (4th year students of theology). The hypotheses were two-tailed and tested at the 1% level of significance.

The results showed that in almost all the 10 scales, there was a positive correlation between the present behaviour (PB) and the personal ideals (PI) of the seminarians in the two seminaries. Correlations are significantly low in both schools on scales (10) *Piety*, (9) *Mortification*, (4) *Diligence and responsibility at studies and work*, and (6) *Observance of seminary rules and regulations*; that is, in four out of the ten scales. The correlations between the seminarians' PB and their SI are generally not significant; negative correlations are found especially among the students of philosophy. Among the students of theology, their SI and their II correlated positively on scales (1) *Respect for elders/Authority*, (3) *Success in Life*, and (7) *Obedience/Hierarchy*. Uzor sees this result as reflecting the closeness the seminarians feel to the "new status" of the priesthood. This high positive correlation between SI and II was not reflected in the relationship PI-SI and PB-SI. This apparent anomaly, according to Uzor, is due to the fact that the seminarians were not convinced of what they were taught in the seminary; their present behaviour was out of fear and conformism[31].

The research is a bold step in looking into the nature and extent of this conflict between the Igbo frame of reference and the Christian one. It has the merit of being the first empirical research to address this problem. The results, however, were not as promising as the propositions suggested: the hypothesised conflict between the cognitive world of the Igbo seminarians and the Christian frame of reference present in the seminary did not appear markedly evident. The general trend of the results appears to be that Igbo seminarians do not feel very much conflict at being both Catholic seminarians and Igbo young men.

The reasons for this apparent lack of definiteness come from the limitations of the study. A clearer view of the problem could have been obtained from the pooled results of all the valid protocols (441 of them) or at least a random selection of a larger sample, in addition to the comparative analysis of the 2nd year students of philosophy and 4th year students of theology and the BMS and

SWS seminarians respectively. This limitation is significant because it means that the sample on which the study was carried out is too small to permit wide-ranging conclusions.

Uzor presents the pooled statistical results of the two seminaries from the 2nd year students of philosophy through 4th year students of theology in appendix B5 of the unpublished edition and in appendix A3 of the published version. A closer look at the statistics gives a better picture of the extent of the supposed conflicts of the Igbo Catholic seminarians on all the ten scales. The relevant relationships are PB-SI, PI-SI, and PI-II, since these three relationships indicate the degree of conflict/harmony between the Christian ideals proposed in the seminary formation and the ideals of Igbo society in the life of the seminarians, i.e., their present behaviour (PB).

In both schools there are significant positive correlations in PB-SI and PI-SI on scales (1) *Respect for elders/authority*, (3) *Success in life*, (6) *Observance of seminary rules and regulations*, and (7) *Obedience/hierarchy*. Among the students from Seat of Wisdom Seminary (SWS), there are significant positive correlations in PB-SI and PI-SI on all the scales except on (5) *Traditional religious belief*, and (9) *Mortification*, and this concerns only PI-SI. In Bigard Memorial Seminary (BMS), Positive correlations are significant on scales (2) *Family ties*, (4) *Diligence and responsibility at studies/work*, (5) *Traditional religious belief*. Positive correlation on scale (8) *Chastity/celibacy* is only on PB-SI, and on scale (10) *Piety* it is only on PI-SI. This means that in BMS, there are positive correlations in PB-SI and PI-SI on six out of the ten scales, and on eight out of the ten scales in SWS. On PI-II, PB-II and PB-PI relationships, there are positive correlations on all the ten scales and in both schools.

When the research is considered from the pooled statistical result of all the valid protocols, the general tendency is that the two seminaries show more harmony than conflict in the relationships PB-SI, PB-II, PI-SI, and PI-II. The scale on which there is almost no correlation in both schools and on relationships PB-SI, is scale (5), *Traditional religious belief*[32]. It is revealing also that on the same scale, the correlation on SI-II relationship in both schools is close to zero[33]. This suggests that Igbo traditional religious belief and Christian-institutional ideals are equally accommodated in the cognitive-motivational system without one influencing the other. This compartmentalization means that either one can be activated at any time without difficulty.

While these statistics show the presence of some conflicts or tensions between the Igbo frame of reference and the Christian one in the life of seminarians, the degree of it varies greatly in the sample; this suggests that some other factors are present. If Uzor had done his analysis from this pooled result, the picture of the situation would have been clearer. A further question would have been raised: why are there more positive than negative correlations in his research? We shall address this question when we revisit the research in the second part of this study.

The structure of the tensions between the Igbo frame of reference and the Christian one as presented in the values of the priestly vocation does not seem to be something peculiar to the Igbo culture; it is to be found in every culture. No matter how Europeanized Christianity appears to be in its expressions, the heart of its message remains countercultural to some aspects of European and North American culture. In a recent study on the newly ordained priests in the United States, for instance, one of the cultural trends mentioned that is creating tension for the priests is their attitude to sexuality. In a culture that values individual autonomy, it is not a surprise that the cultural attitude to sexuality tends to be liberal, permitting individual judgement on the matter. It is a constant area of tension for the priests, and it makes pastoral work more difficult[34]. Amid the sexual scandals in the ranks of the American Catholic priests, it is now argued vehemently that homosexuality is not to be considered an objective disorder but a mere orientation[35]. This position derives from the same cultural value of autonomy and independence. The same cultural value is also at the root of the uneasiness American priests feel towards Church structure, authority in the Church, the complaint about lack of private space in their lives, and the claims of the lay people to be given more and more space in the leadership of the Church[36]. It is not surprising that, with the growth in radical individualism in the American culture[37], younger priests and seminarians in America tend to return to pre-Vatican II ecclesiology[38] as a way of managing this tension.

Therefore, the total self-giving which lies at the heart of Christian vocation, and priestly vocation in particular, is in conflict with many aspects of Igbo, European and North American culture. If it were not so, priests and seminarians from these parts of the world would have less difficulty living it. On the same note, the decline of vocations in these countries could be seen as an indirect indication that the values of the priesthood are in serious opposition to the cultural values in vogue. That is why A. Shorter remarks that conflicts between the Christian message and cultures cannot be eliminated completely, and because of this, "no culture can be called definitely Christian"[39].

More fundamentally, tension is an integral part of any developmental process[40]. What is rather crucial is to identify the kind of tension a person is experiencing: whether the tension is a result of having renounced one course of action or commitment for another[41], or whether it is a tension of frustration which is "an emotional state characterised by a more or less persistent and behaviour affecting apprehension and uncertainty, resulting from a functionally significant lack of satisfaction of a present need"[42]. The persistence and behaviour-affecting nature of the tension of frustration are what actually lead to the development of a conflict in which "the individual is prompted to respond simultaneously in different and incompatible ways"[43]. When the conflict is largely subconscious and persistent, it can affect behaviour to the point of psychopathological manifestations and even physical illness[44].

Notwithstanding these limitations, the goal he had in mind was achieved, namely *"to create awareness* for this dimension in the formation of priests"[45]. What it could not show very clearly is the presumed strong presence of the so-called cultural alienation, which breeds inconsistencies in the life of Igbo priests and seminarians.

The Priesthood as a Symbol of Power in Decline

The point of departure of this hypothesis is that the African Church in general and the Church in Igboland in particular, inherited clericalism from the missionaries[46]. It is a model of the Church in which the priesthood is a symbol of power: the priests command and the lay faithful must obey. This clerical culture projects the image of the priest as one that has and exercises much power, both temporal and spiritual[47]. But according to A. Ekwunife, this power-image of the priesthood began to decline from the early 1970s with the government take-over of mission schools. He is strongly convinced that,

> ... the 1970 state schools take-over and the consequent National policy on education was an official demythologisation of the mythical powers of the Catholic schools and her priests in Nigeria. In other words, the event seems to be an open de-thronement of the image of the catholic priest as a man with unlimited power (power 'plenitudo') and the en-thronement of secular authority as possessor of supreme authority[48].

This hypothesis holds that some of the shadow sides of Igbo priests' life are results of this social change, that is, the decline of the image of the priesthood as a symbol of power. Things are no longer as they used to be:

> Since then to the present moment, the image of the priest in

Nigeria as a powerful figure in society has continued to deteriorate. It has been subjected to attack from various quarters (Christians and non-Christians; professionals and non-professionals). The recent waves of planned robbery of the priests' houses coupled with the flogging of innocent priests after robbing them are symptoms of this sagging image[49].

A. Ukwuoma in his own research on the sources of stress in the lives of Nigerian priests, remarks that the government takeover of mission schools brought a big change in the life of the priests. With it was gone the "power base" of the priest, that he "can no longer hire or fire teachers or dictate the moral code of the society as he used to. With this loss of power came increased threat of anti-clericalism"[50].

Ekwunife believes that the Nigerian priests and seminarians are making strenuous efforts to regain the old power of the priesthood, and in so doing, they engage in irresponsible activities that are inconsistent with their vocation, such as acquiring strings of titles and amassing wealth which is then displayed arrogantly and imprudently. Academic titles and wealth are impressive where the majority of the people are illiterate and poor[51]. Some priests write books and force the lay faithful to buy them whether they can understand them or not. They may associate with rich people, but not for spiritual assistance. There are many unnecessary celebrations of anniversaries, like one year of priestly ordination, during which the parishioners give gifts to the priest. One hears such phrases as "wooden anniversary" or "bronze anniversary", caricaturing these celebrations of one, two or three years of priestly ordination. The frequency of such celebrations led the Bishop of Awka diocese, Most Rev. Simon Okafor, to endorse the suggestion of the Presbyteral Council on the modalities for the celebration of ordination anniversaries in order to check the abuse. In his address to the Plenary Fathers Meeting held on September 2, 1998, he issued the following directives:

> Public celebration of ordination anniversary should be reserved to Silver and Golden Jubilee celebrations. The diocese organises every year for common celebration for this event both for clergy and religious working in the diocese on the first Wednesday in May every year. Other anniversary celebrations, e.g. 5th, 10th, 15th should be made 'spiritual' and 'private' only. We have to avoid all forms of squandermania and show of opulence even in the midst of hard times of our people[52].

All this made Ekwunife to believe that "Nigerian priests seem to prefer the image of worldly lords charged with the duty of displaying worldly excellence and wealth[53]. The power of wealth can be exercised in dehumanising ways. For example, there are priests who agree to sponsor some girls in the school on the tacit condition that the girls submit to them sexually.

But nowhere is this search for power more real and almost absolute than in the exercise of spiritual powers in the healing ministry that is booming in the country now. Many priests are involved in this healing ministry, and the abuses of it are so great that the Catholic Bishops' Conference of Nigeria had to issue guidelines for its practice[54]. People flock around priest-healers, who are conscious of the tremendous power they possess and exercise over the people. Sometimes this power is maintained "through the exploitation of the superstitious and the irrational, of which distressed faithful are easy victims"[55]. Without denying the good done to society and to the Christian church by these priest-healers, Ekwunife draws attention to the inconsistencies observable among the healers themselves which suggest that the search for power is motivating many of them. These inconsistencies include: the healers often disagree on the principles they use in their healings; they criticise each other and discourage their clients from visiting other healers; many of them insist on testimonies after each healing session; some even charge fees. And then Ekwunife asks a penetrating question: "why is it that of all the gifts of the church as enumerated by St. Paul in 1 Cor. 12: 4-11, healing was singled out as the only authentic mark of a true priest?"[56] The lay faithful have consciously and subconsciously classified the priests by their power of healing: those who can heal are "real and powerful priests" and others are just ordinary priests. Some seminarians are preparing themselves to get into this stream of power, however well they do it.

It is not only power that may motivate a particular priest-healer; money is also another powerful factor. Almost all the priest-healers are rich. People make donations and promises and fulfil them in gratitude for favours received. It turns out then to be a very strong combination: the exercise of mysterious spiritual power and getting rich. In addition to this,

> [there is also] the tendency to use spiritual weapons on helpless, often good-willed parishioners either to enforce discipline or redress a wrong done to the priest by some Christians. These spiritual weapons often take the form of cursing in the name of God, denial of holy communion to erring Christians, threat of hell fire and brimstone, excommunication *ipso facto* (canonical or non-canonical), public disgrace, in the name of Christ and so on[57].

Ekwunife's hypothesis therefore not only explains the unhealthy desire for temporal goods among some Igbo priests, but also their highhandedness in the exercise of authority. These are efforts to reinstate the power of the priest.

Educated Laity: Threat to the Power of Priests

Among the changes that have taken place in Nigerian society, as they affect the structure and functioning of the Catholic Church, the increasing number of educated lay members of Christ's faithful is central. A good number of the lay people are becoming aware of their rights as members both of the civil society and of the Church. They realise that the image of *Uka Fada*, "Father's Church" popular in the past, in which the laity was a passive spectator in the affairs of the Church, is losing its fascination and ground. As the church "belonged" to the priest then, he could do as he liked. D.D. Dodo narrated an incident in which a priest slapped a layman because he was angry. "Those who were around feared that the layman would revenge but instead, he went and knelt down and prayed thanking God that a holy man slapped him. That was the time the priest was the Alpha and Omega in the Church in Nigeria"[58]. It was the pre-Vatican II Church in which "the distinction between the clergy and the laity was heavily stressed"[59]. The ecclesiology of that period paid little or no attention to the laity. Today, things have changed, but how far the changes have affected the Church in Nigeria, and in Igboland in particular, is an important question.

The Second Vatican Council brought about unsettling changes in the priest-laity relationship in the Roman Catholic Church. The Church is now understood as a community of Christ's disciples in which all share in the priestly, kingly and prophetic functions of Christ[60]. The lay people should now work alongside the hierarchy; they are no longer mere spectators or the objects of the pastoral care of the priest. This new ecclesiology, founded more on communion than on the power of office, affects both the laity and the clergy in Nigeria, but differently.

> For the layman, the new dispensation brought about by Vatican II and the 1983 Code of Canon Law in terms of his definition and role in the Church are welcome development and he is eager to be given the opportunity to perform; but for the priest, it is an intrusion, an invasion of his traditional power, and he is not ready and willing to allow the layman play his new role. This results in conflict of interest, confusion and suspicion[61].

The former status quo has been upset and conflicts emerge between the laity and the clergy. The knowledge gained by a growing number of lay people and their realisation of their dignity and position in the Church, is experienced by some Igbo priests, like their counterparts in other parts of the world, as threats to their privileged position of power[62]. Not only that, many of these educated members of the laity have assumed positions of power in the civil society and "have gained new self-confidence and sophistication. They cannot tolerate inactive and inefficient clergy anymore"[63]. Priests no longer have a monopoly of knowledge and power.

New questions of practical and cultural importance are being raised, and in many instances priests feel inadequate and unprepared to handle them. It is no longer the time when the priests had the last word, to be swallowed whole; their commands used to be obeyed with military precision. These days, some of their preaching and commands are challenged. Questions of practical significance are put to them constantly, especially by the educated youth. Feeling inadequate to handle these challenges, some tend to resort to using intimidation as if the Church is still the "Father's Church". This method saps the energy of the priest, precisely because it is defensive. Secondly, it does not address the problem of the questioner who is merely seeking understanding. A typical example: a Catholic girl falls in love with a Protestant man and decides to marry him. Her mother vehemently objects to this because she does not want to be barred from receiving Holy Communion as is the usual practice in many dioceses in Igboland. The girl, a university undergraduate, demands that the priest explain to her why she should not marry the Protestant, since marriage is her fundamental and natural right. Moreover, she is not sure she will get a Catholic husband. The priest merely tells her that she should obey the Church's teaching. In addition, he threatens her that if she refuses to obey, her parents will also suffer for it. The girl snubs the priest and tells him that he can go to hell along with his Church. She warns him to make sure that nothing happens to her mother because her mother has the right to receive Holy Communion. Her decision to marry is hers and not her mother's. This kind of attitude was unthinkable in the past, but not now.

Some lay people read Canon Law and the Popes' Encyclicals and are well versed in the scriptures. They scrutinize the priest's homilies and assess them in terms of their effectiveness. When they do not yet have the courage to confront the priest openly, they gossip about his ineffectiveness and his moral life; in the past such gossip would make one feel remorse.

On many occasions, some priests tend to underestimate the extent of the changes taking place in the society and they seem to feel inadequate to meet the new challenges with new methods and new understanding. This situation generates stress in many of them and shakes their self-confidence and so also their enthusiasm and zeal in the ministry. Listening to the participants in the research he carried out on stress in the life of Nigerian priests, Ukwuoma writes:

> Priests are finding it hard to accept the hard reality that nothing is "too hallowed" to change. Change is hard and the current changes have taken a toll on the priests' emotional health. For the participants, it is shocking and devastating that nothing is respected or considered sacred anymore in Nigeria[64].

In summary, this hypothesis holds that many priests are unable to handle the challenges of the new priest-laity relationship proposed by the ecclesiology of Vatican II, and have become more defensive.

Observations on the First Hypothesis

The first hypothesis holds that the inconsistencies seen in the life of Igbo priests could be explained by the impact of the socio-cultural milieu and its changes. We have tried to present the essential points in three areas. Now, we intend to evaluate this hypothesis as a whole.

The hypothesis is based on the self-evident truths that man is fundamentally a *homo socialis* and *homo culturalis*. Men construct their social world and are at the same time shaped by the same world. "The product acts back upon the producer"[65]. In a certain sense everyone is a product of his culture or the social environment in which he is born and bred[66]. Every culture with its long tradition provides its members with stable and guaranteed principles of existence, which contain answers to the questions of ultimacy, expectations, basic concerns and needs of individuals, and the accepted ways for their pursuit and fulfilment. Each culture has a picture of its ideal persons, men and women, against which individuals assess themselves and are assessed by others. The members of a particular culture carry out this assessment almost unconsciously because they have internalised the cultural values and symbols present in what P.L. Berger and T. Luckmann call their "common stock of knowledge"[67]. That is why every action or behaviour of an individual has a cultural dimension to it[68]. It is the reason why H.S. Sullivan insists that the psychiatrist or psychologist should take seriously what the society teaches one to expect. He must take into consideration the social definition of situations in his practice[69]. L. Sperry also strongly recommends that the beginning point of every psychological research must be the experience of the persons concerned, their needs, concerns and expectations[70] which generally derive from their social heritage.

The first hypothesis therefore claims that the Igbo socio-cultural values make a great impact on Igbo priests. If a priest is chosen from among his brothers and sisters[71], he obviously carries with him what he has absorbed from his people. In his post-synodal apostolic exhortation, *Pastores Dabo Vobis*, John Paul II recognizes this when he affirms that "God always calls his priests from specific human and ecclesial contexts, which *inevitably influence them*; and to these same contexts the priest is sent for the service of Christ's Gospel"[72]. Thus, the 8th Synod of Bishops was on the theme of "The Formation of Priests in *the Circumstances of the Present Day*"[73].

On the impact of the socio-cultural situation of the Igbo priests, there should be a general agreement. However, it does not have to be stretched further than necessary. When it is taken to imply that men as products of their culture or society cannot but be what their culture or society makes them to be, we are running into an area full of difficulties. But this is precisely the risk in this hypothesis. Though cultures and societies shape individuals, it is equally clear that the form and extent of this influence varies from one individual to the other. In the same culture we get people who passively absorb the popular values of the culture without questioning, but we also get people who resist some of the same values. In modern society, especially in the industrialised countries of Europe and North America, for example, there are persons who follow the values of absolute freedom of the individual and unbridled economic profiteering without ethical restriction. But there are others who champion the counter-cultural cause as a protest against the excesses of modernization[74]. In Igbo culture, there is the camp of those who defend cultural values insisting on the sacrosanct nature of the Igbo tradition. These belong to the group of cultural revivalists in this age of aggressive assertion of cultural identity. There is also the camp of those who, based on the social and human costs of keeping certain values of the culture as they are, demand their transformation for better human and social development. This latter group while accepting the evident truth that consciousness is necessarily tied to the original cultural formation, also believes that consciousness can and does undergo some transformation[75]. This shows there do exist subcultures within a particular culture. For example, G.A. Arbuckle distinguishes three subcultures within the culture of the

Roman Catholic Church today. They include the pre-Vatican II Church subculture, a Vatican II subculture, and a restorationist subculture, that is, those people who feel that "the Church has drifted away from orthodoxy and want to take it back to the power structures and attitudes of a pre-Vatican II Church"[76]. Such a situation raises the question of what makes one individual tend to belong to one subculture instead of the other.

This argument reckons also with the fact that in the contact between cultures, some individuals absorb the values of the foreign culture easily while others resist it. This resistance can take two forms: one form is a rigid maintenance of the former status quo despite the challenges of the "new". It is the choice usually made by the fundamentalists. The other takes the form of conscious resistance of unhealthy aspects of the invading culture. This latter group is more open to change. To some Igbo priests, for example, the decline of the image of the priesthood as a symbol of power has become an opportune moment for self-questioning and self-reorganisation in terms of their authentic priestly and Igbo identities. But for some others, there is an unending lamentation over the loss of the "good old days" and a subconscious but active effort to recapture the lost glories of the past[77]. There exist those Igbo priests who recognize and happily employ the services of competent lay persons in the building of the Church. But there are also others who are frustrated with the educated lay persons and grudgingly refuse to do anything with them.

The Igbo man's goal to achieve and succeed in the life he has chosen (as in the family) is a genuine quality which is lived by the priests who dedicate themselves to living the values of the priesthood and edify their people. These priests tend to be more sensitive to the cultural and economic reality of their people. But why is there a lack of zeal and enthusiasm in some others? Why is it that in some priests this desire to succeed leads rather to over-emphasis on work for material gain, while in some others, the goal becomes to imitate the selfless Christ more closely for the edification of the people of God? Why is it that while the Igbo people's generally industrious and tenacious character helps some of them to withstand the difficulties and contradictions in their environment, it leads others to a manipulative strategy of enriching themselves at the cost of scandalizing the people of God? Why is it that the social respect generally accorded to the Igbo priests has been well utilized by some as an occasion to draw the people to God by enhancing and maintaining their hope and trust in God in difficult social and economic conditions, while it has been used by others to benefit themselves personally and even to intimidate and oppress the people entrusted to them?

These discrepancies point to one conclusion: though the socio-cultural context of the Igbo people certainly influences the Igbo priests, the range of its influence varies from priest to priest.

All this goes to show that the human being is an active participator in his development; he is not merely impacted upon by his culture or society. The nature of the individual's receptive capacity to the impact of his cultural or societal values appears to be a relevant variable in order to balance out the proposition of this hypothesis. It implies then that the hypothesis of socio-cultural influences, however self-evident, may not, by itself, explain the problems exhibited by the Igbo priests.

Second Hypothesis: Stress and Lack of Satisfaction in the Ministry

This hypothesis contends that some of the difficulties manifested by the Igbo priests are results of stress and lack of satisfaction in their ministry. These two factors affect the emotional status of the priests and so lower their morale and enthusiasm in ministry. I have chosen to examine the result of two researches carried out in this area concerning Nigerian-Igbo Catholic priests; no others have been done, as far as I know. The first research was by Joseph

Brendan Chukwunonye Okorie. The theme of his research, which was published in 1995, is: *Social Interest, Lifestyle, Stress and Job Satisfaction of Nigerian Catholic Priests*. The other research was done by Augustine T. Ukwuoma. The title is: *Being a Priest in a Changing Nigerian Society: Psycho-Social Analysis of the Nigerian Experience*. Both researches are on stress, but Okorie extends also to job satisfaction.

The Research of J.B. Chukwunonye Okorie

Okorie set out to do his study based on the experience of stress and lack of satisfaction in ministry among the Nigerian priests[78]. A high level of stress and dissatisfaction in ministry are supposed to account for the "priests' increasing indifference about the ministry"[79]. Stress and lack of job satisfaction are believed to stem from the priests' *lifestyle* and *social interest*. These two concepts belong to Adlerian individual psychology.

A person's lifestyle for Adler would be "the system principle by which the individual personality functions; it is the whole that commands the parts"[80]. It is the basic principle that defines the uniqueness of the individual. A person's lifestyle constitutes his basic disposition toward life in general so that he "perceives, learns, and retains what fits the style of life, and ignores everything else"[81]. The concept of social interest on the other hand emphasises the network of interpersonal relationship in which the person lives and through which his personality is shaped. By means of this social interest, the individual overcomes his selfish interest and works for the betterment of the whole society as a compensation for his inferiority[82]. While the concept of the lifestyle designates the unique personality of an individual, the concept of social interest depicts the inclination of a person toward society.

The theoretical model of stress used in the research is that of R.S. Lazarus[83] which sees stress as the outcome of the interaction between a person and the environment. The production of stress is dependent on the individual's appraisal of the environmental situation as either too taxing or too demanding. Therefore, the external condition is mediated by personality-variables. So a given situation can be judged by an individual as too stressful and by another person as challenging.

J.B.C. Okorie's research is, therefore, to find out the relationship between "major variables of lifestyles and social interests with stress level and personal job satisfaction of Nigerian Catholic priests in their ministerial vocation"[84]. The fundamental hypotheses of the research are: first, that Nigerian priests are experiencing stress and dissatisfaction in their ministry; secondly, that this stress and dissatisfaction are related to their lifestyle and social interest. These hypotheses are expressed in three questions:[85]

i.   What is the relationship between the predictor variables of social interests and lifestyles and the outcome variables for stress among Nigerian Catholic priests?

ii.   What is the relationship between the predictor variables of social interests and lifestyles and outcome variables of job satisfaction of Nigerian Catholic priests in the ministry?

iii.   What is the relationship between the reported stress level of Nigerian Catholic priests and their levels of personal job satisfaction?

The instruments used include the Lifestyle Personality Inventory (LSPI) to measure lifestyle; the Social Interest Scale (SIS) for the measurement of social interests; the Derogatis Stress Profile (DSP) to assess the stress level; and, the Minnesota Satisfaction Questionnaire (MSQ) to assess the level of satisfaction in their lives[86]. He also used 14 personal interview questions, 4 of which are more open questions while 10 demanded a "yes/no" response[87] in order "to gather more information from the priest participants concerning other areas of priests' lives in the ministry that are the sources of stress"[88].

The sample of his research consisted of 111 priests from the Owerri ecclesiastical province randomly selected from the 200 that returned questionnaires. But the in-depth interview was carried out only on 20 priests. The basis of the selection of these 20 priests was not stated and it seems to be an independent sample. The research was done at a .05 level of significance[89].

On the first question, the research findings show that there is no significant relationship between Adlerian lifestyle or social interest and the level of stress among the priests of Owerri Ecclesiastical Province[90]. Significant predictions were noticed, however, on the DSP subscales of "driven behaviour" and "hostility"[91]. A multiple regression analysis showed that the subscale, "displaying inadequacy" predicted driven behaviour[92]. Overall, however, "no relationship exists between the two independent variables of social interest and lifestyle and the dependent variable of stress among Nigerian Catholic priests"[93].

Regarding the second question, the findings show that "the lifestyle of a priest is not relevant to the prediction of how satisfied the priest will be with his job, and that the addition of social interests does not significantly add to the prediction of job satisfaction"[94]. Among the three subscales of the MSQ, Intrinsic Satisfaction, Extrinsic Satisfaction, and General Satisfaction, a significant relationship was found between lifestyle and extrinsic satisfaction[95] which indicates that their satisfaction is generally dependent on the praise they receive from others for a job well done[96].

On the third question, the findings indicate once again that "no relationship exists between stress and job satisfaction among Nigerian Catholic priests"[97]. The level of stress found among them does not reach statistical significance. But 60% of the amount of stress found among them derives from their driven behaviour[98].

The research therefore could not prove the hypotheses it set out to test. Okorie's remaining hope was the result of the in-depth interview in which the 20 participants voiced their difficulties. From these, some stressors were identified and classified according to their frequencies. These include, in order of significance, workload, church authorities, and parishioners/students[99].

Observations on Okorie's Research

A fundamental limitation in Okorie's research is the anthropological starting point underlying Adlerian individual psychology. The main thesis of this anthropology is that every man fundamentally feels inferior and all behaviour of men can be traced back to this factor. All life is a struggle to deal with this basic inferiority by striving for superiority, which leads to the development of a particular lifestyle. The goal of life is therefore the perfection of the individual, but in the sense of dealing with his inferiority feelings[100].

This anthropology, which emphasises personal striving for superiority, cannot adequately assess the life of Catholic priests whose whole existence should be marked by a fundamental thrust to theocentric self-transcendence. The "transcendence" present in Adlerian psychology is transcendence of one's inferiority. The priesthood cannot be placed at par with other jobs or professions[101]. The lack of enthusiasm and the indifferent attitude which Igbo priests exhibit toward the ministry, may therefore not be properly understood using a theoretical framework that contradicts Christian anthropology in many ways. Surprised by the negative results of his research, Okorie sought out possible explanations including:

> The Catholic priesthood is generally believed to be a vocation for people who willingly seek to render selfless service to God and humanity. Therefore, satisfaction is

almost presumed because these men chose the priesthood as a religious vocation. They do not seek wealth or opportunities for promotion to higher positions, but to serve God and God's people[102].

Though he states the meaning of the Catholic priesthood in this citation, he explained the "selflessness" of the priests in terms of extrinsic satisfaction: Okorie thinks that they are more selfless *because* their satisfaction comes from the praise they get in serving the people.

This does not mean that there may not be stress in the life of Igbo priests or that they are all happy in their lives. Stress is possibly there. We rather mean to say that it is not yet demonstrated that lack of enthusiasm in ministry manifested in the life of Igbo priests can be accounted for by the presence of stress or dissatisfaction in ministry defined and measured within a theoretical framework that does not consider the anthropology of the priestly vocation.

Notwithstanding this limitation, the research reveals some important issues related to the characteristics of the Igbo man: the fact that he tends to lay excessive emphasis on work. He tends to exhibit driven behaviour which may be understood as a basic defence against feeling of inadequacy. All these seem to be related to the Igbo man's strong need for achievement and personal autonomy. The fact that extrinsic satisfaction is somehow relevant in this research again points out the Igbo man's search for social recognition of his achievements. Unfortunately, Okorie did not see these important points because though his research was actually on Igbo priests, he did not focus on their being Igbos.

The Research of Augustine T. Ukwuoma

Since J.B.C. Okorie's research could not explain the dissatisfaction and low morale observed among the Nigerian-Igbo priests he studied, A.T. Ukwuoma decided to fill in what was lacking in

Okorie's research[103]. He therefore hypothesized that "the social and cultural changes that have taken place in Nigeria in the past 30 years significantly affect the stress experienced by priests"[104]. The social and cultural changes to which stress among priests is attributed include: the loss of the power-base of priests consequent upon the government's take-over of schools and the increasing involvement of the laity in the administration of the church; the departure of the missionaries, so that the indigenous priests had to raise funds for the building of the church in an economy that never recovered from recession; the growth in church membership since the end of the Nigerian Civil War in 1970 and the increase in number of indigenous clergy which has created a generational friction between the few older priests and the many younger ones; a growing cultural self-confidence with the result that people now ask more questions than they did at the time of the missionaries[105]. These socio-cultural changes are supposed to be stressful to the priests. The high level of stress among Nigerian priests lead to a lowering of morale, frustration, and general dissatisfaction with their work[106]. The aim of the research is therefore "to examine the lives and ministry of Nigerian priests in order to identify the factors they perceive as stressful"[107].

Ukwuoma chose a qualitative method of researching this phenomenon. The sample was only 15 Nigerian priests. Each participant was interviewed using 4 more or less specific questions. From the interviews, he clustered the implied stressors into five domains. These include: the domain of Church Law and Structure, the domain of Priests and Parishioners, the domain of Socio-Cultural Changes, the domain of *Omenala*, and the domain of Friendly Fire.

Within the domain of Church Law and Structure, the participants perceive as core stressors the evangelical counsel of obedience, which is generally felt as blind and fearful; celibacy heightened by the people's sensitivity to priests' dealings with women; physical and emotional loneliness; rigidity, or what he calls "more-Roman-than-Rome" attitude of the Nigerian Church hierarchy that closes its eyes to the urgency of inculturating Christianity in the culture; and, finally, the abstract nature of seminary training that "is all Schillebeeckx and Rahner"[108] and which does not prepare young priests to face the practical issues of life outside the seminary.

The stressors perceived by the participants in the domain of Priests and Parishioners are[109]: the parishioners' expectation of the priest to be a "jack of all trades", that is, "to be good administrators, orators, miracle workers, building-contractors, good fundraisers"[110]; the "Fish Bowl Effect" that is, the feeling that the parishioners are always watching them: "whatever they did was virtually of public interest, there is no place to hide a mistake"[111]; thirdly, the workload is so great that some are not happy "that some parishioners think of them as having a vocation and not a job"[112]; they cannot plan their work on a day-to-day basis because "the nature of the priest's work is that he is on call 24 hours a day to be able to respond to parish emergencies"[113]; feelings of being torn between conflicting demands as "when they had to choose between following directives on certain issues and following their conscience"[114]; the burden of having to raise funds for building needed structures when the people had got used to getting things done for them freely by the missionaries, and because the economy is in bad shape most of the time; and finally, the constant feeling that they are responsible for the souls of the people entrusted to them, which, while true, may be taken in a false sense.

In the third domain, that is, the domain of socio-cultural changes[115], the first stressor mentioned by the participants is the diminished influence of priests in society and the fact that people do not believe priests as easily as in the past; the second is the growing insecurity among the priests in the wake of anti-clerical attacks on priests and the robbing of rectories; stress also comes from the difficulty in ministering to people who are greatly deprived; and lastly, the income of the Church decreases as the people get more impoverished. It becomes very difficult to maintain the rectory.

The fourth domain concerns the *Omenala*[116], that is, the customs of the people. The stressors emerging from this domain include first, the conflict of living in between two worlds, "being genuinely Christian and truly Nigerian"[117]; secondly, the stress that comes from the demands of the *Ikwu n'ibe* especially financial demands; and finally, priests experience stress in training their younger relatives who live with them in the rectories. These are usually called *ụmụ fada*. These boys need attention, psychological and material, from the priest.

The last domain is titled "Friendly Fire", "a military term referring to a soldier shooting at his own men or an ally"[118]. This domain concerns the stress emanating from priests' relationship with each other. These stressors include inter-generational frictions where the older priests caricature the younger ones as inexperienced. In retaliation, the younger priests refer to their older counterparts as stingy, self-centred and authoritarian. The third stressor comes from the politics of *ịzụ ahịa* among the priests during which gossip and slandering of each other before higher authorities are given free rein. A corollary of the fourth stressor is the unhealthy attitude developed by some priests by which they choose to criticise their fellow priests in public. Lastly, stress comes from the unhealthy competition existing between the priests.

Ukwuoma draws two general conclusions from these findings: first, that some of the stresses experienced by priests have their origin in the nature and circumstances of Catholic priesthood; and secondly, that the socio-cultural environment of Nigeria creates additional stress for the priests[119].

Observations on Ukwuoma's Research

Ukwuoma's study is relevant to the extent that it highlights the presence of stress in the life of the Nigerian-Igbo priests and the *sources* of this stress. He seems to have achieved the objective he set out to investigate, that is, identifying the factors that the priests perceive as stressful to them in their environment. These stressors are clustered in the five domains, as we saw earlier. The stress deriving from these external stressors is supposed to account for the low morale and diminished enthusiasm in the life of some priests.

It is revealing to see the different areas of life that trouble the priests in Nigeria, which they perceive as sources of stress for themselves. Some of the stressors are more general – like the hazards inherent in living the priestly vocation – while others are more specific to the Nigerian situation. Though the author presumes that his data apply to the whole of Nigeria, most of his interpretations seem to be based on the Igbo culture, although he does not mention which part of the country the participants come from. Moreover, the sample is small and the interpretation is vague because no attempt was made to give a precise estimate of the percentage of the participants under each of the domains treated.

Apart from this, the research does not fully respect the theoretical model of stress it adopts, namely, the Appraisal Model of stress developed by R.S. Lazarus. This model holds that stress is always an outcome of the interaction between personality-variables and the environment. In other words, to understand well the level of stress in a person, it is important to consider the personality-constellation of the individual in relation to the environmental stressors. To study only the environmental stressors and propose some changes in the environment implies that the individual is passively at the mercy of the environment. It is for this reason that the research presents a picture of Nigerian priests as men who are not in control of their lives; they are pulled from all angles: from the superiors/bishops to the parishioners, down to the impersonal events of the everyday living. It is as if the priests are pawns.

Underlying this research therefore is an anthropology which sees man as a puppet of the society; the society is to blame for the woes of the priests. This is in sympathy with the secular humanistic thought that man should be freed from society because it does not allow him freedom; the society oppresses him. This is both an unrealistic and dangerous anthropological view which, according to Robert Ardrey, has for many decades "induced us to believe that human fault must rest always on somebody else's shoulders; that responsibility for behaviour damaging to society must invariably be attributed to society itself; ..."[120]. It is an anthropology that contradicts the Christian view of man and his relationship in the world. Christian anthropology sees man as actively involved in his relationship with the world. This relationship is at the same time connected to the transcendent God who creates man and gives him charge over the earth. Man is not merely passive in society; he is also called to be active in the construction and reformation of society.

Observations on the Second Hypothesis

The second hypothesis, that there is a relationship between stress and dissatisfaction in ministry and low morale or diminished enthusiasm among Igbo priests, contains some truth. Though the research of Okorie could not prove this, the results of his in-depth interviews have been revealing. These results have received further confirmation in the research of Ukwuoma.

It is generally accepted that when one is too stressed, one can lose control of oneself and of the situation; one gets agitated and loses concentration. The experience of helplessness and incapacity to cope with many demanding tasks generally heightens one's anxiety-level. Heightened anxiety drains psychic energy. Prolonged experience of this nature can lower one's morale and enthusiasm to face the challenges of life. Accepting all this, one may ask: why is it that the so-called stressing situations can be perceived as too stressful by one person and as challenging by another? This is a relevant issue to be tackled in order to do justice to the nature and level of stress in the lives of Igbo priests.

Stress is part and parcel of human life; it can never be removed from the act of living. For this reason, Hans Selye, who was among the pioneer researchers in this area, distinguished two forms of stress: *distress* and *eustress*. Distress is negative and unhealthy while *eustress* is good and healthy. According to him, the difference lies in the way the person takes the stressful situation since under the same stressful condition *eustress* causes less damage to the person than distress[121]. James Gill remarks that *eustress* is the stress of winning and achievement while distress is the stress of losing, disappointment and desperation[122]. In *eustress*, one feels challenged and is determined to follow the challenge to the end. But in *distress*, the feelings of incapacity and helplessness already forecast doom and despair. The one missing question in both the conclusion of Seyle and Gill is: why is it that one person experiences *distress* and the other *eustress*? When Seyle says that it depends on "how you take it", the question remains: what is it that makes a person take it in a *distress*-like manner and the other in a *eustress*-like manner?

While it is evident that stress could lead to lowering of morale and diminished enthusiasm among the priests, it does not seem justified to argue only from the side of the stressors and leave out the personality-constellations which mediate the stressful situations and, as it were, determine *how* the person takes it: whether as *distress* or as *eustress*.

Third Hypothesis: Problems in Formation

The third and final hypothesis states that the formation in the seminaries does not prepare the seminarians well for their future lives as priests. It maintains that the model of formation is generally outmoded, pre-Vatican II, and too westernised. It does not succeed in forming convinced priests. Because of this, the seminarians after ordination feel like fish out of water and are incapable of dealing with the practical challenges of priestly ministry. Moreover, the number of the seminarians is very large; formation cannot be easy with such large numbers.

This hypothesis lacks documentation in the form of empirical research. However, it is a widely shared opinion and confirmed mainly by the problems which the priests exhibit after ordination. A.K. Obiefuna, the archbishop emeritus of Onitsha archdiocese, observed that:

> From external evidences there is a woeful manifestation of immaturity in our priests and this notwithstanding the long line of degrees after their names. This dichotomy between mere academic degrees and human maturity calls for urgent attention in our formation of priests in our seminaries[123].

Even the priests themselves often see themselves as lacking in adequate preparation; they experience themselves as "people who have been moulded to fit adequately by the 'ideal pattern' of the seminary text books, and retreat masters, but are incapable of properly serving their people in their integral needs. Some others confess to being estranged from the modern world, with a clericalist and sacristy mentality, and a ghetto world view"[124].

Considering that the embarrassing behaviours of some of the priests are so widespread, Okolo believes that the image of the priesthood which the seminarians have will not be different. He asks:

> ... plans for money and donations in kind such as anniversaries and launchings of kinds among the clergy, with newly-made monsignors, wittingly happy with almost interminable receptions, at times well schemed beforehand

by the clergy themselves and with newly consecrated bishops looking forward to reception rounds among their people in the diocese, etc., what sort of image of priesthood and priestly life do we expect our young seminarians to have or form?[125]

Since this hypothesis lacks empirical documentation, we shall rely on the writings of different authors in exposing its content. We shall approach it from three areas: the goal of formation, the method of formation, and the seminary environment

Goal of Formation

Those who hold this hypothesis maintain that often the goal of priestly formation is not always clear to those who form the future priests nor is the meaning of priestly vocation clear to the seminarians themselves. This is seen in the contradictory lives some priests live after their ordination. The proponents of this hypothesis believe that formation-houses seem to have been turned into places where members of the priestly bourgeois class are trained. Whether this is a conscious and systematic project of the formators or not, the image of the priest learned in these houses of formation appears to be that of one who is powerful and who belongs to an elite group in society[126]. This is a continuation of the clericalism inherited from the European missionaries. Being called from among men and inducted into the seminary that is secluded from the life of ordinary people gives a narcissistic feeling of being someone special, on the path to joining an elite group. With a sense of entitlement some consider themselves called to be priests "even when the human and spiritual gifts necessary for any authentic vocation to the priesthood are clearly absent"[127]. Nwatu reports how seminarians reflect this attitude of entitlement when they are sent on apostolic work in the parishes:

> There have been instances of seminarians coming to rural areas for the summer vacation apostolic work and giving the local Christians a run around for all kinds of conveniences. They come believing that it is their divine right to be served and waited on by the people, with all their *wants*, however profane or vain, provided with servile precision[128].

Thus, some seminarians and priests become irresponsible in their lifestyles and pastoral ministry: they live ostentatiously, amass wealth and spend it imprudently as a measure of success[129]; they exercise authority like despots and are removed from and insensitive to the concrete reality of their people[130]. The image of the Church created in the eyes of the people through the bourgeois lifestyle of priests is that of "affluence and of a rich Church with the personnel that lacks no material thing"[131].

In the face of the increasing affluence of the priests, Nwatu is afraid that "priestcraft" is getting into the African Church. In the African cultures, "priestcraft can be said to be reminiscent of the antics of local *juju-men* (*dibias* and *babalawos*) who capitalize on people's religious fervour, fears and temptations to accumulate inordinate wealth. If this is an acceptable type of inculturation, then the authorities in Rome have a justification for distrusting the inculturational initiatives of the African clergy"[132]. To illustrate this return of the priestcraft in the African Church, he cites two actual cases of a young priest and a seminarian:

> A young priest, three years into his first appointment after ordination, erected a magnificent bungalow with interior plumbing and conduit wiring; one of the best in his village at the time but telling the justifiably curious public that the house was financed by his brother. A seminarian was sent to Europe as a teen-ager to read theology in preparation for ordination. A few years later, as a man in mid-twenties and now a deacon he returned briefly to his home town and erected a storied house worth anywhere between fifty to one hundred thousand U.S. dollars[133].

It is therefore understandable that, carrying with them this image of the Church and of an elitist priesthood, some priests have lifestyles that are inconsistent with what people generally perceive to be the authentic meaning of priestly vocation. If they live like kings among peasants, they are only living out what they have learned so well. Some priests justify these arrogant lifestyles as compensations for the "sacrifices" they make in having no family or children of their own as celibates[134]. It would be inhuman, they reason, to deny them these things in addition to what they had denied themselves already. This is another side of that sense of entitlement which lies at the heart of the elitist image of the priesthood in vogue in some of our seminaries.

The Method of Formation

If the goal of formation is, perhaps subconsciously, to produce Church-elites, people of the upper class in society, it is not surprising that the method of formation should be heavily intellectualistic. Since knowledge is power, the formation of the mind of the seminarians takes precedence over the formation of the whole person. The quality of a student's intellect determines his place in the group. Education becomes a symbol of power and a means of dominating others.

> Education is reduced to an unhealthy competition, and also an instrument of domination. It becomes source of power. "Knowledge is power," says Francis Bacon. Everybody is busy struggling to acquire more, to get things under control. To become the president of Nigerian Association of Philosophy Students (NAPS), or the first auxiliary; to become the editor-in-chief of Torch, Fountain, Wisdom Searchlight; to be loved by the lecturers and the Bishops. These are diverse machineries and levels of control[135].

Often, the model of formation adopted is one which emphasizes the institutional and instructional, which believes in imparting exact and correct information about Christian values, but without adequate attention to the personalization or internalization of those values, because the emphasis is on the objective truth and not the total humanity of the subject who searches for and knows the truth[136]. It is taken for granted that a clear intellectual understanding of what it means to be the Church and to function as a priest is enough to make a good priest, thereby equating abundance of education and information with priestly maturity. Such a model does not prepare the candidates to meet with the novelties that will confront them concretely because "the facts, the observations, the multiple concrete circumstances must correspond to the frame of reference, must fit and find their explanation in it"[137]. And in the circumstances of the Igbo culture, an excessive emphasis on intellectual formation tends to distance the seminarians more and more from the people and from the realities of their life. This distancing is often interpreted by some as superiority over the people. Some seminarians think themselves more as academics than as pastors[138]. Thus, the seminary intellectual formation "has remained the gateway to power"[139].

The method of formation in some of these seminaries does not sufficiently aim at forming convinced priests. Conviction can only result when a person has consciously personalised or internalised the values of the priestly life[140]. But with the tacit and perhaps subconscious goal of forming special members of an elite group in both the Church and civil society, the emphasis is on acquiring more and more information and increasing one's intellectual armamentarium.

The Seminary Environment

Within this framework, the seminary is perceived by some seminarians as a privileged place to be striven for. The seminarians who perceive the seminary this way tend to use all strategies necessary to remain and to persevere to the end.

> A good number of students are hypocritical in their behaviours. They do not have the true concept of vocation. They want to be priests at all costs and so they must hide their identity lest they be discovered. They show their true colours after their ordination[141].

In some of the seminaries, some of the formators give the impression of being demigods in whose hands rests the destiny of the seminarians. The very large number of seminarians makes the matter worse: it heightens the competition to reach the end. Thus, fear of expulsion reduces some of the seminarians to unhealthy dependency and conformism[142]. The game of hide-and-seek is creatively devised and played out skilfully. The primary preoccupation for some is to reach ordination and not to construct a meaningful life based on one's convictions. Overall, it would seem the seminarians are well-taken care of so that they are sheltered from the scourge of hunger and the insecurity that has become the normal experiences of ordinary Nigerians[143]. But in return for this, some of the seminarians, especially those who invest everything they have and are in reaching ordination, feel they are entitled to special treatment.

On the other hand, having lived in conformism for the long period of seminary formation, some priests after ordination can and do feel like birds liberated from a cage. Now, no one can question what they do and no one may police them. Some wake up after ordination filled with previously repressed anger at those moments when they felt they suffered intimidation and suppression in the seminary. They can become unruly as a way of retaliating for what they have gone through at the hands of the seminary and diocesan authorities. Some carry grudges against some formators whom they believed had it in for them during the formation period.

Observations on the Third Hypothesis

The third hypothesis seems to offer a clearer diagnosis of the situation. First, it presents the heart of the problem: the interaction between the seminary-formation and the seminarian. For some seminarians, to be a priest is to move upward in the social ladder, and the formation they receive in the seminary may subconsciously reinforce this belief. The desire "to arrive" rather than to construct a meaningful life as a priest who works for God and for the people, becomes a primary motivation. If this is so, self-knowledge and internalisation of priestly identity are not important.

Secondly, the formation still suffers problem of adaptability to the reality of the Igbo person which the seminarian is: it is still heavily intellectualistic such that even some seminarians believe that the more mystifying the jargon one speaks, the more an elitist aura surrounds the one; not to be intelligible can be taken as a virtue. Thirdly, formation programs are sometimes devised without proper study and identification of the concerns, needs, and expectations of the seminarians. The effect then is that it may not be clear what the programs set out to address in the seminarians. Most of the time there are no basic assessment tools to evaluate how well the programs have really functioned.

Fourthly, some programs may be introduced without adequate provision for their lasting impact. For example, the Spiritual Year program was introduced in the dioceses to give the seminarians more spiritual and human formation before they go to the major seminary for their philosophical and theological studies. But there is no provision made in the major seminaries for the continual nurturing and monitoring of the growth experienced during the spiritual year. To the best of my knowledge, it does not seem that the record of growth seminarians made during their spiritual year is transferred to the major seminaries they are posted. The major seminary is still impersonal with an incredibly large number of seminarians. The values presented in the major seminaries could contradict the ones seminarians had learned in the spiritual year. In addition to this, the spiritual year seminaries in the various dioceses follow different programs. Since these seminarians eventually meet in one major seminary, it is difficult to establish continuity with what they had learned in the spiritual year. Some dioceses do not even have spiritual year seminary. It is not clear which program they run. This hazy and uncoordinated situation leaves the seminarians with the impression that the spiritual year is just a strategy to trim their numbers and delay them. With this disposition, the spiritual year program could fail to achieve its objective and become just an obligatory step towards the major seminary.

On the whole, formation in our seminaries still remains more monastic than apostolic. It is still a hangover from the legacies of the missionaries. Few changes have taken place but these are often spasmodic and not really coordinated within the whole formation system. We postpone the discussion on this topic to the third part of this study. Let us briefly look at the diocesan and religious priests and seminarians in Igboland.

Diocesan and Religious Priests in Igboland

Although the priesthood is one, it has two primary forms, namely, the diocesan and the religious. The religious is further divided into the monastic and the apostolic[144]. In this section, we intend to examine the place of the religious priests and seminarians in Igboland and bring out the differences between them both in their structures and in the people's perception of them, and the specific difficulties they have.

Religious and Diocesan Priests: Structural Differences

The priesthood of the diocesan priest and that of the religious are exercised differently. A diocesan priest is primarily a pastor or a parish priest, and he exercises his priesthood mostly through "a ministry of word, sacrament, and pastoral leadership within a local church community, whether on the parish or the diocesan level"[145]. Monastic religious priesthood is exercised in the monastery under the jurisdiction of an abbot and "is focused on the *opus Dei* or liturgy"[146]. According to Rausch, the priesthood of apostolic religious priests is mainly prophetic. That means it is a priesthood "focused on preaching and evangelization"[147]; it is a kerygmatic priesthood[148]. Their ministries originate from and are directed to respond to needs that transcend local boundaries and jurisdictions. This therefore required them to move about "like the apostles"[149]. Mobility is their basic characteristic. Thus, "what distinguishes a priest exercising a prophetic priesthood from one whose ministry is focused on the leadership of a stable local community is availability for mission"[150].

The majority of Igbo religious priests belong to the apostolic religious orders, the foremost of which are the Holy Ghost Fathers or the Spiritans, the Vincentians, Claretians, the Missionaries of St. Paul, the Sons of Mary Mother of Mercy, to mention but a few. Their vow of poverty is presumed visible in the fact that they are required to hand over whatever gifts they receive to their community. Their apostolic orientation also prepares them to be disposed to be transferred elsewhere at any time. With such a possibility, it will be difficult for them, in principle, to engage in the so-called "empire-building".

Formation in religious life maintains a continuity which seems greater than that of the diocesan priests. They move from postulancy through novitiate, to temporary vows, apostolic experiences, perpetual vows, and ordination. Initiated into community life at the very beginning, they are offered the opportunity to experience it at each stage of their formation, and this continues for their whole lives. The formation of the diocesan priest, on the other hand, lacks this continuity. For instance, there is very little continuity between the programs run in the diocesan spiritual year seminaries and in the major seminaries. Secondly, there is a sharp dichotomy between the structured common life of the seminary and the unstructured pastoral life of the diocesan priest; and who knows how many diocesan priests are able to manage well the kind of freedom they have after ordination?

Because of the presence of the diocesan priests everywhere in Igboland, easily distinguished from seminarians and religious priests by their caped white cassock, the religious are somehow less visible. Empirical research about them is not available; at least, the present author does not know of any. In comparison to the diocesan priests and seminarians, their number is very small.

And it is because of the imposing presence of the diocesan priests in Igboland that I.M. Onyeocha, himself a religious, writes that the religious priests are experiencing a conflict of identity. The issue is this: the diocesan priests have cape with their cassocks to distinguish them from seminarians; the religious do not. This makes some religious feel like second-class priests. To resolve this problem of status,

> ... some have resorted to overdressing with cassocks, sashes and pectoral crosses solemnly combined to match. It is not exactly clear whether that has completely solved the problem of status or whether it has created its own problem

of trying to be like little bishops apart from their red buttons[151].

Apart from this, Igbo religious priests and seminarians also have difficulty in following the evangelical counsels, especially poverty and obedience. For example, their way of life requires that they hand over gifts received to the community, as well as share things in common. But though the relatives contributed to training them, and sometimes still support them even after their final profession and ordination, their vow of poverty prevents them from rendering financial assistance to their families. Thus, M.C. Onyejekwe admits that when it comes to this point, the vow of poverty pinches the religious "very intimately"[152]. There are those among their ranks who have refused to be pinched and have started to "live in luxury and exuberance, so interested in flashy and costly materials"[153]. Others may choose to establish profitable connections outside their communities, and through those connections, set up some projects in their families.

Since Igbo people love their autonomy, and tend to be republicans in political organisation, "the radical practice of religious obedience in the traditional mentality presents a problem and is highly resented"[154]. Paradoxically, Onyeocha observes that among the religious themselves, the exercise of authority can become an obsession. At every point, the person in charge "must be seen to be in charge by taking on everything and running the whole show like his own private estate. Anything less would take the face of insubordination and can lead to problems for the offender"[155].

There are structural differences between the Igbo religious and diocesan priests and seminarians. At the same time, there are some similarities in the nature of their difficulties. For instance, as Igbo people, both the religious and diocesan priests and seminarians love their independence. But when they are given authority, they tend to be highhanded in exercising it. This can be testified from the parishes to the religious houses of both men and women. It is a paradox that calls for a deeper understanding.

Popular Perception of Religious and Diocesan Priests

There is a general impression among the Igbo laity that the religious priests are more serious in their priestly vocation than the diocesan priests; that is why, some claim, many young men prefer to get into diocesan priesthood where it appears that things are more lax and boundaries are blurred. Religious priests, exemplified by the Holy Ghost Fathers[156], are regarded as "real priests" while the diocesan priests are often seen as "family priests" since they are usually presumed to be free to render financial assistance to their family and relatives. Thus, some parents dissuade their children from becoming religious priests, and some even persuade the religious brothers or priests to transfer to the dioceses since diocesan priests, seen as "family priests", have the opportunity to care for the needs of their family members, unlike the religious priests[157].

Because of the large number of the diocesan priests in Igboland, the presence of the religious priests is not felt much. In fact, they are not many, and so have limited contact with the people, often within a school environment. Out of the 137 parishes in the Awka diocese, for instance, only 1 is being managed by religious priests, the Holy Ghost Fathers. Nsukka and Enugu dioceses have more presence of the religious priests and brothers. However, religious women are more visible because they are found in many hospitals, motherless babies' homes, and in certain Catholic schools, for example. Religious priests are more present in those parts of Nigeria where there are not many diocesan priests or they are on mission in other parts of the world.

That notwithstanding, the people generally see religious priests as more authentic, and they are perceived as more detached than the diocesan priests because they are not, in principle, required to have things of their own. Right from the day of their ordination, people realise that they are different because the members of their religious congregation receive the money and other gifts given to them. This, in principle, should dispose their family members to expect little from them in terms of financial help. Secondly, the people see them as "real priests" because they do not live in the place where they grew up; they are often sent to distant places for mission, which concretely presents them as having truly left their families for a religious cause. Some return home with almost nothing when compared with any diocesan priest from the same town or village. Thirdly, the religious priests do not often have territories where, as individuals, they are in charge, so that their relatives can come and visit or even stay. Their community lifestyle demands that there be more than one person, wherever they are. They are therefore perceived by the people as priests who have really given something up for the sake of God, especially their freedom and independence. Some lay persons are inclined to exonerate religious priests from the embarrassing behaviours found among priests. Sometimes, if a diocesan priest is devoted or spiritual, people who do not know him often ask whether he is a religious priest; even those who know him might say that he behaves more like a religious priest than as a diocesan.

The impression that the religious priests are more authentic than the diocesan priests is not limited to the Igbo people; it is widespread. It used to be, and perhaps it is still, the feeling that the diocesan priest, heavily immersed in the world, is more like the rest of men "in the world" and closer to the profane, while the religious, by his religious consecration, has left the world and taken God more seriously. Because of his immersion in a busy ministry, the diocesan priest was considered to be with little or no spiritual life[158]. To leave the diocesan priesthood and join a clerical congregation or monastic life, was encouraged because it indicated "a spiritual step up in the line of perfection"[159]. In the meantime, the word "secular", used to describe the diocesan priest's immersion in the lives of the faithful, sometimes is understood in a pejorative sense of being "worldly" and "lax" about priestly values. Some people appeal also to the principle that diocesan priests make mere promises to their bishops but the religious take vows. This subtle distinction could give the impression that the commitment of the diocesan priest is less binding than that of the religious. Some people actually understand it this way and so believe that the diocesan priest is "more free" than the religious; freedom not in the sense of vocational maturity, but in the sense of being free to do what he wants.

These are the impressions which have endured through the centuries and decades. Ultimately, they indicate that the formation of the religious priest is more effective than that of the diocesan priests. While there is no need to fight over whether the religious priest is better than the diocesan priest, it is necessary to verify this out, find out how they are better and why they are so. This will offer us a more valid ground to understand the formation of the diocesan seminarians in order to provide them the kind of formation that will help them be happy priests in the future with the desire to serve God's people entrusted to their care.

Summary

We have presented the views of various authors about the shadows of Igbo priest. We also presented the differences between diocesan and religious priests and the perception people have about them. The important conclusion from this chapter is that the formation of priests, religious and diocesan, makes a significant difference in their lives. Formation involves selection, discernment, and training of the candidates. In the next chapter, we shall carry out an empirical verification of seminarians' expectation of the priesthood. The reason for this is that if the formation they receive has been effective, it would be able to modify their expectations of the priesthood, making them more realistic and mature. The implication is that most of the incongruous lifestyles of priests today derive from their expectations of the priesthood which were either not discerned properly or not touched during the time of their initial formation.

III

What are Igbo Seminarians Looking for in the Priesthood?

Life, Expectations, and the Priesthood

Life is full of expectations, and we all have abundance of them about almost everything. A child growing up has certain expectations of his or her adulthood. When one finishes secondary school and is about to enter the university, he or she nurtures certain expectations of what the university promises. Those who are engaged or are getting married fantasise about their future family: the home, the children, the marital life, and so on. Those in relationship expect certain things or attitudes from their friends. These expectations are so powerful that the joys and dangers of future lives may have their root in the nature of expectations people might have had about a particular reality or event.

A young man training to become a priest has certain expectations of the priesthood, and these expectations constitute his ideals. Now, every seminarian has his ideals of the priesthood. But it is possible that those ideals may or may not reflect the reality of the priesthood. When a seminarian's ideals reflect the truth of the priesthood, they are said to be mature, otherwise they are immature. Psychologically, whether a seminarian's ideals of the priesthood are mature or immature may be inferred from how they are represented in his cognitive-motivational system.

Human behaviour takes place in time[1]. This means that the three dimensions of time – the past, the present and the future – co-determine human behaviour[2]. But this chapter is concerned with what and how the seminarians *expect* their future life as priests to be. Expectations imply desires and hopes and both terms have their place in the future[3]. Therefore, the relevant time-perspective involved is that of the future.

Time-perspective "consists of mentally represented *objects* localised in different time periods"[4]; it is the totality of the individual's understanding of his psychological future and his psychological past existing at any given time. While past time-perspective concerns objects that belong to the field of memory, future time-perspective has to do with set goals as well as means-end structures of human behaviour[5]. Ideals as the goals which the individual strives to realize, are localised in the psychological future. Each person has some ideals towards which he or she lives. These ideals represent what the person *should be* and not what he or she is, and as such, they are goals towards which one strives[6].

To live a life of self-giving in love of God and service of humanity, is the goal of Christian life and especially of priestly life and ministry. This goal, the *telos*, is constituted by the values of the priesthood. As the ideal toward which the individual seminarian in formation looks up to, it is temporally localised in the future as the kind of priest he *wants to be*; it is the future towards which the seminarian is going. It is therefore important to find out what a seminarian *really* looks for in the priesthood.

Future Expectations affect the Present

Ideals or goals to be realized are cognitively localised in the future. The seminarian envisions the kind of priest he wants to be and sets that as his goal. It constitutes his ideal self which exercises its power in his motivational system through the hopes that underlie it. These hopes, present in the ideals, lie in the future but exercise influence on the present: they determine the plans to make and also how to manage both the time and the resources available[7]. J. Batten emphatically notes that, "all constructive and healthy plans, actions, and accomplishments are fuelled by hope. It is the central elixir of life itself"[8]. But expectation is the stuff of which hope is made: "We can only express, target, and pursue hope through and by expectations"[9]. For this fundamental reason, the manner of anticipating one's future, i.e., the way a person expects his future "overarches and orders every experience and behaviour"[10]. The future dimension of a person's life is so important that when it is blocked, either as absence of possibilities, or as repeated experience of failure to arrive at a meaningful goal, the individual experiences distress and a kind of disorientation[11].

Every action in the *now* seeks its direction from the anticipated future. Actions of the present are goal-oriented. Thus, B.M. Dolphin observes that, "we live out our lives in the present, both as individuals and in our relationships with others, in the light of a variety of ends or goals towards which we are moving or failing to move at this particular moment in time"[12]. Thomas Merton emphasises that each person's life is shaped by the end he lives for, and that we are made in the image of what we desire[13]. J. Nuttin notes that every human behaviour is *integral*, incorporating the overt behaviours of the present *and* the cognitive-motivational aspect, which inhabits the goal or meaning the individual is trying to accomplish[14]. As the *fundamental stance* of the person, the *telos* toward which the person strives, the ideals give direction and meaning to the person's actions in the present[15]. Thus, the ideal self, as that which the individual wants to become, gives the reason for enduring specific renunciations for the sake of realising the ideal[16].

From a humanistic perspective, K.M. Sheldon and T. Kasser express the impact of the future on the present in a different manner in their distinction between higher-level and lower-level goals. A higher-level goal refers to the dominant or central goal which the person aims at achieving or becoming in the future by engaging himself in some specific activities at the lower level. The lower level-activities are means or instruments for the realisation of the higher-level goal. Thus, these authors speak of vertical and horizontal coherence: the activities which a person performs in the present (horizontal activities), receive their impetus and modulation from the higher-level goal (vertical) the person strives for[17]. In other words, the vertical operation, which is the ideal or goal the person aims at, to a reasonable degree determines the choices and decisions carried out in the present (horizontal operation): "Strivings are midlevel goals that represent what people are characteristically trying to do in their everyday behaviour. In contrast, possible selves are higher level goals that represent what people hope to become (or avoid becoming) in the future"[18]. Coherence between vertical and horizontal operations yields psychological dividends in the increased sense of commitment to the chosen ideal.

Psychologists who follow the expectancy-value models show that there is a close link between the future expectations of persons and their actions in specific situations[19]. This link specifically concerns anticipated positive or negative outcomes consequent upon a particular course of action. Anticipated outcomes are commonly generated from the underlying general motives and values of the person. The contents of a concrete situation are linked to the affective system through the dominant motives and values of a person. When this happens, anticipated positive and negative affects are aroused within a means-end structure. The affects become the motivational base for the particular action that is taken[20]. This is the reason why future expectations and the valences attributed to them "combine multiplicatively to determine the strength of a person's tendency to approach a goal"[21].

In many psychological works that treat of the impact of future expectations on the present, the nature of the goal or value striven for is often overlooked. Their concern is mostly with the structural processes that link expectations to the particular actions or activities[22]. For example, K. M. Sheldon and T. Kasser view the impact of the future goal on the present actions, and the congruence between the two, in terms of the organismic needs of the individual. Goal-systems are congruent "when goals feel genuinely chosen and are expressive of intrinsically satisfying values such as growth, intimacy and community"[23]. In essence, a goal-system is congruent if the goals are consistent and congruent with the inherent needs and growth tendencies of the individual[24]. This orientation also determines the scales they used in assessing the psychological health that should result when there is congruence in a goal-system[25]. Goals chosen and pursued for organismic needs become intrinsic goals and those chosen and pursued for merely external rewards and praise are considered extrinsic[26]. That is the reason why, in their example of the person whose goal is "to become famous",[27] these authors do not see the need to raise fundamental questions like: in what does being famous consist? And depending on the answer, a further question arises: is "being famous" all there is in life?

In another article, K. M. Sheldon and A. J. Elliot acknowledge that "a complete model of optimal goal functioning will need to address not only the why of striving, but also the *what* of striving"[28]. The "what of striving" refers to the content of the goal. But all they mean is whether what the person is striving for is intrinsic or extrinsically satisfying to him. Personal satisfaction determines the validity of a goal. Thus, one can choose to be famous as a criminal if this is intrinsically satisfying to him. The specific strivings in the present would then include, for instance, learning different forms of manipulation or studying gang life and activities. The individual is the sole determinant of the validity of what he should pursue as short or long-term goals.

This approach is intended to ensure value-free orientation in psychological research. But it is not a realistic position, because every psychological theory has its underlying philosophical assumptions about the ultimate goals of human life, moral codes, and practical implications[29]. These assumptions may be explicit or implicit.

Underlying the values of priestly vocation is the Christian view of the ultimate goal of human life. The Christian response reveals a wider horizon of goods to pursue and, more importantly, it "logically becomes the context in which other values take their place"[30]. Studying the impact of the future expectations of life as priests on the present actions of the seminarians therefore goes beyond statements on how the priesthood is subjectively satisfying to the seminarians; it includes whether *what* the seminarian expects and is striving for is valid for a Catholic priest, present or future.

Lived Life and Future Expectations

By "lived life" we do not mean simply "past life". It means the life the person lives which includes his past and present. It refers to a person's general psychological maturity which is expressed in his psychodynamics. In the Christian vocation, "lived life" means how the person is currently living his life as a Christian, whether he is guided by Christian values or not. Thus, it is important to know whether there is a relationship between the lived life of the seminarian, i.e., his existential maturity, and the expectations he may have of his future as a priest. If a positive relationship exists between them, then the type of expectations a seminarian may have of the priesthood could reflect, to a reasonably high degree, the way he lives or shall live as a priest.

It was noted above that human behaviour is integral and that the actions of the present derive their orientation from the goal. The future goal does not actually exist in the present; it is mentally present to the individual in a representational way. The perception of the goal and the expectations of it are predicated upon the psychological patterns he had already developed in the past as a unique individual[31]. In other words, the nature of a person's future expectations bears the mark of his personality. W. Lens observes that this positive correlation between the individual's personality variables and his future expectations is overlooked in many theories that study the functional relationship between cognitive variables (expectancy, instrumentality) and the affective ones (valences, incentive values)[32]. It is to be expected that a seminarian's expectations of the priesthood would positively correlate with the way he concretely lives the values of priestly vocation because his life reveals his personality.

Empirical research confirms that there is a positive relationship between the life an individual lives or his psychological maturity and the expectations he has regarding any goal he sets for himself. Psychological maturity stresses the degree of the person's development: it indicates a person's degree of impulse control, moral development, nature of interpersonal relationships, and cognitive preoccupations[33].

L.M. Rulla and his colleagues adopted this conceptualisation in their research on Christian vocationers. From this conceptualisation, they developed the *Index of Developmental Maturity* (IDM), which they used to assess the degree of the vocationers' developmental maturity before entering Christian vocation. This index "expresses the degrees of compliance, identification, and internalisation of an entering vocationer as they can be inferred by his capacity to handle, to control his major conflicts"[34]. They also developed the *Index of Vocational Maturity* (IVM), which expresses "the degrees of compliance, identification, and internalisation which an individual has at the moment in which he actually enters a vocational setting"[35]. The IVM index assesses the amount of consistencies and inconsistencies at the entrance into a vocation.

The total number of Christian vocationers was 91 and they included religious males and females and seminarians. The statistical analysis shows a phi-coefficient validity of .6304, P <.0001[36]. This study concludes that the degree of developmental maturity of the individual vocationer positively correlates with his vocational maturity. Which means that the level of developmental maturity, the general psychological maturity of the individual, clearly affects the maturity and immaturity of his ideal self[37].

In a similar research, the authors assessed the existential maturity of 103 Christian vocationers after four years of formation. Existential maturity refers to the subject's maturity in *concretely* living the values of the Christian vocation. It was assessed by a depth-interview carried out on each subject and the result of his *IDM*. This study found a high degree of correspondence existing between the potentiality of growth in the individual at entry into the vocation and the degree of maturity attained after four years of formation[38]. In other words, those subjects who were psychologically more mature upon entry into the vocation tended to live the vocation better because they had a potentiality to assimilate the values of the Christian vocation. On the other hand, those who were psychologically immature lived the values of Christian vocation in a lesser degree.

In light of the present study, these results show that the level of developmental maturity relates to the way the individual perceives his vocation, and to his choice of it. In other words, the way a person perceives his future life-goal as a priest should positively correlate with the degree of his psychological maturity. The more he is psychologically mature, the more he will tend to have an objective and free ideal self, and the contrary is the case if he were psychologically immature. The results of the second research show that this trend is reliably stable even after four years of formation such that those who have mature ideal self live better than the way those who have immature ideal self live.

When the two researches of L.M. Rulla and his colleagues are combined, one readily sees that the way a person perceives the ideals of the priesthood correlates positively with the way he lives these ideals: if his ideal self is objective and free, then there is high probability that the seminarian will live a better life as a priest with less inconsistencies; if his ideal self is immature, then it is highly likely that he will live immaturely with lots of inconsistencies.

This hypothesis was proved in another research undertaken by C. O'Dwyer on the imagined future of Christian vocationers. The result of this research shows that "the mature not only live better; they also write much fuller stories when they imagine the future; the immature live less well and are more constricted in imagining the future"[39]. In other words, the existentially mature tend to imagine their future more completely and more realistically, while the immature tend to look at their future in a way that does not reflect the true nature of the values of the Christian vocation.

These researches sufficiently prove that there is a relationship between the life the individual lives and the expectations he has of his future ideals. In the following sections, we shall present the method and the findings of the empirical investigation of the nature of the expectations Igbo seminarians have of the priesthood.

Research Method and Results

Basic Assumptions of the Research

The present study assumes that the difficulties and incongruities in the life of Igbo priests could be indicating that their self-ideals as Catholic priests are in some way lacking in maturity. This means that the values of the Catholic priesthood have not been received well enough in their motivational system so as to become the dominating influence on their concrete choices and actions. If the values of the priesthood do not occupy a central place in the motivational system of a priest, it is likely that other motives would dominantly influence his daily choices and decision so that a style of life he may have adopted, consciously or unconsciously, may be in opposition to the priestly life he has chosen.

But whether the values of the priesthood are well received in the motivational system of an ordained priest is dependent on his expectations of the priesthood as a seminarian, and these expectations are mostly influenced by his personality and how the values of the priesthood are presented by the formators in the seminary and other priests whom the seminarians meet during the time of their apostolic work experiences or during holidays. However, it is the personality of the seminarian that plays a decisive part in deciding which values to be attended to and those to be left out in his value-system.

Thus, it is obvious that the more or less discrepancy between the seminarians' expectations of their future life as priests and the values of the Catholic priesthood will be reflected in their concrete life. Consistency in living priestly life is more to be expected when there is greater agreement between seminarians' expectations of their future life as priests and the values of the priesthood. Expectations about one's future usually are connected with the structure of a person's personality[40].

Strategy and Hypotheses of the Research

We stated earlier that it is often taken for granted that religious priests are more authentic in their lives as priests than the diocesan priests. This belief implies that the self-ideals of the religious priests might be more authentic, that is more mature, than those of the diocesan priests. In other words, the values of the priestly vocation might be clearer to the religious priests than to the diocesan priests not just intellectually, but that they have been appropriated more in their psychological system. Stretched further, it implies that the way the religious train their priests is more effective than the way diocesan priests are formed. That is to say that the diocesan priests are less mature in their vocational ideals than the religious priests. Is this mere impression or an empirical fact?

To get to the heart of these problems, it is necessary to obtain information regarding the self-ideals of the Igbo religious and diocesan seminarians in as direct a way as possible, and compare them. When comparisons are made, the two groups serve as "controls" for each other, within the same culture.

This strategy is useful for two reasons: first, it investigates the effectiveness of the formation-methods used in training the Igbo diocesan and religious seminarians. Different religious congregations apply different formation-methods which makes it hard to generalise about them. This should not constitute a problem because the effect of any kind of formation should appear in the nature of the self-ideals of the seminarians, whether religious or diocesan. Secondly, this strategy may help to reveal the nature and extent of the influences deriving from the Igbo culture and society.

This study is essentially exploratory. Two hypotheses have been proposed; they are non-directional and are framed as questions.

i.   Are the self-ideals of Igbo Catholic religious seminarians more valid than those of the Igbo Catholic diocesan seminarians?

ii.   Could there be a specific way vocational maturity and immaturity express themselves among Igbo Catholic seminarians?

Research Approach

A projective approach has been chosen to explore the two hypotheses. This approach is deemed promising for certain reasons. First, previous researches done on Nigerian or Igbo priests have usually used questionnaires or objective psychological tests[41]. This method has the advantage of gathering data in a standardized manner and may be administered in many ways[42]. But the disadvantage it has in psychological studies is that "information such as underlying motivations may not be obtained"[43]. Moreover, objective instruments "may miss many character traits that may be real limitations"[44] of the person.

The disadvantage of relying wholly on objective methods in psychological research is that supplied-response formats are usually answered by "yes/no" or some similar response. These responses offer little insight into why the subject responds the way he does[45]. And even if the subject provides reasons for his or her response, it should not be taken for granted that the person's justification exactly and completely explains it. The reason for this apparent scepticism about human behaviour is that "on the one hand, individuals can be victims of unconscious constraints (the affective unconscious) and, on the other hand, their own reasons do not always permit them to become aware of the deeper reasons for their own intentions (the cognitive unconscious)"[46].

In general, projective methods of research are based on the hypothesis that "manifestations of the human being's behaviour, from the least to the most significant ones, are revealing of his personality – that is, the individual principle of which he is the carrier"[47]. When he or she actively and spontaneously structures an unstructured material, the individual reveals his or her structuring principles "which are the principles of his psychological structure"[48]. According to Murray, the power of a projective test is due to two tendencies in people, namely, the tendency "to interpret an ambiguous human situation in conformity with their past experiences and present wants, and the tendency of those who write stories to do likewise: draw on the fund of their experiences and express their sentiments and needs, whether conscious or unconscious"[49]. Even in those situations in which a person 'decides' to write stories which would seem obvious to him, "they are nevertheless highly personal products and correspondingly revealing of his needs"[50].

A faithful use of a standardized projective test, therefore, can provide information about a person "which, in the terminology of contemporary psychology, would probably be called *personality traits, habits,* or *styles*"[51]. It reveals the general principles a person usually employs in structuring events, which derive from his or her personality-structure[52]. The use of projective instruments in seminary formation does not only bring out what is uniquely of the individual, his fundamental structures, psychic themes, weaknesses and strengths, but it also highlights those features of the individual that "preclude both the ability and availability for a meaningful, successful formation"[53]. This is the kind of information anyone who forms seminarians would like to have, but which, most of the time, eludes the researcher who uses only non-projective methods.

This study seeks information about the self-ideals of Igbo seminarians. To obtain such information, a projective method is deemed suitable because it offers the individual seminarian free rein to present his ideal future from *within*, that is, from the configuration of his motivational system including the conscious and the subconscious aspects[54].

Instrument and the Variables Measured

The present research uses a single instrument which investigates the expectations of the Igbo diocesan and religious seminarians about their future life as priests. The instrument, developed by C. O'Dwyer in 2000, is very simple but has been shown to have a great power in revealing maturity and immaturity in Christian vocationers. The instrument can assess the nature of the ideal future of the seminarians as an expression of the degree of their maturity in living the Christian values of the priestly vocation. It is both valid and reliable[55]: the validity is shown by the fact that it really measures what it sets out to study, which is the maturity of the ideal future of Christian vocationers as correlated with their existential maturity. Test-retest stability of each variable, combination of single variables, and the total number of positive and negative points was also carried out at a one-month interval, and the agreements were very high[56]. This degree of its test-retest stability demonstrates its reliability. In addition to the potency, validity, and reliability of the instrument, the variables it measures have been variously confirmed to be relevant to the self-transcendent ideals of the priestly and religious vocations[57].

The narrative nature of the instrument is another reason why it is appropriate for this research. Every narrative is linked to the context in which the narrator lives and acts. This makes his narration intelligible, because his story reflects the story of the community in which he lives and from which he acquired his personal identity[58].

The fundamental anthropological context of this instrument is that of the Christian vocation[59]. As a projective instrument in narrative form, it is also capable of saying something about how this fundamental Christian anthropological context interacts with specific cultural contexts[60]. This is important for a research on Igbo seminarians who live simultaneously in two contexts: Igbo and Christian. Their stories will in some way express their Igbo identity as well as their Christian identity, and the way maturity and immaturity may express themselves in their ideal future. Therefore, it is understandable how the instrument can be transcultural and useful in delineating areas of strength and vulnerability of Christian vocationers from different cultural backgrounds. Such information is necessary for the inculturation of Christian formation.

The stimulus of the test consists of the instructions asking the subjects to write the story of their future as they would imagine it to be from today until the end[61]. The variables measured by the instrument are fifteen and are grouped into two, namely the Experience-of-Discipleship Variables: Promotion, Abasement, Piety, Power, Security; and Cost-of-Discipleship Variables: Aggression, Chastity, Harm Avoidance, Humility, Obedience, Place, Poverty, Responsibility, Self-Discipline, Succorance[62]. This grouping was based on the insight of B.M. Dolphin that some of the variables reflect the *rewarding* or attractive aspects of the Christian life while others are related more to the *sacrificial* or demanding aspects. The former are five in number, and are called experience-of-discipleship variables, while the remaining ten belong to the latter, and are called cost-of-discipleship variables[63]. The 15 variables were recorded and scored as by O'Dwyer and then recorded on a scoring sheet according to the scoring rules[64].

The Research Design

This research work is a comparative study of two groups of Igbo Catholic seminarians: the diocesan and the religious. It seeks to compare the two groups as to the validity of their self-ideals according to their scores on the stories of their imagined future vocational life as priests. The two Igbo groups shall also be compared with an international group, which consists of the male group in the research of O'Dwyer.

The research design is, therefore, extensive because it seeks to gather information about the characteristics that are common to a group of persons, and not about individuals[65]. It is otherwise known as the nomothetic approach in research[66].

In this research, it is assumed that the existential maturity of the Igbo Catholic diocesan and religious seminarians finds expression in their expectations of life as future priests, revealed in the stories of their ideal future. The independent variable is the group to which they belong and the dependent variable is their scores on the variables of the story of the imagined future or of combinations of these variables.

To obtain a high degree of objectivity and accuracy in this research, it was necessary to "minimize uncertainties, ambiguities, or interferences affecting the relationships between the variables"[67]. For this reason, the control of variables was rigorously carried out in the following manner:

i)   Selection bias was controlled by making sure that all participants agreed to take part in the study. The rectors of the concerned seminaries and houses of formation were personally met and their permission obtained to speak to the students before distributing the sheets containing the instructions. A total of 500 sheets and a personal letter of invitation to participate in the study were sent out and 223 were returned, from which 88 were discarded because they were not scorable[68]. The remaining 135 protocols were used in the actual analysis.

ii)   Control of the variables was also carried out in relation to the instrument by making sure that all the participants were given the same "instructions" for writing the story of the imagined future.

iii) All aspects of the research were scored "blind" in order to control rater-bias. The returned protocols were collected from the seminaries and religious houses by an independent person, and given codes by the same person. They were then mixed up and given to the researcher who scored them. After scoring them, he handed them over to the independent person who knew, according to the code he devised, which protocol belonged to which group. The scores for the subjects in the international group were the original scores used by O'Dwyer in her research. They were made available to me by the appropriate authority of the Institute of Psychology, Gregorian University, Rome.

iv) Research among seminarians might generate anxiety because of the fear that the results could be used to decide about their vocation. To control that, each participant was assured of absolute confidentiality throughout the research. This was stated in the personal letter written to each of them and was also verbally emphasized to them when I spoke to them before distributing the "instructions". In some of the seminaries and formation houses for the religious seminarians, the rectors spoke to the seminarians assuring them that the research result was not going to be used to evaluate them. In order to maintain this confidentiality and anonymity, only a little demographic information was requested from the participants: (1) Name of their Father's Father, (2) Name of their Mother's Mother, (3) Age, (4) Class in Theology, and (5) State of Origin.

The Sample

The sample of this research is composed of 187 subjects who are basically divided into four groups: Igbo Catholic diocesan seminarians (N=75), Igbo Catholic religious seminarians (N=60), the Entire Igbo group (N=135), and the International group (N=52). All of the subjects are Christian vocationers. These groups shall now be described one by one.

The Igbo Groups

Igbo Catholic Diocesan Seminarians: (N=75)

This comprises Catholic seminarians who are *Igbo*, and who are training for the *diocesan priesthood*. All of them were in the final phase of their formation journey, the theological studies. They practically came from three major seminaries in the Onitsha and Owerri Ecclesiastical Provinces: Bigard Memorial Seminary, Enugu, Seat of Wisdom Seminary, Owerri, and Blessed Iwene Tansi Seminary, Onitsha. A total of 300 sheets containing the instructions were given to them. After the blind scoring, it was discovered that 122 protocols had been returned and 47 had been discarded as not scorable, and the remaining 75 were valid. Their age is 27.865 ± 2.570.

Igbo Catholic Religious Seminarians: (N=60)

This group comprises all Catholic seminarians who are *Igbo* and who are training for the *religious priesthood*. They are also in the final phase of their formation journey, the theological studies. They are all Igbo, and came from about 9 clerical religious congregations whose houses of formation are located in different parts of Nigeria. From the Eastern part of the country, participants came from the Congregation of the Holy Spirit or Holy Ghost Fathers (CSSP), the Claretian Missionaries, the Congregation of the Mission (CM) or the Vincentians, the Capuchins, the Congregation of Sons of Mary Mother of Mercy (SMMM), and the Emmanuelites. From the North, they came from the Missionaries of St. Paul. From the West, they came from the Redemptorists and the Vocationists. 200 sheets containing the instructions were given to them. After the blind scoring, it was discovered that 101 protocols were returned by this group, 60 of which were valid and 41 had been discarded as non scorable. Their age is 29.250 ± 4.205.

The Entire Igbo Group: (N=135)

This group comprises all the Catholic diocesan and religious seminarians who are *Igbo* and who are doing their theological studies. It constitutes the whole number of the Igbo diocesan and religious seminarians in this research-project. Their distribution according to the States is as follows: Abia State (5.2%), Anambra State (35.5%), Ebonyi State (6%), Enugu State (13.3%), and Imo State (40%).

The International Group: (N=52)

This group consists of subjects who are not Igbo and who come from different parts of the world: Armenia (1), Australia (1), England (1), Germany (2), India (3), Ireland (9), Italy (22), Poland (2), Romania (7), Slovenia (2), and Uganda (2). All of them are males and Christian vocationers, seminarians and priests. Their age is 28.135 ± 6.651. This group formed the male group in C. O'Dwyer's research.

It might be objected that there is no ground for comparing this group with the groups from Igboland since all of them are not seminarians. The objection is appropriate, but can be answered by recalling the remarkable discovery in the research of B.M. Dolphin[69], M.P. Garvin[70], and C. O'Dwyer[71]: that age, years of formal education, and theological studies make no significant difference on one's degree of existential maturity. The results of their research demonstrate strongly that existential maturity is not merely a function of age, long years of formal education or long years of theological studies as common sense would ordinarily make one to believe; some other significant factors are seriously in play.

The Results

Remarks on the Interpretation of Data

Interpretation of data is based on whether a variable is present or absent, distorted or ambivalent, and on the combination of variables. A variable is present if it receives a net score of +2 points or higher and absent if it does not receive a score of at least +2 in the Story of the Imagined Future. A variable may be absent in four ways, first, in the form of omission (where the score = 0); secondly, when it receives only a fleeting mention (where the score = +1); and thirdly, when it is present but prevalently distorted (where the score = -2 or lower); fourthly, when there is a major ambivalence in a variable, that is, when it receives both positive and negative scores including at least two negative points.

A variable is distorted when it has a net score of −2 or worse. This means that the individual has included in the story of his ideal future a desire that is objectively in conflict with the values of Christian vocation[72]. For example, if the priesthood is presented as a way of having a prestigious career, that would be a distortion of the variable Promotion. A distortion can be minor, that is, when it is mentioned in a fleeting way or with an uncertain meaning; in which case, it receives a score of −1. A major distortion receives a score of −2, indicating that it is definite or recurrent[73]. In the present research we are concerned only with major distortions; O'Dwyer showed that minor distortions are not significant[74].

A variable is considered ambivalent when it receives both positive and negative scores. This means that the person includes in his story contradictory expressions of the same variable, some in harmony with the objective values of the priesthood, and others in conflict with the same values. Ambivalence in a variable can also be either minor or major. Minor ambivalence means that a particular variable receives a score of −1 in the presence of any positive score of the same variable, and major ambivalence means that the same variable receives a score of −2 together with some positive score[75]. The present research examines only variables with major ambivalence; O'Dwyer also showed that instances of minor ambivalence are not significant[76].

Distortion and ambivalence express conflicts in the stories of the ideal future, expressed as either negative scores (in distorted variables) or as both positive and negative scores (in ambivalent variables). Examination of the maturity and immaturity of the ideals of future vocational life takes into consideration all of the 15 variables of the story of the imagined future, the experience-of-discipleship variables (5) and the cost-of-discipleship variables (10). Maturity is indicated by a more complete vision of the priestly vocation and immaturity by an incomplete vision. Completeness is measured by the Algebraic Index of Maturity (AIM), which is defined as "the number of variables scored as present in the story of the imagined future, minus the sum of variables with major distortion or major ambivalence"[77]. This represents the person's strength minus his weaknesses. The criterion of maturity is that a story must have an AIM ≥ 7; immaturity corresponds to AIM < 7. In other words, we apply the criterion given by O'Dwyer[78].

Immaturity in the form of psychopathology (expected in a minority of persons) was found by O'Dwyer to express itself frequently as overt passivity in vocational living, a tendency to hope for an easy vocational life without a corresponding effort[79]. The Fairy Godmother Index (FGI) or the "index of passive expectations of fulfilment" algebraically sums up this tendency on each story of the imagined future. The criterion of division is that a story with an FGI ≤ 1 is considered to show this tendency while a story with an FGI >1 does not show it.

The Findings

Igbo diocesan and religious seminarians are compared on the single variables and the result shows that Igbo religious seminarians differ significantly from Igbo diocesan seminarians on the variables Power and Security[80]. The variable Power involves the exercise of power or authority in a spirit of service as befits a Christian leader, and not for the sake of domination. It also implies a filial trust in God as source of strength in moments of trial. Security, on the other hand, means trust in divine providence rather than narcissistic self-sufficiency. Thus, it basically implies a relationship with God as the one who provides[81].

The comparison between the international group and the Igbo seminarians all taken together shows some difference: the international group is better than the entire Igbo group on two experience-variables, Power and Security, and on one cost-of-discipleship variable, Harm Avoidance[82]; the Igbo group is better than the international group on two cost-of-discipleship variables, Chastity and Responsibility[83]. The subjects in the international group and in the entire Igbo group in whose stories each variable is present are counted and compared. The result shows that the number of subjects in the international group for whom the variables Power, Security, and Harm Avoidance are included as ideals of the priestly vocation is substantially greater than the number in the entire Igbo group[84].

When Igbo religious seminarians and Igbo diocesan seminarians are compared with the international group, Igbo religious seminarians are more similar to the international group than to the diocesan seminarians, in the total number of variables present and in the number of experience-variables present. On the other hand, Igbo diocesan seminarians are different from the international group in the sense that they have less number of total variables present and experience-variables present[85].

The examination of the total number of variables present confirms the two patterns revealed by examination of the single variables, which are, that the Igbo religious seminarians are better than Igbo diocesan seminarians on experience-of-discipleship variables, and that the international subjects are better than Igbo seminarians (both groups taken together) on experience-variables.

When the groups are compared on major distortion and major ambivalence, the result reveals that the international group includes more frequent distortion of the values of the priestly vocation. This result shows something that is common to the two Igbo groups, namely, that they have a lesser tendency to distort the values of priestly vocation than the subjects in the international group[86]. In other words, the vocational ideals of the international group are more conflicted than those of the Igbo seminarians. There are no significant differences between the groups for major ambivalence.

I then put together the whole data in order to assess the overall maturity and immaturity of the subjects. The number of those who are immature, that is, those with AIM < 7, is 47 among Igbo religious seminarians, and 59 among Igbo diocesan seminarians. These constitute 78.3% and 78.7% of the Igbo religious and diocesan seminarians respectively. The AIM index confirms what the two Igbo groups have in common namely, that there is a notable incompleteness in the vision of the priestly vocation among them. This is found in 78.3% of the Igbo religious seminarians and in 78.7% of the Igbo diocesan seminarians.

The FGI index used to discriminate between the deviant and non-deviant immature, also showed another quality that the two Igbo groups have in common, namely, that immaturity does not tend to express itself in overtly passive expectation of fulfilment in vocational life, a kind of passivity that is often connected with psychopathology[87]. This tendency is found in 15% of the Igbo religious seminarians and in 12% of the Igbo diocesan seminarians.

Immaturity rather takes an active form among Igbo seminarians, both diocesan and religious. If we subtract the percentage of the subjects with mature vocational ideals in each group (as measured by AIM ≥7), and also those showing signs of psychopathology (those who have FGI ≤ 1), we get the net percentage of immature subjects who are actively pursuing ideals which have limited correspondence with the objective ideals of the priestly life. These subjects constitute 63.3% of Igbo religious seminarians and 66.7%

of Igbo diocesan seminarians.

These results indicate no significant difference between the Igbo religious and diocesan seminarians in terms of the overall maturity of their vocational ideals. They rather reveal what they have in common firstly, that a large percentage of the two Igbo groups have incomplete vision of the priestly vocation. Secondly, among the immature subjects in the two Igbo groups, a larger number is active while quite a small number is immature in an overtly passive sense. That is, a small number has difficulties that are psychopathological.

A comparison of the Igbo groups with the international group reveals that 40% of the subjects in international group have mature ideals of their future vocational life as measured by AIM. This is against the 21.7% of the Igbo religious seminarians, 21.3% of the Igbo diocesan seminarians, and 21.5% of the all-Igbo group. On the other hand, the FGI index shows that 27% of the subjects in the international group are overtly passive toward their vocational commitment, as against 15% of the Igbo religious seminarians, 12% of the Igbo diocesan seminarians, and 13.3% of the entire Igbo group.

The results for the FGI show a significant difference between the international group and the two Igbo groups, taken separately or together[88], that is, that the immature Christian vocationers in the two Igbo groups show an overt passivity in their stories of the future more rarely than those of the international group. In other words, there are more cases of psychopathology in the international group than in the Igbo groups, taken separately or together.

Verification of the Hypotheses

The findings of this research can be summarized as follows:

i.   Igbo religious seminarians are better than Igbo diocesan seminarians on experience-of-discipleship variables (in particular Power and Security), but are about the same on cost-of-discipleship variables.

ii.   Subjects in the international group are more mature than Igbo seminarians on experience-of-discipleship variables. The relative weakness on experience-variables is found more among Igbo diocesan seminarians than among Igbo religious seminarians. Igbo diocesan seminarians are better than Igbo religious seminarians and the international group on the variable Responsibility.

iii.   The overall maturity of vocational ideals (measured by the AIM) is about the same for the Igbo religious and diocesan seminarians. On the other hand, subjects in the international group demonstrate a more complete vision of the priestly vocation than Igbo religious and diocesan seminarians, as shown by higher values of the AIM.

iv.   Though the international group has in general more mature ideals of the Christian vocation, they have more conflicts than Igbo religious and diocesan seminarians. This is seen in their greater tendency to distort variables.

v.   Immature subjects in the international group are more often passive, while immature subjects in the two Igbo groups (taken separately or together) are more active. This finding implies that the FGI, as a measure of overt passivity and so of psychopathology, is not equally valid everywhere[89]. This index seems to be sensitive to cultural variation, and therefore, may not be very useful in identifying pathology in a culture like the Igbo with its strong work habits and high sense of responsibility.

vi.   When all these results are put together, the picture of the Igbo Christian vocationers becomes clearer: *they work hard and can be dedicated to their duties, but their spiritual motivation can be weak.* This is indicated first, by their weakness on experience-variables and their strength on the variable Responsibility; secondly, by the small number showing overt passivity as indicated by the FGI.

First Hypothesis: When Igbo religious and diocesan seminarians are compared as to the completeness of the ideals of their future priestly life, using the Algebraic Index of Maturity, we do not find any significant difference. When the two Igbo groups are compared with the international group on the same index, the result shows that both the Igbo religious and diocesan seminarians are alike in having a less complete vision of the priestly vocation. Thus, neither of the two Igbo groups has more valid ideals than the other. This means that the vision of priestly vocation as one in which one makes a *total* gift of the self is relatively weak in both the Igbo religious and diocesan seminarians. But as regards the balance between the two aspects of the Christian vocation, i.e., the receptive and the sacrificial aspects reflected by experience-variables and cost-variables respectively, then Igbo religious seminarians differ from the Igbo diocesan seminarians in including more experience-variables. This result indicates that in their self-ideals as future priests, Igbo religious seminarians are more conscious of their future priestly life as a vocation dependent on the personal experience of and relationship with God as the foundation of their life and apostolate, more than are Igbo diocesan seminarians.

As to the first hypothesis, therefore, the results of the research show that the overall maturity of the self-ideals of Igbo religious and diocesan seminarians is about the same; however, Igbo religious seminarians are more attuned to the spiritual basis of their vocation than their diocesan counterparts.

Second Hypothesis: In general, the results of this research show that the international group has a more complete vision of the values of priestly vocation than the Igbos. Out of the 52 subjects in the international group, 40% have mature ideals of their future vocational life. This is against 21.5% of the subjects in the entire Igbo group (21.7% for the religious seminarians and 21.3% for the diocesan seminarians). In addition to this, subjects in the international group include more of the experience-variables than the subjects in the entire Igbo group. In other words, Igbo subjects tend to trust more in their active efforts in living their lives as priests than in their personal relationship with God.

In the international group, vocational immaturity is expressed more by overt passivity in Christian vocation as compared to the Igbo seminarians: 27% of the international subjects, 15% of Igbo religious seminarians, 12% of Igbo diocesan seminarians, and 13.3% of the entire Igbo group, expect that their future vocational commitment will be easy with less effort as shown by the FGI. On the other hand, immaturity expresses itself among the Igbo seminarians in activeness: 33% of the international group, 63.3% of the Igbo religious seminarians, 66.7% of the Igbo diocesan seminarians, and 65.2% of the entire Igbo group, are active but immature in their vocational ideals. The difference between the international group and the entire Igbo group, as measured by the FGI, is significant. The result shows that Igbo subjects are more active people than the subjects in the international group. This result converges with the attitude of the Igbo subjects toward experience-variables, and suggests they tend to trust more in their own efforts and power.

A closer look at the research as a whole reveals certain unresolved ambiguities. The active tendency of the Igbo subjects in Christian vocation seems to go into the pursuit of goals that do not fully correspond to those of the priestly vocation. The percentage of those showing overall maturity in their vocational ideals in the entire Igbo group is relatively small: 21.5%. This is the percentage of the Igbo subjects who have a more complete vision of the Christian vocation and anticipate that the commitment demands continuous struggle and effort on their part. The percentage of those Igbo seminarians who have an incomplete vision of Christian vocation, and also have the tendency to be passive in their vocation, is only 13.3%. These are clearly passive subjects in relation to their future ideals; seminarians with difficulties that could be psychopathological. If we add up these two percentages and subtract it from the entire Igbo group, we have the percentage of those Igbo subjects who have immature vocational ideals but are active in their vocation. These are the majority.

This group constitutes 65.2% of the subjects in the entire Igbo group. Since these subjects are actively oriented towards the

Christian vocation but are, at the same time, immature in their vocational ideals, it implies that they are actively pursuing goals that do not fully match the ideals of the priestly vocation.

Low values of the Algebraic Index of Maturity reflect *covert* passivity, while the Fairy Godmother Index assesses *overt* passivity. Covert passivity means that the subject is making a relatively restricted selection of the aspects of the Christian or priestly vocation that are important to him, and omitting other aspects. High values of the AIM express a more complete gift of self while low values of the AIM express a selective emphasis on some aspects of vocation which the subject himself finds more gratifying. Such selection and omission is like the attitude of some people who prefer to eat biscuits and coca cola or *akara* and bread rather than eat a balanced meal that is good for health. What came out clearly in this research is that *covert passivity* more than overt passivity characterizes the two groups of Igbo seminarians. How do we understand them? Many do not have mature vocational ideals and they are not clearly passive. They are very active, but their activeness is directed to the pursuit of other goals than the goals of Christian vocation.

C. O'Dwyer argues that passivity consists in attempting to evade the normal dialectical tensions of life. It can be obvious and therefore *overt* or disguised and therefore *covert*[90]. The individual who is overtly passive is inclined to see inactivity as a virtue; he needs to wait patiently for a quasi-magical resolution of his difficulties. The wish is entertained that the realisation of the ideals of Christian vocation will happen upon him and with no pain or tension. This wishful optimism drives him toward inactivity and encourages the effort to avoid the normal tensions of life.

On the other hand, the *covertly* passive Christian vocationers strive to achieve their goals *actively* employing whatever means within their reach. However, instead of seeking to realise the totality of the values of the Christian vocation, they select a few of them and reinterpret others according to their personal needs. Making this arbitrary selection of some goals and avoiding others, they become passive to those other goals not selected. It is like the Christian vocation has to be lived the way the person "feels it good for himself". Thus, their activeness is ambivalent.

In the entire-Igbo group 65.2% of them falls into this group of covertly passive Christian vocationers, and among the international subjects, the number is only 33%. In essence, these subjects are in Christian vocation but could be pursuing goals that are basically their personal ambition.

Thus, in comparison with the subjects in international group, vocational immaturity is expressed by the Igbo subjects in covert passivity, which can imply an active pursuit of personal desires and needs that may not necessarily agree with the values of the priesthood. These persons may use the priestly vocation as a platform or place to gratify their needs and realise their personal goals or projects. The percentage of the distribution of this immaturity among the Igbo religious and diocesan seminarians is great, and shows that this covert passivity is common to the Igbo subjects.

In response to the second question, therefore, the research-results show that specific to the Igbo Christian vocationers is a kind of vocational maturity expressed as less distortion of priestly values, in comparison with international subjects. Immaturity among them expresses itself in covert passivity, masking itself in active pursuit of some goals which may not agree with the values of priestly vocation. Immaturity in the form of overt passivity is more present among the international subjects than among the Igbo subjects, which means that more subjects in the international group have psychopathological difficulties than Igbo subjects when discriminated by the FGI index.

Synthesis of the Results

An important conclusion to be drawn from the data of this research is that vocational immaturity has cultural nuances: among the Igbo subjects, it is expressed more in covert passivity. Immaturity in vocational life in form of overt passivity is more present among the subjects in international group than among the

Igbo subjects. This implies that the formation of people from different cultures must respond to cultural variations[91], a need which was again expressed by some Fathers in the 8th Synod of Bishops[92], but which received scanty attention in the formal documents of the Synod[93].

The data also show clearly that culture is more influential than the structures of formation. The two Igbo groups, religious and diocesan, seem more alike than different. It is true that the religious seminarians are more aware of the receptive aspect of their vocation than are the diocesan seminarians, but the two Igbo groups differ very little in the overall maturity of their ideals or in their tendency to covert passivity while both Igbo groups differ more clearly from the international group. In the remaining chapters of this work, we shall expand the implications of these data especially on the formation of Igbo priests.

Part II

Implications of the Empirical Data

IV

Igbo Priests and their Struggles: the Cultural Factor

The results of this research reveal not only the challenges of forming Igbo seminarians, but also the struggles Igbo priests go through, which could be expressed as the tension that exists between Igbo cultural values and the values of Christianity in the various ways they take flesh in their personalities. These struggles are expressed indirectly in the immature expectations Igbo seminarians have of the priesthood. The mediation between Igbo culture and Christian values takes place in the personality-configuration of each person, from which the meaning of these expectations could be understood. Thus, it is important to understand the general psychological structure of the Igbo young men who have opted or are opting for the Catholic priesthood. A more direct way of doing this is to examine the various areas of Igbo culture that constitute dominant values, attitudes, ideals, and needs, which Igbo men and women pursue as giving them meaning and a sense of belonging to the Igbo community. Doing this will expose some of the psychological roots of the attitudes of Igbo priests and seminarians, and also challenges formators to think about and develop a better way to help Igbo seminarians understand themselves and the life they desire to live. First, we shall attempt a psychological portrait of the Igbo people. Secondly, we shall bring out the indicators of this culture from the stories of the Igbo seminarians in this research. Thirdly, we shall see how these indicators are reflected in other researches done on

Igbo priests and seminarians. From this, we shall explore the difficulties Igbo priests have in trying to be both Igbo and Catholic priests. Finally, we shall attempt a psychological understanding of why these difficulties are experienced differently by priests leading to greater or less maturity or immaturity.

Psychology of the Igbo People in Brief

The Paradox of the Igbo

A good way of approaching a psychological understanding of the Igbo people is to analyse what C.J. Uzor has called the two principal paradoxes of the Igbo as expressed in their history.

> The Igbo were the most vocal group in Nigeria in advocating not only for [Nigerian] national unity and independence from colonial tutelage of Great Britain but also the Pan-African Movement, and at the same time they were the only group that eventually decided to secede from the Nigerian Federation. Secondly, the Igbo was the group that most vehemently resisted the white man's rule and way of life in Nigeria, but today they are the most anglicized and 'westernized' group of people among Nigerians[1].

The second paradox includes their tendency to prefer European languages to the Igbo language. In comparison to other ethnic groups in Nigeria, the Igbo is the only people who cannot speak their own language very well without adding foreign words here and there. It is enough to watch any movie performed in the Igbo language to understand the situation.

To these two paradoxes, I shall add another two that are relevant to the life and ministry of Igbo priests: Igbos have been described as "ultra-democratic" or "radical republicans" in their social and political organisation as expressed in the aphorism, *Igbo enwe eze* [the Igbo do not have kings][2], but they can be autocratic in exercising authority, as can be seen among their clergy. Secondly, Igbo people have no traditional concept of permanent celibacy because of their belief in *Ndụ ọma* [good life] as the goal of life and the maintenance of family lineage in their progeny, which makes procreation a religious duty[3]. At most, the Igbo traditional religious system "demands limited and seasonal celibacy"[4] from the priests especially at the moments of sacrifice; yet, there are many men and women who opt for a celibate life as Catholic priests and religious men and women. We shall attempt a general understanding of these paradoxes in the light of the psychological portrait of the Igbo people, which has emerged from the research conducted on them.

From Uzor's analysis, these paradoxes can be understood by recognising some of the psychological and social characteristics of the Igbo people, which derive from their belief-system. First, the Igbo, like many Africans, believes that the goal of life is *Ndụ ọma* [good life] and that the human person stands at the center of the universe, connected with the supreme being, deities, ancestors and other life-forces. Therefore, he or she feels a responsibility to make the best out of life; success in life, which should also be relevant for the community, becomes fundamental, and one is ready to run any risk to achieve it. Secondly, the Igbo loves his autonomy; he is "the king and master in his own house and in his own affairs. When he needs assistance he asks for it, but before then he minds his own business and expects the other to do likewise"[5]. Therefore he resists any form of domination and does not have a tradition of centralised government; which made it difficult for the colonial master to conquer the Igbos as easily as they did other groups in Nigeria[6]. M.C. Onyejekwe sees this independence expressed in another of their cherished aphorisms: *I na-enye m nri*? [Do you give me food?][7], emphasising that the Igbo does not have a reason to submit to the "rule" of another or be dependent on another. From all this Uzor concludes:

> This explains his paradoxical openness to new ideas, new vistas and new frontiers, such as Christianity and Western culture. The paradox expresses itself in his aptitude to embrace Christianity and Western culture and at the same time staunchly resisting both, saying yes to 'One Nigeria' and at the same time seceding from it in the Biafra war, being community-loving and at the same time

individualistic when it comes to achievement and status-seeking[8].

The Igbo can then be described as a people who love *novelty* and who cherish *autonomy*. These two basic characteristics combine so well in them: the one disposes them to go for anything that will bring them success and comfort in life irrespective of the risks that are involved; thus they are open to all kinds of change.

> For a people who have a special bent for individual and group achievement and status, change can only be a welcome phenomenon: every change carries potentials for new avenues to status, opens up new alternatives to existing goals and/or enhances the opportunities open to a greater number of aspirants[9].

Their sense of autonomy makes them fearless; also, it makes them feel equal with some people and superior to others but never inferior, no matter who the other person is[10].

This irresistible urge for the *new* as a way to status and booster of prestige is not always to the advantage of the Igbo; it has a shadow side, which can be seen in the life of the Igbo as an individual and as a group. I dare to call it the fundamental fragility of the Igbo person, because it hinders their efforts to attain lasting stability especially as a group.

The same attitude is expressed in their understanding of art. Achebe observes that the Igbo does not engage in private collection of works of art except such "personal ritual objects like the *Ikenga*"[11], because such collections "will impose rigid, artistic attitudes and conventions on creativity which the Igbo sensibility goes out of its way to avoid"[12]. When any work of art has been completed, the Igbo tends to eliminate the product otherwise "the impulse to repeat the process is compromised"[13]. It is thus that even in their cosmology, the "gods could fall out of use; and new forces are liable to appear without warning in the temporal and metaphysical firmament"[14]. It is in this line of thinking that Mbefo understands progress as "newness and parting with inherited habits"[15], without stating the basis on which to judge which inherited habits are to be dropped and what new way of life is to be adopted.

Thus, what seems to be constant is process or motion, and in social life, this finds expression in the continuous search for achievement, social status and social relevance. These, in their very nature, are always changing like fashion, because what is today a symbol of achievement and social relevance will become obsolete tomorrow. For instance, models of cars and houses change often; they may not guarantee the kind of stability that societies seek for. "'Relevance'", as P.L. Berger rightly observes, "is a very fragile business at best"[16], and is even more precarious today with the increasing trend of secularisation, which creates a hunger for the latest experience and an equal disgust for what has been tasted. If achievement and social relevance are held to be constant values among the Igbo people, then the Igbo can do anything to get them, not excluding manipulative practices[17].

Love of novelty can promote more and more experiences but not necessarily much reflection and critical judgement; it can favour an uncritical flirtation with new models of anything, including ideas, but without necessarily submitting them to patient and rigorous criticism that aims at long-term goals. To carry out such critical assessment, one would need some stability in the form of enduring standards. Because these stable structures and standards are often not respected especially in the recent times, the Igbos are the most changed people in Nigeria. Let us illustrate this with the problem of the Igbo language.

With the exception of the Igbo, as already noted, every other group of people in Nigeria can speak their language without adulteration with foreign words. According to C.J. Uzor, Igbo language suffers this fate for two reasons: first, the Irish missionaries and the colonialists decided to suppress it because it was not worthy enough, being the language of a primitive culture. Secondly, the natives themselves opposed the proposal to incorporate some local elements in the English School Certificate Examination curriculum because it would mean giving them an inferior position in relation to the Europeans; the English language was seen as a symbol of superiority so that "the more grandiloquent one is in the use of English, with a lot of –isms and –ities nicely spiced with a good dosage of Latin words, the more erudite and intellectual one is taken to be"[18]. Though he acknowledged the responsibility of the Nigerian elite in this matter, he was inclined to maintain, in line with the fundamental premise of his study, that they behaved the way they did because they had been cognitively modified by the Europeans so that they equated "their equality with the white man with the *knowledge* of the latter's background and culture at the expense of their own native culture"[19]. The question he did not answer is why this is so widespread among the Igbo that "when others from the same tribe spoke and conversed in their native languages, he preferred to speak to his fellow Igbo in English and looked with contempt on any one who spoke to him in his own native language"[20]. This suggests that there are other factors beyond epistemological reorientation of the Igbo elites.

It seems to me that the efforts of the Irish missionaries and the colonialists to suppress the language of the natives largely succeeded among the Igbos because it gratified the Igbo person's desire for symbols of social relevance and, perhaps, of superiority. The interaction between cultures follows systemic laws of relationship: if the Europeans have the tendency to dominate and feel superior to other cultures[21], and come in contact with a people who seem to have identified some level of superiority in having anything represented by the Europeans, subconsciously a psychological deal is struck: "I give you my European culture and language and you feel superior before others, but then, you forget your language and culture because they are inferior!". This systemic equilibrium between the Europeans and the Igbos holds till today: the Igbo has such a strong tendency to identify with whatever comes from the western world no matter how inferior it may be. That is why shoemakers, for example, can make their products in Nigeria but mark them "Made in Italy", and sell them at exorbitant prices. If something is costly and has a foreign trademark, then it must be superior, just as some tend to believe the more one makes oneself obscure in speaking the European languages, the more one appears educated[22]. When E.G. Ekwuru wrote about how to promote the true spirit of "Pan-Igboism" and work towards a synthesis of the Igbo culture after colonialism, he completely neglected the other cultures of Nigeria and focused on the synthesis between the Igbo and Western cultures[23], as if to mean that the Igbo does not need to struggle for a synthesis with other cultures in Nigeria! This might appear to be a slip of the pen, but it might, indeed, represent an attitude of the mind that seems to identify with anything that is western. It is then understandable why the Igbos, though they resisted the white man's rule, are the most anglicized and westernised of all groups in Nigeria.

Basic Attitudes

The high premium the Igbos place on autonomy and social status also clarifies other paradoxes. Social status, acquired and maintained through achievement, is the most vital means of asserting one's autonomy. Concretely this implies that every person wants to make his mark in society; everybody wants to make his own name as an individual, but he must receive social recognition for this. Thus, the community is indispensable for the Igbo and forms an integral part of their culture, but its value seems to be first and foremost to serve the individual's self-affirmation. Thus, as one moves away from the immediate nuclear and extended family into the village and town or country, the Igbo seems to become more and more reluctant to engage oneself in any collective development for the sake of the larger group, unless for the gain of honour and social status for oneself and one's kin. The state of the Catholic Church in Igboland will illustrate this clearly.

The tendency of some Igbo priests is to initiate personal projects either in their own towns or in the diocese, and in so doing, carve a niche for themselves. There are Church-related projects that are difficult to coordinate at the central level; each functions independently of others and not in relation with others. Some use the name of the bishop to get funding for a particular project but eventually personalise the project. In other instances, an establishment meant for a diocese or several dioceses is converted into a personal one. I suppose it is for the same reason that most healing priests find it difficult to coordinate their activities and help each other; each often goes his own way and may even discourage his clients from visiting others.

At the political level, this issue is clearly demonstrated in the presidential campaign of 2003 in Nigeria, where at least four presidential candidates emerged from among the Igbos while other groups were represented by one major individual at a time: incumbent president Olusegun Obasanjo came from the Yoruba, and Alhaji Buhari represented the Hausas. From the Igbos came Jim Nwobodo, Alex Ekwueme, Ike Nwachukwu, and Emeka Odumegwu Ojukwu[24]. Four Igbo candidates vied for presidential position in the primary elections of All Nigerian People's Party. None of them could agree to step down for the other. And Uwalaka wisely asks: "How could the Igbos ever dream of winning a presidential election, when they cannot get a consensus candidate?"[25] The problem is that each of them feels he is capable because "an Igbo does not recognise anybody as his chief or superior and so does not see why he should entrust his welfare into the hands of another; he believes that what you can achieve he too can achieve"[26], a mentality that often makes him overestimate his ability[27] and fail to acknowledge the capability of the other.

Because of this difficulty in accepting their giftedness and limits, the Igbos are also divided among themselves. This dilemma is the greatest obstacle to the realization of the sovereign State of Biafra. Most of the writings on Igbo seem to emphasize that these attitudes of Igbos could be traced back to the amalgamation of Nigeria and the impact of the Nigeria-Biafra war[28]. While these historical events can explain certain aspects of Igbo life today in reference to other Nigerians, it does not seem to explain enough the basic attitudes. It is true both in biological and social anthropological studies that basic structure which defines a living being, biological or social, is hard to change. Minor changes can occur that may entail certain modifications which may not affect the basic structure[29]. This is also why certain basic aspects of a personality's structure are difficult to change because they constitute the definition of a person's sense of self. Change can occur, but to a limited degree.

The point I am daring to make here is that the psychology of Igbo people retains the dispositions that determine the extent that the perturbations suffered from colonialism and Nigeria-Biafran war would affect the Igbo people. What is rather needed today among the Igbo is a deeper understanding of their giftedness and limitations, and minimize the effects of their weaknesses as a people and as individuals. That is always the goal of development for individuals and groups.

There is some truth in the saying that Igbo people are "ultra-democratic" or "radical republicans". At the same time, the shadow side of this attribute haunts the Igbo people: it leads to a situation that tends to fragmentation rather than a social and political condition guided by the spirit of dialogue and humble acknowledgement of personal abilities and limits. The urge to achieve for oneself and one's family and edge others out often results in the inability to pull resources together and make a meaningful and lasting project possible, as a group. This is a situation that is painful to any Igbo person and to all those persons who sincerely acknowledge the giftedness of the Igbo people.

This is why the Igbos, among the peoples of Nigeria have most difficulty in organizing themselves as a group[30]. Since the individual and his family often take precedence over the larger community, and short-term experience and satisfaction over long-term ones, any person in power can utilise the Igbo against his own people as long as money is given to him. It is among the most significant factors that led to the downfall of Biafra[31], and it is still widespread among the Igbos.

> [The] political events in the country have shown that among all the tribes in Nigeria, the Igbos are the most

disunited group. Most of the Igbo leaders so far have demonstrated beyond all reasonable doubts that they put their selfish and clan ambitions over and above that of the entire Igbo people. Within the present reality of Igbo politics, every Igbo seems to manifest a social character of self-contradiction, which makes him a traitor to his tribal identity and a great enemy of his tribal collective progress and development[32].

The possession of more money, big buildings, expensive cars, and honours, confers on him a status over and above others among his townspeople. Corruption among politicians and the police is not rare. As much as the Igbo can be angry at their plight in Nigeria, the look inward to what they have done to themselves is also important. Uwalaka leads this examination of consciousness with a series of questions:

> What of the Igbo sons and daughters who conspire to abort the projects meant for Igboland or get the contracts for projects and do not realise them? What of our sons and daughters who have the privilege of being governors in Igbo States in the past and the present? How many of them have displayed real love and commitment to Igbo interests? How many of them have used their offices to uplift the Igbo man? How many of them had not left Igbo land leaner, drier and emptier? How many of them have not left Igboland poorer and more distressed? How many of them due to selfish-interest have not conspired with outside forces to abort or destablize Igbo common agenda?[33]

It comes down to acquisition, monetary achievement, honour, and having an edge over others. Thus, due to the importance the Igbos attach to social recognition and achievement, I.R.A Ozigbo suspected that the requirement of celibacy would not deter young men and women from responding to vocations to the Catholic priesthood and the religious life as long as these vocations are perceived as avenues to achievement and social prestige.

The ordination ceremonies and the rousing receptions

which accompany them, leave deep impressions on the young. Despite the prohibitive demands of celibacy and personal poverty, the priesthood and the religious life have been generally perceived by the Igbo as sure avenues of social mobility. The relatively high economic security and social prestige which the Catholic priests and nuns enjoy have attracted many a Nigerian youth to the priesthood or the sisterhood[34].

Adibe confirms this suspicion of Ozigbo in his research on how Holy Orders/Consecrated Life are understood and lived by Igbo Christians. According to him:

> The Sacrament of Holy Orders and the profession of Sisters and Brothers has social status symbol attached to it. The relations of the ordained and the professed boast about this by the big receptions given their sons and daughters who had reached the goal[35].

This also helps to explain why none of the subjects in the present research made mention of missing marriage or having family of his own.

Leadership and Territorial Consciousness

The sense of personal autonomy maintained through achievement and social recognition generates what I can call "territorial consciousness", which is the mentality that one is in charge of one's life, family and business, and all persons should mind their own affairs. Within the family, the authority of the father is unquestionable, and sibling-relationships are guided by gerontocracy, which also extends to the way villages relate with each other. Democratic discussions and respect of other people's autonomy occur when matters get to the umunna [Kinship], village or town levels. At these levels, those persons who have the talent, respect, wealth, and the ability can lead the people[36]. However, in recent times, it is to be doubted if ability, talent, respect or intelligence determine who leads the people. Wealth seems to have an outstanding influence over any other value in determining who leads.

Thus, I feel that two models of leadership can be observed among the Igbos: the male leadership of the family which tends towards complete control, and the more democratic and conciliar system which obtains more outside the family. It is understandable then that a carryover of the model of leadership in the family into the *ụmụnna* (or village or town level), will be resisted vehemently by any Igbo. V.C. Uchendu aptly describes it: "The Igbo saying that 'everyone is a chief in his hut' must be understood in its proper context. What is meant is that a dictatorial leader of the Igbo is inconceivable. A leader may be a dictator if he likes, but his leadership must be restricted to his household"[37].

If the Igbo clergy tend to be highhanded in their exercise of authority, it suggests that the leadership model they generally adopt is the one of the family in which the father exercises too much control. In other words, it is possible that some of them perceive the areas of their pastoral work as their territory, where they can exercise authority to the full. With this mindset, the ecclesiology which assigns a significant position to the priest in the parish, can be easily misinterpreted as a validation of this mentality, so that the Church indeed remains the "Father's Church" even after the Second Vatican Council.

In the light of this sketch of the psychology of the Igbo people, we re-examined the stories of the Igbo religious and diocesan seminarians in this research to see if their culture is manifested in them, in order to trace the cultural root of the finding of this research, that Igbo Christian vocationers exhibit immaturity by means of covert passivity[38].

Igbo Cultural Values in the Stories of Igbo Seminarians

Every group of persons has consistent patterns of behaviour in its members, which guarantee some equilibrium in it. The behaviour of any one member of the group in any one context, according to G. Bateson "is, in some sense, cognitively consistent with the behaviour of all the other individuals in all other contexts" so that "the inherent logic of one culture differs profoundly from that of others"[39]. This is what differentiates a culture from another, and it is shown in the *regularity* or *pattern* in their thinking and behaviour. These make any human community an organised entity like any individual[40]. The "regularity" or "pattern" is due to the functioning of what B.J.F. Lonergan calls *"schemes of recurrence"*[41], which enables human beings to understand occurrences of certain events or actions. Human actions, for example, are recurrent and regular, and "the regularity is the functioning of a scheme, of a patterned set of relations that yields conclusions of the type: if an X occurs, then an X will recur"[42]. An Igbo proverb alludes to this same situation when it affirms that *Ihe agwọ mụrụ aghaghị ito ogologo* [What a snake gives birth to is always long]. Lonergan observes that once schemes of recurrence have begun to function, they tend to perpetuate themselves and even resist change[43]. The probability of their survival rests on the occurrence of any of the components of the scheme itself.

This implies that the recurrent themes in the stories of the Igbo seminarians in this research could represent some patterns found among them as people from a single culture. They suggest areas of concern, expectations and desires that are common to them, which can be helpful in understanding the phenomenon of their formational needs.

Recurrent Themes in the Stories of Igbo Seminarians

Three themes were found to be recurrent in their stories. In order of frequency, they are: first, those concerning achievement and social recognition; secondly, those dealing with justice and the alleviation of poverty; and thirdly, those relating to family concerns.

The theme of achievement and social recognition pertains to desires and efforts that reflect the need to accomplish something and increase one's self-regard in society[44]. This is expressed recurrently in their desires to go for studies overseas and obtain many degrees; to be lecturers especially in secular universities rather than in major seminaries; to be famous for writing books and articles and attending national and international conferences;

to aspire to be historic bishops and accomplished major superiors; to establish foundations that will immortalise their names among the people they serve. All this entails hard work and determination. It is therefore understandable that in both Igbo diocesan and religious seminarians, the variable Responsibility scores the highest among all the cost variables and the second highest in all the 15 variables after the variable Promotion. When compared with the international subjects, Igbo vocationers score higher on this variable.

The theme of justice and the alleviation of poverty is the second in the stories. It deals with resistance to and open confrontation of oppression, including the alleviation of poverty of the individual future priest and of the people. This comes out in the desire to fight against subjection of oneself or others, to engage in large-scale agricultural production to feed oneself and others, to care for the underprivileged and the abandoned, and to establish educational foundations to educate them.

This theme has its root in the Christian principles of service to the poor. However, it seems also to express the desire for autonomy, for self-definition and self-management; the desire to assert oneself and reject subjection or dependency as an individual and as a group. Thus, the recurrence of this theme highlights the fact that of all the 15 variables in the story of the imagined future, only the variable Aggression, which assesses the manner in which a subject behaves in a confrontational relationship, is negative in both the Igbo religious and diocesan seminarians[45]. This shows that not only is aggression strong among them, it also tends to be generally expressed in an unhealthy manner. This suggests that it is a significant area of conflict for Igbo seminarians.

The third theme relates to family concerns. This is expressed in the fear the Igbo seminarians have of not being able to assist their family members financially; of not being available all the time to settle family disputes; of being unable to take care of their nieces and nephews; and in preoccupation with the unity of their families. This theme means that blood-relationship is very strong among the Igbos as it is in African people[46]. It is striking that not even one of the subjects made reference to not marrying and having children, considering the fact that these are very important elements in the Igbo traditional value-system.

The frequencies and the differences in the stories of the two Igbo groups reveal that the theme of achievement and social recognition appears in the majority of the subjects, appearing in 51.6% (n=31) of Igbo religious seminarians and in 65.3% (n=49) of Igbo diocesan seminarians. This theme ranks as the most prominent desire in the sample. It appears more frequently in the stories of Igbo diocesan seminarians than in the religious seminarians, while the theme of justice and struggle against poverty is more salient in the religious seminarians, present in 23.3% of them as against the 17.3% of the diocesan seminarians. Family concerns are expressed equally in the two groups: in 16.6% of the religious seminarians and in 16% of the diocesan seminarians. The chi-square tests on each of these themes show that the differences between the two Igbo groups are not significant; in other words, the recurrence of these themes is about the same in the two groups.

The theme of justice reflects the desire for personal dignity and autonomy, which extends to the freedom of the people. It indicates a rejection of any real or imagined sign of subjection to another person. Personal autonomy calls for the capacity to be oneself and to have personal regard. And from the strength of the first theme in the stories, it seems that the most conspicuous way the Igbo seminarians get it is through achievement that receives social approbation. Subjection to another person and poverty would not only mean lack of achievement but also a betrayal of one's being and destiny among one's people.

> Since suffering and poverty are no virtues to be aspired and actually are considered almost a curse, every effort is directed towards eliminating or avoiding poverty and suffering. That one has succeeded in overcoming poverty must be visible in one way or another. The commonest manifestation is in material possessions as well as in a

good measure of social well-being...[47].

Thus, it may well be that Igbo diocesan seminarians, as future diocesan priests, by virtue of their lifestyle, have the possibility of gratifying their need for achievement and social recognition, more than do the Igbo religious seminarians or priests who live in communities. This can lead to feelings of injustice among the religious, and a vicarious identification with the oppressed, and may be probably the reason why this theme is more frequent among the religious seminarians.

The results of this research concerning the influence of Igbo cultural values on Igbo priests and seminarians seem to agree, directly or indirectly, with some of the findings of some other studies. We shall now re-examine the empirical researches done by J.B.C Okorie and C.J. Uzor which have been reviewed in the second chapter of this study.

Parallels in J.B.C. Okorie Research

Okorie's research was on the relationship between stress and satisfaction in the ministry among Igbo priests. Two important findings of his research converge with the present study: first, his results showed that the subscale "displaying inadequacy" predicted "driven behaviour" among Igbo priests[48], of which 60% of the stress found among them was accounted for by driven behaviour[49].

These three factors – feeling of inadequacy, driven behaviour, and stress – are not unconnected with the need to achieve and be somebody in society, especially if the need is as strong as it is among the Igbo seminarians. To clarify the data further, we look at the second important finding of his research, which is that, out of the three subscales of the Minnesota Satisfaction Questionnaire (MSQ), namely "intrinsic satisfaction", "external satisfaction", and "general satisfaction", a significant relationship was found only for *extrinsic satisfaction*[50]. This implies that their satisfaction as priests usually comes from outside themselves, from the social approval they receive for doing their work[51]. What do these data actually mean for the Igbo priests?

M.R. Leary and colleagues had hypothesised that self-esteem functions as a sociometer which detects and measures "the degree to which the individual is being included versus excluded by other people (the person's *inclusionary status*) and the motive to maintain self-esteem functions to protect the person against social rejection and exclusion"[52]. It serves as a subjective index that monitors how far a person is bonded with his significant social group through the clues that "connote disapproval, rejection, or exclusion"[53]. Thus, people would tend to aspire and excel in those areas that "will enhance their inclusion by certain other people. As a result, they adopt other's standards, and their self-esteem is affected by performance in domains that others value"[54]. It also implies that the feeling of being excluded from the group lowers self-esteem and increases the feeling of inadequacy[55].

If the Igbo people value achievement and social recognition, it suggests that these become significant aspects of the self-esteem and symbols of inclusion or exclusion from their community, as we shall elaborate shortly.

In another research, a relationship was found to exist between affect and the way people look at their goal: there are those who believe that "their happiness is contingent on attainment of the goal" and "those who do not believe this"[56]. The former are called *linkers* and the latter *nonlinkers*. Linkers are prone "to focus on nonattainment of goals whereas nonlinkers focus on the present"[57]. Because linkers preoccupy themselves primarily with outcomes, they tend to worry a lot and are vulnerable to stress-related illness[58] whereas nonlinkers are interested in "the intrinsic quality of their present performance"[59]. One has to imagine the psychological strain of linkers when the outcomes are also invested with social relevance! The value of the person is measured by his achievements that have received recognition by society. Such a condition will not only strain individuals; it will lead to a fragile sense of self and to defensiveness.

These ideas make more sense in cultures like the African in which community or being together, occupies a central place. In African cultures, the individual is defined in terms of his community: "I am because we are"[60]. This means that whatever Igbo society, for instance, legitimises as an indicator of one's degree of social inclusion, will be salient to the self.

The results of J.B.C. Okorie's research become clearer: achievement and social recognition have high value among the Igbo people; they symbolise the degree of one's social importance and inclusion in the community. At the same time, the strength of this need to achieve and be socially recognised could put one on a slippery psychological ground. The value of any achievement heavily depends on its social importance, the absence of which increases a feeling of inadequacy[61], which, in turn, suggests that social approbation is lacking, because one is not performing well enough. The individual perceives it as lack of social importance, and therefore, lack of achievement, and so he is *driven* to work harder in order to achieve. In this state of social demand, the work can be seen as too tasking, too demanding, too stressful; this drains energy away. The situation heightens the feeling of inadequacy, and the circle repeats itself.

The fact that the theme of achievement and social importance is the most recurrent even over and above family concerns shows the power it has over Igbo seminarians. It reveals the amount of psychological strain many Igbos may be experiencing, the effects of which can be observed at the individual and social levels.

The Contributions of C.J. Uzor's Research

The basic thesis of Uzor's study was that the current form of Christianity present in seminary formation is too western that it leads to a kind of alienation of Igbo seminarians from their culture through the process of acculturation. This situation was expected to produce intrapersonal conflicts in the seminarians. However, the empirical findings of his research did not really prove this thesis.

Uzor was surprised that his survey did not clearly show the expected intrapersonal conflict among the Igbo seminarians he studied. He had anticipated marked signs of conflict in the seminarians due to the nature of seminary formation. The result rather showed first, a strong positive correlation between present behaviour (PB) and the personal ideals (PI). Secondly, there is generally a positive correlation between Igbo societal ideals (SI) and the institutional ideals (II) of the seminary. Thirdly, from the pooled statistics, there are mostly positive correlations on the relevant variables on the PB-SI, PI-SI, and PI-II relationships.

He sees the strong positive correlation between PI and II as a proof that seminary formation modifies the mind of Igbo seminarians, making them to adhere more and more to the ideals of the seminary institution, almost to the same degree they move away from their own Igbo culture. Conflicts were expected to result from this, but that was not very much evident from the results of the research[62]. Instead, there was more agreement than conflict. He decided to interpret his data utilising a smaller sample of 2nd year students of philosophy and 4th year students of theology of the two seminaries, and separately. Even at that, there is still a positive correlation between SI and II among the fourth year students of theology in both schools than among the second year students of philosophy on scales (1), *Respect for elders/authority*, scale (3) *Success in Life*, and scale (7) *Obedience/Hierarchy*.

His interpretation of the harmony of the SI-II among the fourth year students of theology on these scales is that the variables match with the aristocratic image of the priesthood prevalent among Igbo priests and in the seminary formation.

> [The seminarians] are at the threshold of a new status: they are beginning to inhale intensely the air of becoming authorities and members of the hierarchy. In addition, the prospects of attaining the new social status, - a further step up the ladder of success in life – where Respect and Obedience are considered more rights than privileges, are very likely to arouse a highly positive evaluation of these scales[63].

Also, the fact that the correlation between SI and II among the second year students of philosophy on these three scales is less positive than among the fourth year students of theology implies that the closer the former get to ordination, the more their sense of being a success in life and respectable in society would pervade their life and thoughts.

If the agreement between SI and II on these three scales was indicative of the aristocratic image of the priesthood, it would suggest that the seminarians held these as their ideals, and expected them, consciously or subconsciously, to be realised in the Catholic priesthood. In other words, there is greater congruence between the cultural ideals of achievement and social recognition and the ideals of priestly vocation which seminarians have, which, perhaps, they see in Igbo priests. This interpretation agrees with the data of the present research regarding the primary place given to achievement and social recognition by the Igbo religious and diocesan seminarians. It also explains why their vocational immaturity is expressed mostly as latent or covert passivity. The fact that all the seminarians in the present research are students of theology close to ordination adds validity to the data.

If the results of C.J. Uzor's research are viewed from this perspective, it will become clearer why, on the whole, there are greater positive correlations in the relevant relationships of PB-SI, PI-SI, and PI-II than negative ones: it suggests that many of the seminarians do not experience intrapersonal conflict because the greater part of their needs and cultural ideals or goals are perceived as realisable in the Catholic priesthood as presented and lived by Igbo priests. The data of the present research further clarifies the issue: 63.3% of religious seminarians and 66.7% of diocesan seminarians are actively in pursuit of goals or ideals that do not fully match the goals of the priestly vocation. This percentage feels no serious dialectical tension because their personal needs and ideals are expected to be met in the priesthood. The positive correlations therefore may not be taken literally as an indication that the majority of the seminarians have internalised the values of the priesthood as a matter of acculturation. What seems to have happened is that the cultural frame of reference, in terms of success and achievement, has in the majority of the seminarians, modified the values of priestly vocation, subconsciously investing them with cultural meanings.

The absence of any correlation on scale (5), the scale of *Traditional Religious Beliefs*, is a special case and calls for deeper understanding. The scale has 19 items out of which one would expect conflict between the Christian view of life and Igbo religious beliefs on 12[64]; instead, the correlation is close to zero[65], strongly suggesting that the seminarians hold these traditional religious beliefs and the Christian world-view in different cognitive compartments, so that neither influences the other.

Here we seem to be dealing with the phenomenon of two or more frames in the same mind, that can be activated whenever the need arises, leading to what some authors have called "frame switching", in which "an individual shifts between interpretative frames rooted in different cultures in response to cues in the social environment"[66]. This interpretation throws light on some of the attitudes found among Igbo Christians, priests and lay alike. It is what the Fathers of the African Synod express as "Rosary in the morning and witchcraft in the afternoon"[67]. A devoted Christian woman had no child. She visited a traditional medicine man who diagnosed her problem as her pride against the gods, and suggested she slept with a madman as a sign of humility. She did that, but did not conceive. It was only after this that she felt the need to consult a priest. Throughout the process, she did not feel any conflict except the anxiety of not having a child of her own[68]. It seems that it is the same phenomenon of frame switching that is operating when some priests get involved in burying crucifixes and heads of goats during exorcisms, without any feeling of conflict[69].

It is a natural thing that people carry with them different frames and can switch between them as the need arises. With this disposition, human beings can learn and adjust to different cultural and social situations. However, since human beings have an intrinsic propensity to unified thought and avoid any form of "cognitive schizophrenia"[70], it is also possible that compartmentalisation is a subconscious solution to different aspects of thought that have not been reconciled. This does not apply to thought alone, but to the whole self, because there is anxiety when one's thought lacks some fundamental reconciliation. When this occurs, compartmentalisation could become a kind of splitting in order "to alleviate affective ambivalence"[71].

The puzzle in Uzor's research can be understood better and resolved now. He seems to have discovered something surprising and important, beyond what he set out to prove, namely that the ideals of the priesthood as perceived by Igbo seminarians are very much in agreement with many of the ideals of the Igbo society. Because this is the situation, it does not seem that many of them would feel they live between two worlds; the seminary life and the priesthood can be perceived as a further extension of their cultural ideals and a congenial place to realise their dreams in society. Igbo seminarians who actually feel the normal tension of renunciation for living the values of the priesthood would be in the minority. From the results of the present research, those with mature ideals would constitute 21.7% and 21.3% of the religious and diocesan seminarians respectively.

Now, we can draw some practical implication of this information on the concrete lives of Igbo priests, bringing out their struggles and the challenges they face.

The Basic Struggle of the Igbo Priest: to Belong

The basic struggle of Igbo priests and seminarians could be expressed in form of questions: how does one become both an Igbo man and a Catholic priest? Is it possible to struggle to achieve and receive social recognition as an Igbo without hurting oneself deeply as a Catholic priest? How could one live the priestly values of simple lifestyle without feeling inferior before one's counterparts in the Igbo society? Is the Catholic priesthood enough to make the desire for one's own family and children something that can be given up without regret? These questions express the deep desire to belong to the Igbo society and, at the same time, remain an authentic Catholic priest. They reveal a kind of dilemma that I call the dilemma of belonging, which every Igbo priest must seek to resolve in one way or the other[72]. The data of this research highlights different factors that constitute this dilemma, and the research findings of Okorie give some insight on the effects of this struggle in the lives of many Igbo priests. Our intention in this section is to expose the reality and nature of this dilemma and the various ways people tend to deal with it.

Covert passivity among the Igbo seminarians suggests the presence of some kind of homelessness that could be felt by ordained priests in a culture in which social validation of one's value is significant. From the findings of the present research, it seems that a good number of Igbo priests, like the Igbo seminarians in our research, perceived the priesthood, during their formation period, as an avenue to realize their dreams which may or may not be in consonance with the priestly life. Sometime after ordination, the pursuit of the so-called projects of ego-enhancement, which lies at the root of incongruous lifestyles among priests, would no longer satisfy. Disillusionment follows and reveals itself in the form of a dilemma, the dilemma of belonging.

Igbo society, like many societies in Africa, is fundamentally communitarian in the sense that the identity of the individual is intrinsically connected with his belonging to the community. Interdependence rather than independence is the social ethic. Belonging to a specific community within the Igbo society goes beyond the fact of birth; it includes the recognition of one's place in society, and one's achievements that have been socially validated. They range from founding and raising a family of one's own to the possession of distinguished and respected positions or titles in the community. At the present time, public signs of prosperity such as gorgeous buildings, expensive cars, and flagrant display of wealth in public functions like fundraising ceremonies, have also assumed the symbolic status of achievement.

Thus, there are three ways, it seems to me, a person ratifies his or her belonging to a specific Igbo community beyond being born an Igbo. These are: founding and raising one's own family, appropriation of one's place in the community, and achievement that is socially recognised.

To Marry and Beget Children

Marriage is central among the Igbos and it constitutes the centre of the social network, formed from the nuclear family through the extended families to the different lineages that become the clans and towns[73]. Each marriage is expected to be fruitful, that is, to have children with at least one male child who is supposed to be the bearer of the family's name and carry it on to future generations.

A childless marriage is a failure. Sometimes a man may be very wealthy, but if he has no children his economic success may be regarded cynically as a wasted effort[74]. To ensure that descendants are not lacking "all sorts of marriages and unions (polygamy, nnuikwa = woman-heir-single-parent, nwanyi ilu nwanyi = woman-woman marriage, husband-helper, etc) are allowed"[75] in certain areas of Igboland.

If childless marriages are failures, marriages without male children are in deep crisis. Since descent is traced patrilineally,[76] there must be a legitimate male child who will take over the maintenance of the ancestral lineage from his father. Thus a couple, in the search of a male child, may end up giving birth to more than ten girls. But "not even an uncountable number of female issues can make up for a baby boy!"[77] In situations in which a marriage has only girls, the community of the man sometimes induces him to take another wife to see if God would bless them with a male child[78].

The aspiration to get married and have children – and male children in particular – is built on a world-view that sees the survival and continuation of a family or community in their posterity.

Every family maintains a successive line of male representatives, stretching from the land of the living to that of the dead. When no son is there to maintain the link it is assumed that the lineage is virtually moribund. That is a curse and the worst calamity that can happen to any Igbo family.[79]

This clearly indicates that both marrying and having children are not private affairs of the two persons concerned;[80] they are matters involving the whole community, including the dead ancestors. No Igbo man would like to disappoint his ancestors by breaking the lineage. And for this reason, to have family and children has assumed a social and religious significance: they indicate success in life and social worth and communion with one's ancestors[81]. They are also indices of virility on the part of the man and fertility on the part of the woman. So, in addition to boosting one's self-esteem in the society, marrying and having children are significant factors that enter into the definition of both sexual and gender identities.

The consequence of this aspect of the Igbo culture is that a childless man or woman remains psychologically insecure and existentially unfulfilled. For the man, his social standing and his manhood are in question; for the married woman, her apparent "infertility" casts doubt on her womanhood. Thus, behind this cultural demand to remain faithful to the ancestral lineage, procreation has assumed the psychological function of achievement and its absence creates some psychological injury.

Appropriation of One's Place in Society

African societies are generally communitarian. The individual "does not and cannot exist alone except corporately. He is simply part of the whole"[82]. Thus, every African can say "'I am, because we are; and since we are, therefore I am'. This is a cardinal point in the understanding of the African view of man"[83].

This African way of life means that each individual is connected to every other member of his or her community. It is a relationship that goes beyond the fact of birth to embrace shared beliefs, values, and cultural and religious mores. Socialisation takes place according to these shared systems of beliefs and practices. As E. Ilogu testifies concerning the Igbos: "Boys and girls gradually learn to perform the various functions belonging to their particular groups, and through that process, learn early how to contribute to the well-being of their community. They also learn early what things are done and what things custom prescribes as not done"[84]. Thus, an African grows up to know the place of the woman, man, mother, father, elder, diviner-priest, medicine-men, chief, titled men, etc. in the society. Africans live in a unitary universe, and so they see these roles not in isolation as "areas of specialisation", but in their relationship with the whole community and the whole cosmos. As long as the different nodal points of community relationship are functioning well, harmony is maintained in the cosmos, which embraces the world of the human beings and that of the spirits. By implication, the dysfunction or malfunction of one aspect affects the whole community. The recognition of and respect for one's place in society leads to social cohesion. In doing so, the individual claims his belonging to the community, and the community in its turn makes legitimate claims on the individual. Thus the individual and the community mutually create and recreate each other in a circular way.

The place of the Catholic priest in the community is different from the place of the chief of a town or the father of a family; the position of a man is different from that of a woman, and so on. These are clear to the Africans and are interconnected with each other; the action of any one person has a ripple effect in all segments of life. In this unitary vision of reality, crossing of boundaries or aberrant behaviour is seen and interpreted as a disruption of the harmony existing in the community and between the community and the spiritual world. Thus, certain behaviours are not seen as mere moral sins; they are considered as sacrileges that disrupt the cosmological harmony. For this reason, it is not enough to confess; expiation must be carried out to restore order[85]. In the industrialised cultures of Europe and North America, one who commits incest, for instance, is prosecuted and punished according to legal prescriptions. In traditional African societies, such an act is more than a breach of codified law; it is often believed to bring disharmony to the community: to the family, living and dead, and to the cosmos. In most cases, the offender loses his belonging to the community by being temporarily ostracised until sacrifices and other forms of expiation and propitiation have been carried out.

There have been certain incidents of priests and religious women who left their vocation but found it difficult to marry within their own communities. Some parents believe it is a sacrilege for their daughter or son to marry an ex-priest or ex-sister. Canonical dispensation and temporary vows make no sense to them. A would-be father-in-law was said to have fainted when he realised that his daughter's suitor was an ex-priest. The marriage ceremonies could no longer continue. In another occasion, a mother cried that her son should never marry an ex-sister because, "I do not want to incur God's wrath on my family", she said. This is probably the reason why the majority of those Igbos who have left the priesthood or religious life are more comfortable in Europe and North America, and some are married to white girls or to the Igbo girls who have lost much of this aspect of African religious consciousness. In the industrialized parts of Europe and North America, it is much easy for priests or religious to leave their vocations and marry, because it is part of the exercise of one's basic human rights.

Underlying these attitudes of the African-Igbo is a strong belief that priests and religious have been consecrated to God; and that is their permanent place in society. Some Africans urge the return to the unitary vision of reality of Africa as against the dualistic tendencies of western thought. But when it comes to concrete situations like this, they tend to see the African view as immature and naive. "The people", some argue, "should know that priests are human beings", not realizing that Africans' expectations that a priest or religious be coherent in their lives comes precisely from their unitary view of life, and it will take time, if at all, before it loses its grip in the consciousness of Africans. In the meantime people have to live and find meaning in their lives within this cosmological framework.

Achievements and Social Recognition

The complex structure of the family network among Igbo people is the bedrock of social life and provides the security of belonging that the individual needs for his well-being. Every Igbo man sees himself in terms of his belonging to a particular family and to the larger community; it is difficult to conceive an Igbo man outside this context. But this also means that everything an individual Igbo does has a social significance and must be understood and recognized as such; this forms a significant aspect of the Igbo man's self-identity. Thus, personal achievements tend to be weighted according to their social value; different methods are employed to transfer them into the social realm and confer an appropriate social value on them. It is logical then that Igbo society is structured into classes clearly marked by the degree of wealth, the nature and type of title(s) one has, and the associations to which one belongs[86]. The examination of the concept of *di* [master] and the custom of title-taking among Igbo people will demonstrate clearly how achievements and their social recognition have formed a potent source of belonging to the Igbo society.

The concept of *di* is an effort to ritualise the process of transformation of personal achievement into social status. It indicates that a person has distinguished himself in a particular sector of life, so as to be socially recognized as a «master» in that field. For example, *di-ji* [master farmer] justifies his mastery of farm work by possessing many barns of yam which he shares with his family and communities. *Di-mgba* [master wrestler] has distinguished himself in defending the pride of his family and community in a recreational show of strength. *Di-nta* [master hunter] has demonstrated his expertise in dealing with animals so that meat is available to his people. A *di-ochi* [master wine tapper] is known for his special palm wine. The central idea in this concept is that an ideal Igbo man must be a *di*, a master in a specific area of life, and that this must be socially recognized.

L. N. Mbefo interprets this cultural practice philosophically as "differentiated consciousness" by which Igbo people encourage "masters in different areas to emerge and from an amorphous mass, we experience a variety of possibilities"[87].

Knowing and experiencing oneself as competent is necessary for psychological health; and recognition of areas of competence is also of vital importance if a particular society is to grow, because productivity is enhanced when competent persons take charge of specific sectors of the social life. The social recognition of these distinguished Igbo sons, therefore, is an incentive to the younger ones to work hard and excel in their various activities for their own self-definition and for the good of their communities. This is a basic reason why the Igbos could reconstruct many parts of their land destroyed during the civil war.

However, the strict linkage between achievement/competence and social recognition in Igbo culture, poses a problem regarding the intrinsic value of activities. It creates a situation in which people tend to enjoy more the social impact of their symbols of competence, rather than their own experience of competence. The distinction between experience of competence and enjoyment of the social impact of competence is subtle, but it logically follows from the distinction between the intrinsic value of an activity and the performance of such an activity for some narcissistic end. This is important because one enjoys working hard, even if no obvious social recognition comes, one can still live in peace with oneself.

On the societal level today, emphasis seems to have shifted from authentic competence to the acquisition and maintenance of symbols of competence. This is what has happened in passing from the more traditional Igbo society to the modern one. Many Igbo persons today may not be interested in being distinguished business men, good and seasoned academics or teachers. What matters is getting money as quickly as possible, and raising visible structures in the community as social signs of having succeeded. The same thing seems to happen in the Church that Ozigbo observes the great retrogressive impact this search for social symbols or prestige has had on the Church in Igboland since the local clergy took over the management of the Church from the missionaries.

Many of our church projects are "white elephants." Our love of cement and steel projects, has become gargantuan. Many on-going Catholic projects are evidence of misplaced priorities in quest of prestige. Rather than learn from the costly experience of Europe, our younger churches are being stampeded into an architectural cul-de-sac. If one should look through Igboland, one would find that the beautiful stone churches of the 1930s are now completely unusable and unserviceable[88].

This is the shadow side of communitarian societies where emphasis is heavily placed on the social relevance of things and persons. What appears to be more important to the people today is that which is socially relevant here and now; the long-term implication is hardly considered. In this, the Igbos could be said to resemble the Romans who held that love of glory and praise "should be aroused and kindled, considering it to be in the interest of the commonwealth"[89]. St. Augustine calls it a vice "if the greed for glory is stronger in the heart than the fear or the love of God"[90]. He acknowledged that this desire for glory and honour may not be wholly uprooted from the heart of man; however, it should be overcome by the love of justice and truth, so that in doing things which are right and good in themselves, even if they do not have any social relevance, people will be able to put love of praise and honour to shame.

Personal achievement is also converted into social value by means of taking titles. Economic riches in their various forms are often not sufficient by themselves;[91] they must be ritually transformed into social significance by title taking. As M.A. Onwuejeogwu wrote:

> Wealth to be of any social value and significance has to be transformed into social status by the taking of titles (Echichi). Thus by a graded and systematic 'destruction' of accumulated economic wealth done by a socio-cultural process of public sacrifice and consumption, economic achievement is transformed into social status as indicated in the graded title system and associations characteristic of

Igbo society[92].

In becoming a titled man, "a person's achievement is institutionalised"[93]. He immediately assumes a high status in the society and is henceforth to be recognized and addressed by his title. His belonging to the particular community is then insured and assured. For example, *Onwanetirioha I* [the moon that shines for everybody] points to what he has spent on behalf of others and community development; *Ekwueme I* [he does as he says] indicating that he does not merely brag about having money; he demonstrates it. As can be observed, everyone wants to be the first; no one wants to be "the second." As L.N. Mbefo notes, "Igbo self-understanding does not expect to be second or third. Only the first is enough to support his ego"[94]. Sometimes a man may possess as many as five titles depending on what he has been able to demonstrate economically among the people concerned. And in all the titles he may possess, he is always the first.

This drive to succeed, and therefore to ratify one's belonging to the community through possession of symbols of social status, has been a significant factor in the economic and social development of the Igbo people especially after the Nigerian-Biafra war that saw the devastation of the Igboland. The fact that success is made socially relevant by means of title-taking, adds energy to the drive.

To really have nothing to show publicly as a concrete sign of success in Igbo society reduces one to nothing; his belonging to the community is, at most, limited to the fact of his birth. As L.N. Mbefo notes again, "the non-performer, the never-do-well, is the *'atamgboloko'*" [a useless fellow]. The result, according to him, "is the cut-throat rivalry or competitiveness that other people recognize as the choke that propels progress"[95]. What he does not seem to recognize is the shadow side of this drive: the manipulations and fraudulent practices that permeate their relationships, political organizations and businesses. And these have serious impacts on the life and survival of the Igbo in the current Nigerian setup.

But the Igbo must be a success: from founding and raising a family with children to having demonstrable signs of achievement as symbols of social status. "The Igbo are status seekers. To use a market metaphor, they believe that the world is a market place where status symbols can be bought"[96]. To be an achiever is a primary value and must be socially recognized in order for one to feel belonged fully to the Igbo social system. Otherwise, the person runs the risk of not having a respectable belonging in the community, of not being admitted into the community of good ancestors; in some cases, he may not even be accorded a good funeral because he is an *akalogeli* [a useless person][97].

The Dilemma of the Igbo Priest

The dilemma of the Igbo priest lies precisely in how to negotiate his belonging to Igbo society: through the search for and satisfaction of these desires and aspirations of his people that may not necessarily agree with the priestly vocation or through appropriating his proper place in society, which implies living the values of his vocation? From whichever angle this is looked at, the Igbo Catholic priest faces a real psychological hurdle, namely, coming to terms with his psychological experience of belonging or inclusion in Igbo society. The feeling of belonging through founding and raising a family is ruled out *ab initio* because he is a celibate. If he seeks to assert and maintain his belonging through demonstrable competence and achievement, he runs into difficulties also; and some are already experiencing this difficulty.

Igbo people do not simply accept those socially recognised symbols of achievement from their priest-sons whom they have learned so well to respect because of their vocation to serve God and the people. Being religiously sensitive people, they take serious the public declarations of the priest at ordination. The authentic understanding of the Catholic priest in Igbo society is that he is a spiritual man who carries with him God's love to human beings; someone who protects the people from the vagaries of life, known and unknown, and invokes God's blessings on them; someone who allies with the underprivileged and the poor and protects them from the possible oppression and aggression of the rich and the powerful. This is his area of competence and is socially recognised and accorded respect and honour. Any Igbo priest knows that this is his place.

It may well be that because a large number of Igbo priests have, consciously or subconsciously, given in to the pursuit of the symbols of achievement which the people do not identify with being a priest, e.g. having expensive cars, inappropriate relationships with women, displaying extravagance in wealth, allying with the rich and the powerful, and being highhanded in exercising authority, the people have begun to treat the priests anyhow, attacking them verbally and physically as well as associating them with the rich class of the society. Sociologically, these intimidations and attacks can be said to be the way the society seeks to remind the priests to take their proper place in society in order to maintain societal equilibrium[98]. It is a nonverbal invitation addressed to the Igbo priests by the social system to be true to their vocation. Thus, the pursuit of these symbols of achievement that may contradict the true meaning of the priesthood and the place accorded the priest in society, leaves an Igbo priest who is not quite mature in a dilemma: he does not fully belong to the Igbo society on the same terms as his lay counterparts nor does he fully belong as he could if he lived his vocation in a mature way.

Immaturity hinders some Igbo priests from experiencing a profound sense of belonging to the Igbo society. Some resolve this dilemma by acquiring more material things or more academic degrees; some through establishing businesses and institutions; some also resolve it by founding congregations or religious associations; others through seeking and securing secular and ecclesiastical positions; others still, through complete immersion into the secular society and its mores, disregarding their own integrity and authenticity as human beings and as priests. Others have taken the more regressive path of apathy toward ministry that smacks of passive aggression or that of antisocial recklessness with their ministry and life. Still others have escaped the Igbo society and settled in Europe and North America and identified with those societies, or even left the priesthood and married.

These solutions may not have resolved the real dilemma; they may have served the immediate need of calming the person down, while the real problem is postponed. In this sense, some who have left the priesthood might have even made a wiser decision than those who stay but are not settled because the solutions to the dilemma hitherto applied have been makeshifts. A typical instance is that of a priest who escaped into North America where he stayed for the greater part of his priestly life. As he entered into his sixties, the feeling of homelessness emerged. Eventually he decided to come back home. Coming back to his fatherland did not resolve the problem because he still felt like a fish out of water: his community saw him as involved in a betrayal; he could not even fit into the presbyterium any longer, despite the fact that the priests welcomed him back with open hands.

The dilemma is real; and the authentic way out of it is working towards maturity, towards the personalisation of one's vocation as an Igbo priest. Vocational maturity yields the psychological dividend of knowing and appropriating one's place in the destiny of the world and in the Igbo social system. It restores to the person the peace of his true belonging in society simply because vocational maturity is grounded in the recovery and appropriation of the priest's interiority[99]. There is no insoluble conflict here; a genuine and holy priest will have his own place in Igbo society. Vocational immaturity, on the other hand, leaves the individual with the feeling of homelessness, of being a wanderer in search of a home, inside and outside, which is externalised in the search for symbols of achievement that may never satisfy the yearning for a home.

Psychological Insight into the Struggles

In the last section, we were able to expose the fundamental struggle Igbo priests and seminarians live, which is expressed as the dilemma of belonging. This dilemma is real, and its healthy resolution is necessary for a fulfilling life as an Igbo Catholic priest. The resolution demands some insight into one's expectations, which may be realistic or unrealistic, and their relationship to one's personality. Expectations mostly express the personality of the individual – his goals, desires, needs, and values – and the more unrealistic they are in relation to the priesthood, the greater the possibility of alienation because the process of integrating one's vocational identity into the core of the personality could be undermined. The data of this research reveal that majority of Igbo seminarians training for the Catholic priesthood has expectations that seem to be largely immature or unrealistic, in the sense that the priesthood does not promise to fulfil certain ideals that are culturally relevant. This situation could create problems for the future priests if it is not dealt with, especially through greater self-knowledge and a deeper appropriation of the totality of the priestly vocation. In this section, we shall examine these issues for a deeper understanding of the basic struggles of Igbo priests.

The Danger of Unrealistic Expectations of Life

An effect of these struggles of the Igbo priests is that the flamboyant lives of some Igbo priests seem to enable the seminarians form unrealistic expectations of the priesthood in such a way that cultural ideals of achievement and recognition would appear to be realizable in the priesthood.

Unrealistic expectations are often expressed through idealisation or over-valuation. For instance, "if an individual is subconsciously wishing for a covert gratification of his needs, or hoping that his vocational decision will exempt him from having to meet and deal with the attendant conflicts, he is holding false and unrealistic expectations"[100]. Future life as a priest is then idealized not "as an expression of values, but as a solution to personal problems"[101]. When this occurs, priestly commitment includes a latent condition that personal needs should be satisfied or that personal problems should be resolved. Frustration could set in and enthusiasm diminishes as it is realised that priestly life is neither mere satisfaction of personal needs, nor do personal conflicts go away just by becoming a priest. When expectations do not reflect the reality as it is, the probability of frustration and confusion is high, and incongruities in vocational lifestyle can be the result.

Unrealistic expectations often have their root in the subconscious aspect of the personality, and are expressed in the tendency to select a part of reality or add to it what it does not have. A man wants to marry a wife, but his subconscious expectation is that the woman will be a mother to him. He idealises the woman as a "perfect wife". But the woman cannot be both a wife and a mother to her husband. A man wanted to be a priest but with a subconscious expectation that the priesthood would resolve his problem of affective dependence. When the priesthood could not do that, he got frustrated and left[102].

Unrealistic and false expectations arising from subconscious needs have been linked to the tendency of human beings to pursue a good that is only apparently good, rather than real. In pursing an apparent good, the person is seeking the satisfaction of his or her subconscious needs; in other words, the person is seeking himself or herself and not the good in itself. Entering any vocation, persons *expect* these needs to be satisfied.

The search for the apparent good generally leads people to frustration and inauthentic life precisely because it only "appears to be good", and so it can deceive; and "the more it seems good, the more it will be deceptive"[103]. The more the priesthood or the religious life *appears* to be an object that can satisfy a person's need for social relevance, the more attractive it becomes. The real good, on the other hand, expressed in realistic expectations, leads one to self-transcendence, and therefore, to authenticity[104].

When a seminarian enters the priestly vocation with subconscious needs that largely contradict the values of the vocation, he may not be aware of them; at the same time, he must try to satisfy them in one way or the other since the needs are there in him. If he does not satisfy them directly, he does so in a covert way. Thus, the gratification of a subconscious need for social relevance could be sought *covertly* in the priesthood, through exaggerated identification with the role of the priest and other positions of power in the Church or in society. Such a person may be more interested in being the chairman of many committees in the diocese than in being a priest.

The danger of false and unrealistic expectations lies in the fact that the satisfaction of those subconscious needs does not necessarily address the fundamental question of the value of the person[105], and so the person gets frustrated. Why, for instance, does such a person want higher positions of power and to belong to many committees? It is because at each step, he would falsely hope and expect, subconsciously, that he would be completely satisfied. But then, after some time, the need resurfaces and demands satisfaction; and so, he seeks for something more. In this way, such a person "is led by his false expectations into a vicious circle, which may lead him to abandon his vocation literally, or to the form of 'abandoning', implicit and perhaps partial, which is called 'nesting'"[106].

Unrealistic expectation can also be present at the conscious level. For instance, a seminarian expects that through the priesthood, he will be able to raise the financial condition of his family, and will realise it through making connections within and outside the country. After his ordination, he hopes to be given a rich parish, and sent overseas after a few years. However, with the euphoria of ordination ceremonies over, he is posted to a suburban parish. After eight years in the ministry, none of his expectations has come true. He is frustrated and angry, and even begins to pilfer from the Church's money entrusted to his care, neglect his priestly ministry, and experience loss of enthusiasm and morale. He gets involved in certain moral problems and risks some psychological ones as well.

Realistic expectation of priestly vocation as a future goal or ideal, therefore, implies a more complete vision of that goal at both the conscious and subconscious levels. It means the capacity to discriminate realistically what the priesthood is and what it is not, because it is possible to have false expectations due to the tendency of the human being to seek the apparent good[107].

To have realistic expectations of the priestly vocation implies that the person has a relatively complete vision of the priestly values. In the present research, the overall completeness of the values of the priestly ideals of the Igbo seminarians is assessed by their scores on the Algebraic Index of Maturity. The research results show that the vocational ideals of the majority of Igbo religious and diocesan seminarians are incomplete and so immature. Compared with the international subjects, the expectations Igbo seminarians have of the priestly vocation are more unrealistic and often involve a covert passivity. Igbo religious seminarians are more realistic about the spiritual basis of the priestly vocation than the Igbo diocesan seminarians.

Personal Needs and Selective Attention – Passivity in Life!

Passivity consists in attempting to evade the normal tensions of life through selective attention to the areas of life that one feels that personal needs would be satisfied. This tendency can be obvious and therefore *overt* or disguised and therefore *covert*[108]. The individual who is overtly passive is inclined to see inactivity as acceptable; he tends to wait for a quasi-magical resolution of his difficulties. Imagine the man who believes that the problems of his marriage will resolve themselves at some time in the future, but he does not do anything concrete to solve the problem. "It will work out", some usually say. In the same way, some people entertain the wish that they will one day be good, holy and fulfilled priests or religious; it will happen one day to them with no pain or suffering. This is a mere wishful optimism which favours inactivity and encourages the effort to avoid the normal tensions or pains of life.

On the other hand, *covertly* passive Christian vocationers strive to achieve their goals by *actively* employing whatever means are within their reach. However, instead of seeking to realise the totality of the values of the Christian vocation, they select a few of these and reinterpret others according to their personal needs. Take the example of the man who wants to marry, have children and his own family, *in order to be like others*, but does not believe in being committed to his wife. He selects certain aspects of

Christian marriage and leaves out commitment, or becomes *passive* to it. In the same way, certain priests and religious make arbitrary selection of some aspects of the priesthood and religious life and avoid others or become passive to them. In these two instances, it is like a person wants to be a priest but it has to be the way he "feels it good for himself". This is covert passivity and such persons may be working hard in their priestly vocation, but for a different reason. For instance, a priest works very hard to be obedient but in order to be given the title of Monsignor one day or even made a bishop.

The findings of this research show that 65.2% of the entire group of Igbo seminarians show such covert passivity. In essence, these subjects are in priestly vocation but are pursuing goals that are in part defined by their personal ambitions. It could be that the cultural ideals of achievement and social recognition are central in such persons so that the priesthood appears to be largely perceived in such terms. In the long run, this condition could generate some form of alienation in the individual.

Alienation of the Self and Nesting in Vocation

To be mature in one's vocation implies that the priest or seminarian has been able to make his own the values of the priestly vocation to a reasonable degree[109]. This means that not only is it clear to him what the goal of priestly vocation is, but that these values are to a high degree consistent with the rest of his self, the conscious and the subconscious aspects, so that he is motivated by all the components of his self in realising his ideal. This means that he has developed that "willingness" which is the state in which he no longer needs to be persuaded to make decisions and choices that integrate rather than divide him as a priest[110]. The reason for this is the presence and maturity in the person of what Aschenbrenner calls the original "presumption of perseverance and permanence" of being called to a loving relationship with God in Jesus, as a priest. It is the presumption that God really calls him to the priestly commitment and ministry for the rest of his life, until he dies[111]. The maturation of this presumption rests on the extent the person has made the priestly vocation the center of his life. In which case, the priest who is mature in his vocation lives a life that is integrated to a large extent because "the rudder of such presumptive priestly identity provides a guidance of interpretation that gives clear direction to life"[112]. Because the priestly vocation constitutes the center and meaning of his life, it penetrates all his daily life and activities, providing a solid and enduring orientation to his experiences.

Immaturity, on the other hand, implies a state of contradiction within the person, inconsistency of some aspects of the self[113]. It means, for instance, that the seminarian who is largely immature is not aware of those aspects of his self that are in opposition to the priestly life he wants to live. For this reason, he does not experience conscious tension in those areas, because they are alienated from consciousness; this being the case, they cannot be challenged to growth and integration by the values[114]. A seminarian for whom it is important to be at the center of attention may not be aware the extent he tries to seduce people by his behaviour. Yet, when he is frustrated because he is not recognized, he may tend to blame others who are "jealous of me". He is frustrated but does not know the true source. The observation of L.M. Rulla is clearer, that a person may not only be unaware of his or her inconsistencies but also unaware of the tension associated with them as well as the activities he or she undertakes to resolve or escape from them[115].

Thus, the theoretical contradiction in the structures of the self may not necessarily lead to a conscious experience of uneasiness within the person as long as conditions are favourable. This explains why some priests and religious have constructed a nest for themselves in the vocation where their orientation is principally the pursuit of their personal desires or satisfaction of their needs, while human and vocational growth is abandoned[116].

This is also why some degree of vocational immaturity may be connected to psychological underdevelopment. A prominent desire of the underdeveloped person is to enhance his or her sense of self-identity. Problematic issues in his or her life are removed from consciousness through the mechanisms of isolation, repression, and regression and are carefully masked by such ventures as intellectual pursuits, administrative skills, and other socially recognised symbols of achievement and efficiency[117].

It is this alienated subconscious aspect of the self which is more or less projected onto the priesthood and then seen as an avenue where one's needs would be gratified. A narcissist who feels he is special may project this aspect of himself and perceive the priesthood as a vocation reserved for special people like himself. He works his way carefully to the priesthood because he craves for fame and popularity, and he feels the priesthood will offer him those desires. For such a person, the priesthood is merely a stop-over, a starting point for other higher ambitions marked out for special people like him. The values of the priesthood are then compromised through distortion and/or arbitrary selection of some of them and neglect of others, because what he feels is important to him prevails over the true reality of priestly vocation. Having found the gratification of their needs in the vocation, these persons build a nest in the vocational institution[118]. The finding of this research, that a large portion of Igbo seminarians has ideals that are immature, suggests that there are many nesters among them.

The term "nesting" may suggest overt passivity, but the basic idea is that priestly vocation is being used to satisfy oneself more than to realize values of the Gospel. The needs being gratified might be those of success, recognition, domination, popularity, and so on; they could require much energy, aiming however at subjective satisfaction rather than at Christian values. In other words, "nesting", like passivity, can be overt or covert.

The Personality of the Individual

Okorie and Ukwuoma saw the problems of Nigerian priests as consequences of stress and lack of satisfaction in their ministry, and Uzor would be inclined to see them as results of the intrapersonal conflicts deriving from the fact that Igbo seminarians and Igbo priests are torn between two epistemological worlds: one that is heavily western and dualistic and the other that is Igbo-African and unitary. Other authors link these problems to socio-cultural influences and the ineffectiveness of formation.

It can be seen from the findings of this research and from the re-reading of the research-results of Okorie and Uzor, for instance, that the problem touches all these areas. Their interpretations converge at the basic question of how Igbo seminarians are formed as future Catholic priests. We recognise that two contexts are involved in their formation, namely, the Christian and the Igbo. But it is the personality of each seminarian that mediates between the two contexts. Again, the manner in which these struggles are experienced and lived depends on the personality of the individual priest.

Drawing from the biological insights of H.R. Manturana and F.J. Varela, we know that every individual is a living being with a unique personality. And it is the rule that in the interactions between any living being and the environment in which it lives "the perturbations of the environment do not determine what happens to the living being; rather, it is the structure of the living being that determines what change occurs in it"[119]. In other words, every individual as a unique living system is somehow structurally defined in their personality. This means that all the changes that take place in them, as in any living system, are mediated by the way their personality functions[120]. Whatever changes that may occur, they can either be the results of the structural dynamics of the unique living system or are triggered off by the interactions between the living system and the environment. The environment could be a source of perturbations, but the specific changes that come about within the individual are mediated by his structure. That is why it is usually the personality of an individual that gives structure to any unstructured situation.

Thus, the success or failure of the mediation between the Christian and Igbo contexts in formation rests fundamentally both on the personality of the individual and on the seminary structure which embodies these two contexts. We understand seminary structure here to include the formators and the seminarians and their different modes of interaction, what is taught, the guiding regulations of the seminary, the physiology of the seminary, like the number of the seminarians, accommodation, and feeding. Whatever can be said about the seminary environment, in the final analysis it is the individual seminarian and the way he functions psychologically that is the primary mediator of the formation process. Although all the seminarians live in the same environment, some turn out to have clearer and authentic vision of the priesthood while others do not.

The limitation of the interpretations of the authors reviewed in this work regarding the problems and struggles of Igbo priests lies in their neglect of this factor in formation. The interpretations seem to focus unduly on the seminary environment and underestimate the fact that the seminarian is a unique entity who functions in a certain way that is unique to him. Igbo priests experience enthusiasm, satisfaction, and morale in various ways in their life and ministry. The external situation may remain the same, but the experience varies from one priest to another, due to the personality of the individual. The same thing could be said regarding the experience of intrapersonal conflict: it all depends on how each person sees and receives the challenging process of formation. But it also depends on the kind of formation that is provided.

The actual situation of the Igbo priests and their formation seems to be that little attention is paid to their unique personalities in order to know the kind of help each person would need. Because of this neglect, some seminarians go through the seminary formation with little or no change in the ideals they entered with nor is any substantial help offered them to help them understand themselves and the difficulties they are aware or unaware of in relation to the priestly vocation. Some of their ideals may be in agreement with the priestly life they are pursuing, and after ordination they emerge as incongruities in their lives and ministries. The findings of the present research demonstrate that the majority of the seminarians in theological studies, who are close to their priestly ordination, have ideals that are defined only in part by the objective ideals of the priestly vocation, showing a selectiveness that depends on their respective personality.

These are the psychological issues related to the basic struggle of Igbo priests and seminarians. They do not present an easy situation, but, at least, the problems could be identified so that appropriate assistance could be offered. In the light of what has been said, we shall now assess the state of vocations in Igboland drawing from the findings of this study.

Ꝟ

The Meaning of Vocation Boom in Igboland

In this chapter, we shall address the question of the meaning of the vocation boom in Igboland, the areas that are lacking in the vocational stories of the future priests, and what these are saying to the Church in Igboland.

What Does the Vocation Boom Suggest?

The results of this study reveal something important about the number of vocations to the priesthood in Igboland, especially to the diocesan priesthood: that big numbers do not necessarily indicate vocational maturity. The findings show that a large number of Igbo seminarians has ideals that only partially correspond to the true values of the priesthood. There is a notable omission of the variables of the priestly vocation in their stories of the imagined future. This suggests that some people who strive to become priests in Igboland use the priesthood as a way to pursue other goals besides those of the priestly vocation. This reveals itself as incongruities in lifestyle and ministry, which range from inordinate acquisition and use of wealth, search for power, to abuse of authority; whatever satisfies personal desires, needs, and ambitions.

This could imply that the increase in the vocations to the priesthood among the Igbo people does not necessarily indicate strong religious convictions around which seminarians and priests build their vocational identity. The meaning of the "vocation boom" in Igboland is rather ambiguous. It could seem to suggest an abundance of men who sincerely want to give themselves to God in the service of human beings as Jesus Christ and the apostles did. The results of the present research show that seminarians with such real and authentic ideals are few in number: 21.7% of the religious and 21.3% of the diocesan seminarians. On the other hand, the results reveal a large number whose vision of the priestly life is immature, seminarians for whom the priesthood is at least partly a place to satisfy their ego and social needs: 63.3% of the religious and 66.7% of the diocesan seminarians.

This would mean that the priesthood could be attracting some Igbo young men who may have a strong need to enhance their self-identity[1], young men who may expect to live through the role and the opportunities offered by the priesthood rather than through their own personalities[2]. This is rather a hard observation to make but it needs to be made. The data of this research should alert bishops and directors of formation to be very careful in the selection, discernment, and formation of those who feel called to the priesthood. The situation does not allow for carelessness or inattention to the goings-on in the seminaries.

Weak Spiritual Motives for the Priesthood

The Catholic priesthood is fundamentally a spiritual calling to which the individual graciously responds. But if the spiritual basis of this call is weak, on what foundation would it rest? This is an interesting finding of this research, and we need to examine it in detail.

A major finding of this research is that Igbo religious seminarians include more experience-of-discipleship variables in their stories of the imagined future than do Igbo diocesan seminarians. This means that they are more motivated in their vocational ideals by spiritual motives than the Igbo diocesan seminarians. Further, the research showed that in comparison with the international group, Igbo seminarians (both groups taken together) are more limited in the number of experience-variables included. In this section, we shall explore the meaning of this finding in two ways: first, we shall interpret it as it relates to the religious and diocesan priests and seminarians in general; secondly, we shall present the consequences it might have on the Igbo priests and seminarians, religious and diocesan alike.

Between Igbo Religious and Diocesan Seminarians

There is no significant difference in the total number of cost-of-discipleship variables present among Igbo religious seminarians and Igbo diocesan seminarians: $t = 0.322$, $P = 0.748$. In other words, there are no differences in the way the two groups perceive the demanding aspect of the priestly vocation. However, Igbo religious seminarians include more experience-of-discipleship variables than do the Igbo diocesan seminarians, a trend which became more evident when the two groups were compared with the international group. This means that Igbo religious seminarians are more conscious of the importance of being receptive to God in their vocation: they can depend on the providence of God, and trust in his sustaining power in times of difficulty. It further shows that more than their diocesan counterparts, Igbo religious seminarians have a more solid and balanced spiritual life as an important aspect of their ideals; they expect it to be their fundamental *manner of being* the priest from which their activities derive; they have a more developed interiority than the diocesan seminarians.

In general, this means that for the Igbo diocesan seminarians, receptivity in personal relationship with God as future priests does not receive as significant a place in their ideals as for their religious counterparts. Among the experience-of-discipleship variables, Igbo religious seminarians are significantly better than the Igbo diocesan seminarians on Power and Security. These two variables express the disposition of the seminarian to see God as his truest security and thus to be ready to depend on Him in the uncertain circumstances of life; fundamentally, they indicate a secure anchoring in God. This implies that Igbo diocesan seminarians tend to see their future life as priests more as a personal effort to give security to their lives than as a vocation which is basically rooted in a relationship with God.

The experience of discipleship, indicated by the experience-variables included, is important because it is the reason for accepting the cost of discipleship. If one undertakes to live the cost-of-discipleship variables by themselves, this can be a matter of pride or ambition, because people generally can endure a lot of physical or social privation if this is in harmony with their self-esteem[3]: for instance, "girls may starve themselves to look beautiful, and athletes endure real pain for the sake of success. A scientist may lead the life of a hermit and not find it burdensome"[4]. A Pharisee performs many spiritual feats but for a different motive, namely, to feel good in himself. But a good Christian fasts, gives alms, and keeps vigils, for a different reason, for the sake of his relationship with God through which he feels himself connected to others. Hence St. Paul says, "If I gave everything I had to the poor, and even gave up my own body, but only to receive praise and not through love, it would be no value to me"[5].

Thus, the spiritual motivation stands at the foundation of all privations and renunciations in the Christian life; it is the experience of that love which exists between the God who calls and the priest who is called that gives true meaning to the sacrifices in his life and ministry.

This love of God is fundamentally a gift to be *received*[6]; it is grace, that "*free and undeserved help* that God gives us to respond to his call to become children of God..."[7]. It is the foundation of the Christian vocation and necessarily requires the priest to grow in intimate union with God. Thus the Fathers of the Second Vatican Council insist that it is the intimacy between the priest and Jesus Christ that holds the life and ministry of the priest together[8]. Growing in that intimacy, priests shall be able to discern whether the projects they carry out agree with the mission God entrusted to the Church[9]. For this reason also, the Council Fathers emphasized that greater attention should be given to the spiritual formation of the candidates for the priesthood so that "the students may learn to live in intimate and unceasing union with

God the Father through his Son Jesus Christ, in the Holy Spirit"[10].

In different ways, the preparatory documents for the 8th Synod of Bishops on the formation of priests in the circumstances of today, the interventions of the Fathers of the Synod, and the post-synodal apostolic exhortation, *Pastores Dabo Vobis*, emphasise the primacy of the *intimate relationship* that should exist between the priest and Jesus Christ as the foundation of priestly life and apostolate. Affirming that the spiritual formation "is the center of unity for all preparation for the ministry"[11], the *Lineamenta* hold that formation should be able to lead seminarians "to an intimate knowledge of Jesus Christ and, in him, to a sense of God who is 'rich in mercy'"[12]; the *Instrumentum Laboris* emphasises that "in the life of the priest the *spiritual dimension takes precedence* over every other aspect, no matter how important or essential another aspect might seem, e.g., the apostolate"[13]. This spiritual dimension consists principally "in an authentic relationship of *intimate friendship* with Him [Jesus Christ]"[14], which "implies a *deep experience of prayer…*"[15].

The interventions of the Fathers during the Synod also carry the same emphasis of the primacy of spiritual formation. R.J.R. Umaña of El Salvador asserted that spiritual formation is not only the centre of all formation *but* the reason and principal motivation for the human, intellectual, and pastoral growth of the priest[16]. In his own intervention, the archbishop of Malta, J. Mercieca, notes that the personal relationship with Jesus Christ to which the priest is called by virtue of his vocation, is a gift of the Holy Spirit, and requires that the priest be receptive to it, by developing a profound life of prayer[17]. A. Bala of Bafia, Cameroon, emphasised that the life of the priest must revolve around his attachment to Christ[18].

In the post-synodal apostolic exhortation, *Pastores Dabo Vobis*, Pope John Paul II recalls to the priests that the Holy Spirit is the principle of their consecration and configuration to Christ[19]. This implies that the priest should be open to the special grace given to him by deepening the intimate relationship between him and Jesus Christ. This he can concretely realise by continually renewing and deepening his awareness of being a minister of Christ[20]. Again the emphasis is that the experience of the love of Jesus and the growth in the personal relationship with Him is primary in the life of the priest, and gives direction and meaning to the priest's efforts to love and serve the Church[21]. It is the reception and consciousness of the love of Jesus (experience-of-discipleship) that calls forth from the priest a generous response (cost-of-discipleship)[22]. The relationship between experience of discipleship and cost of discipleship is what the Pope described as the "unbreakable bond between divine grace and human responsibility"[23]. While the two sides of Christian vocation are intimately bound together, the one precedes the other otherwise the sense of human responsibility (expressed in terms of the cost of discipleship) can turn the Christian vocation into a merely private and personal achievement.

The Dangers in the Diocesan Priesthood

The limited presence of experience-of-discipleship in the lives of the future diocesan priests indicates that they are lacking in that which they need most: intimacy with God. A diocesan priest is totally dependent on his intimacy with God for the unity of his life and actions. The religious priest has the support of his community which not only provides him with structure, but also prevents him from unrestrained ambition. It is difficult, for instance, to be very proud of one's intelligence, when one is surrounded by other intelligent persons. Without a deep relationship with God, the diocesan priest can follow whatever ambition he sets out for himself. This is happening already in some dioceses in the world and in Igboland. Secondly, the religious enjoys the company of his community members, and this is a help to him especially in living out the evangelical counsel of chastity[24]; the diocesan priest is most of the time alone and therefore has the greater possibility of being lonely. But such loneliness can be transformed into solitude only if he has a profound relationship with Jesus Christ, "sustained by daily prayer and the Eucharist"[25].

If the diocesan priest is lacking in this "his fundamental mystical-sacramental dimension"[26] especially in this secularized world, this can lead to activism or busyness that lacks integration with the spiritual center of the priestly life and ministry. The tension between prayer and work will be resolved often in favour of work[27]. This has negative consequences as revealed in a study of 239 Catholic priests – 94% being diocesan priests – conducted to find out the relationship between burnout and depression. A significant finding of the research is that there is a close relationship between personal prayer, agreement with the Church's teachings, spiritual reading, solitude and low degree of burnout, less depression and a sense of personal accomplishment[28]. The finding highlights the risk involved in the neglect of the personal relationship between the person called to the priestly vocation and the caller, God himself through the Church. This is also confirmed by the results of D.R. Hoge's research which show that lack of a solid spiritual life represents a serious danger to the priest[29]. For this reason, the newly ordained in the United States strongly recommend the development of a strong prayer life in the seminary without which the active ministry of the diocesan priest risks losing its bearing[30].

A possible reason for this difference between the Igbo religious seminarians and Igbo diocesan seminarians could be traced to the difference in the lifestyles of the religious and diocesan priests. It may well be that the community life of the religious priests favours their being more attuned to the importance of a personal relationship with God and dependence on divine providence as an integral aspect of their dependence on the community. It is true that the diocesan priest belongs to the local diocesan community, relating with the bishop, the priests working in the diocese, and the laity. But in his concrete life as a pastor, he is by himself, within the structure he creates by himself, a structure that is constantly threatened by the countless demands made on him[31]. In many aspects of his life, he receives some guidelines and is then left to decide for himself. For instance, he is allowed to have some material things of his own but only counselled to live with discretion. The religious priest, on the other hand, is dependent on his community to provide for his needs[32]. This spares him the difficulties of having to make decisions and choices. Human beings desire to be free and choose from many possibilities.

However, it is equally true that when persons have many alternatives and feel they are left to exercise unconstrained freedom in choosing, they can become paralysed; they need some guidelines on how to pattern their choices. To avoid this difficulty, "cultural institutions go a long way toward telling people where they can choose and where they cannot, and within the domains where choice is allowed, these institutions determine what the possibilities are"[33].

These two dispositions have practical implication in the life of the religious and diocesan priests and the very consciousness of their priestly identity. The more concrete and structured self-dispossession of the religious in his community life and the vows of the evangelical counsels may favour in him a greater disposition of self-emptying toward God, a conscious awareness of belonging to God like Jesus Christ, and so help him to render his service to mankind from this inner disposition.

The situation of the diocesan priest is different because it is less structured: he makes a promise of obedience to his bishop, and is counselled to live the value of poverty. What these mean precisely in the concrete may remain vague to a diocesan priest. Yet, the evangelical counsels do not make any less demand on him than they make on the religious, if the diocesan priest is to live the profound truth of his priestly vocation[34]. The less structured situation of the diocesan priest may favour in him a greater sense of personal autonomy and of striving for personal security, which may provide him some psychological support, but which may have negative effects on his sense of personal relationship with God as a primary disposition of his being, the solid source of his priestly identity[35]. It is possible that he may devote more time to seeking for his security, and giving insufficient attention to his spiritual life[36]. D. Cozzens rightly observes:

> Finding time for contemplative prayer remains a significant challenge for the diocesan priest. The almost unbearable demands upon his time make this challenge all the more difficult. The call to contemplative prayer remains, nonetheless, as imperative for the diocesan priest

as it is for the priest in religious life[37].

In that sense, it could be asserted that the vocation of the diocesan priest is psychologically more precarious than that of the religious and would demand, by that very fact, more robust psychological maturity from the candidates for the diocesan priesthood. Candidates for the diocesan priesthood need to possess the necessary psychological resources that will enable them live their vocation maturely in the less structured situations of the ministry.

The structured condition of religious communities, on the other hand, could help protect immature individuals from acting out their immaturity. This protection, however, could also be frustrating to the person, since his dissonant needs may not be freely gratified. This could explain some of the findings of D.R. Hoge's research on American priests. First, his research showed that religious priests feel lonelier than diocesan priests; common sense would suggest it would be the contrary. Secondly, religious priests complain more about the present structure of authority in the Church than diocesan priests. Thirdly, more than diocesan priests, religious priests perceive celibacy as one of the chief problems today: only 33% are satisfied with their life as celibates while 53% of diocesan priests are satisfied with theirs[38].

The Entire Igbo Seminarians

When compared to the international group, the Igbo group as a whole includes fewer experience-variables in their stories of the imagined future.

For the Igbo people, two things are of primary importance, namely, the family and achievement or success. An ideal Igbo man must be virile and able to maintain the communion with the living and the dead members of his lineage by founding his own family with children. The Igbo woman is the typical mother who has given birth to males and females. Newly married couples receive a blessing from the elders to fill their house with children; to give birth to males and females and to be taken care of in their old age by their children. This tradition is so embedded in the life of the Igbo people that those who seem to have received a lot of western education still find it difficult to free themselves from it even when they know that something might be medically wrong with the man or the woman so as to create some difficulties in conception[39].

Because one's own family is an integral part of one's self-esteem, it provides one with a solid ground for striving to achieve. The maintenance of his family is a reason for a man's ambition. If a man is successful, but lacks children of his own, he feels inferior and unfulfilled. Thus, these two things – the family and success – increase a person's self-esteem and are necessary to consolidate his or her belonging to the Igbo community.

The Igbo priest, being a celibate, does not have a family of his own or children. He has brothers and sisters and relatives from the extended family, but these do not substitute for his own family and children. What can then happen is that everything he is and has may be invested in trying to be a success, for nature (and also culture) abhors a vacuum. But since he does not have the cultural ground for his achievements as do his married counterparts (that is, his own family), his ambitions and achievements can become merely egocentric. He may invest his achievements in caring for his relatives, brothers and sisters, nieces and nephews, but these remain relatives, so that at some point, a priest may feel he does not belong, especially if the relatives remind him that he does not have a share of their property. In the long run, this may not give him the fulfilment he is seeking or consolidate his belonging to the community; it may alienate him from both himself and from the community.

What should directly enable Igbo priests and other African priests to deal with the issue of lack of personal family and children is a strong intimacy with God reflected in the experience-variables, and manifested in pastoral charity. This requires first, a solid spiritual life; secondly, a conscious broadening of the concept of the family to embrace the family of the Church; and thirdly, the internalization of Church-as-family to such a degree that the Igbo priest truly lives the experience of *spiritual fatherhood*[40]. As the Fathers of Special Assembly for Africa advise African priests: "Africa, which loves family life, reveres the father figure. Do not disappoint her. The Church counts on you to exercise faithfully this spiritual fatherhood without sparing yourself"[41]. When intimacy with Jesus Christ is lacking, the priest risks losing touch with himself and the true meaning of the priesthood. With the Igbo cultural value of being a socially recognized success, priesthood could be turned into "a religious bureaucracy"[42], fruitless and lifeless.

The consciousness and the internalization of the place of the priest in the Church-as-Family would be ineffective in the absence of intimate personal relationship with God nourished by a deep prayer life. It will remain a theological abstraction without a direct impact on the life of the individual priest.

This need for intimacy with God is more urgent for the African diocesan priest than for his religious brothers. The community life of the religious priest already provides him with a helpful structure to develop the consciousness of a religious family, of brothers living together, and serving a common cause. The diocesan priest lacks this structure and must find it in his intimacy with God, which is directed outward to the care and service of the people of God entrusted to his care.

The manner of living of Jesus best fits the diocesan priest: from the depth of His relationship with His Father, constantly nurtured by prayer experiences, Jesus was able to manage the tension between his ministry and his prayer life. Often, very early in the morning, before daylight, Jesus goes to a lonely place to pray[43]. In that intimate union of love with His Father, he could discern the Father's will in the midst of his busy ministry. In this connection, Greshake affirms that, "it is only when pastoral activity is founded upon contemplation that it does not lose sight of its proper goal of leading the community entrusted to it into a personal relationship with God which is particularly expressed in prayer"[44]. This is perhaps the reason why all that Jesus asked Peter, who was to be the future leader of the Church, was: "Do you love me?"[45]. And this question He asked three times, to emphasize its importance. Whatever Peter was to do must flow from his intimate knowledge of and love for Jesus, and nothing else. This is the biggest challenge of the diocesan priests.

Summary

We have seen the status of priestly vocation in Igboland in the light of the data of this study. We saw that not all that glittered was gold: the vocation boom is ambiguous because only less than a third of all those who aspire to be priests express authentic and realistic vision of the priesthood. Majority of them are more driven by personal ambition and aspirations. This confirms the impression voiced out by Most Rev. A.K. Obiefuna, the then bishop of Awka diocese, in 1993, that many persons came to the priesthood as a *means* to pursue and achieve their private ambitions[46].

This sheds some light on the incongruous lifestyles some priests have adopted. Some seminarians, for instance, expect to use the priesthood to feed their ego, amass wealth, upgrade the financial condition of their family, and acquire popularity. It is not surprising that when they become priests, they can steal the Church's money, go after rich people, exploit poor people, erect buildings in their families with money stolen from the church under their care, engage themselves only in things that make them popular. Such persons will very likely neglect certain aspects of their primary life and duties. How do we explain, for instance the attitude of some priests who find it so difficult to visit the sick because they are not disposed or that the road is not good for their car? What of those who steal huge sums of the Church's money to do their personal projects or realize their ambitions, and not see it as immoral or even as a crime?

The situation calls to question the effectiveness of the formation given to our future priests both in and outside the seminaries. If the number of seminarians with unrealistic or false expectations of the priesthood is very high as indicated in this study, something is not working well with the formation models. In Part III of this work, we shall review these formation methods in order to highlight their advantages and disadvantages, and then we shall propose a kind of formation that will be more effective in the present circumstances. It is on the formation of future priests that the danger and the challenges of the future lie.

Part III

Formation and the Future of Catholic Priesthood in Igboland

VI

The Current Methods of Forming Igbo Priests

The central implication of the results of this study is that the formation methods adopted in the training of both Igbo religious and diocesan seminarians do not have as deep an effect on their overall vocational maturity as one might have hoped. In addition to this, the ordinary means of formation, the long years spent in formation houses, age, or academic studies, do not seem to make much difference to the overall maturity of the Christian vocationers. This is observed in both Igbo seminarians and international subjects in the great number of variables omitted in the stories of their imagined future. In this last part, we wish to examine the formation-methods presently used in the seminaries and houses of formation in Igboland and then propose the challenges that face the formation of future Igbo priests.

Two principal models of formation can be observed in the houses of formation in Nigeria. Of the eight models of religious formation described by G.A. Arbuckle[1], the conformity/institutional model seems to apply more closely to most of the formation situations in Nigeria especially in those seminaries which train candidates to the diocesan priesthood. None of the remaining seven models clearly identifies the second formation situation in Nigeria. The Blossom Model comes close to it, but does not fully express it. It seems appropriate to describe the other formation situation in Nigeria as progressive in so far as it arose as a kind of reaction against the institutional model that prevails in the majority of the formation houses. It has been introduced recently in the country and is still under experimentation in some houses of formation.

The Conformity/Institutional Model of Formation

Seminary formation in many African countries including Nigeria is heavily academic[2] and tends to overlook the importance of personal conviction as the heart of authentic priestly identity and freer disposition for mission[3]. The tacit presupposition for such overemphasis on intellectual formation is that Christian life is a body of doctrines to be known, implying that knowing them can make one live them easily. The model of formation generally applied in these seminaries is the institutional model which seeks to give to seminarians as much information about the Christian faith and Christian philosophy as possible. Hence, the curriculum tends to be largely theoretical and somehow western in orientation[4]. Often, undue emphasis is placed on memorising what has been taught in order to pass examinations.

Apart from this, the environment of the seminary is highly structured[5]: a daily timetable is followed strictly, with bells marking the beginning and end of each duty in some of them; much interaction with the world outside the seminary is not encouraged, and where interaction happens, it has to be guided. Seminarians wear their white clerical cassock all day long, unless they are engaged in sports or manual labour; this seems to serve as a reminder to them that that they are separated from the world. Deviation from these structures invites punishment of various degrees. In some seminaries, the atmosphere can be filled with tension and fear, which favours "the psychological illusions attending ordination ceremonies", that is, that "the journey is over", the idea of 'I have arrived!'"[6]. One Igbo seminarian in one research had this comment to make in this regard: "There is in our institutions what I may call 'fear of freedom' which hinders auto-formation. The resultant effect is forming pretentious seminarians and consequently pretentious priests"[7].

As can be expected, this model stresses the *conformity* of the seminarian's ideals to those of the ecclesiastical institution, with the result that priestly identity could remain on the periphery of the psychological system of many seminarians and priests, because it is often "based more on compliance and non-internalising identification than on internalisation"[8]. But in those who are more or less mature in their psychological dispositions, this model offers some help even though not as profoundly as it would be if all the aspects of the person had been considered. At least, it reinforces their moral and religious values, but, perhaps, with little effect on their psychological structure[9] because it does not help them understand how these values function in their motivational system.

It seems that one of the reasons why this model has dominated in the African Church even after the Second Vatican Council is the significant place the elders occupy in African culture: they are revered and obedience is due to them because their life-force is considered to be more powerful, and they are also custodians of the customs of the land and instructors of the young. The culture is structured gerontocratically to the extent that "elder brothers and sisters exercise authority over their younger siblings. Younger sons and daughters are not allowed to get married before their elder brothers and sisters"[10]. Giving advice to Igbo priests and seminarians in a seminar, A.N. Aniagolu told them: "do not take the fact of our people being respectful to Priests and Seminarians – being good Christians they are – instil in you a feeling of arrogance or of a feeling of one set aside as special. *You must remember that you, after all, are a small boy who must give respect to your elders*"[11]. The young make little contribution to decision-making. Sometimes, if they ask questions about certain attitude or decisions of the elders, it is not taken lightly. A more adequate model of formation that can prepare the future priests for the challenges of today's world, should also demand a further reflection and interpretation of the relationship between the old and the young in the African-Igbo culture.

Again, this conformity/institutional model of formation seems to thrive in the developing parts of the world because of the large number of those in formation[12]. This is understandable because in such situation, control of the number is more immediate than the more personal knowledge of the candidates. It dawns on the formators that at the time of evaluating the candidates, they may find themselves at sea at not knowing some seminarians. On what moral ground would they make valid statements about such seminarians? We shall take up this issue in the last chapter.

The Progressive Model

In recent times, some houses of formation in Nigeria, especially the religious congregations and some Spiritual Year seminaries[13], are experimenting with a different model which I describe as "progressive" because it aims at reforming the prevalent institutional model characterised by rigid structures and fear, which (it is presumed), hinders seminarians from engaging themselves in their own formation. This model is in sympathy with the freedom of the seminarians and of the seminary environment. Its objective is to help the seminarians to personalise their vocation through the exercise of personal choice and decision. Hence, it favours the "relaxation of rules" and the enhancement of the authentic self of the individual. In contrast to the institutional model, the formation-environment tries to be as unstructured as possible so as to leave the individuals to be themselves, discover and follow their talents and potentials: there are no bells in some; seminarians may wear anything they like except at liturgies where they are expected to put on liturgical dress. In some houses of formation, only those directly involved with liturgy are expected to wear that. The gap between the formators and the seminarians, which is strictly maintained in the institutional model, is bridged: formators now eat with the seminarians in the same refectory, and in some cases, the same kind of food; the apartments of the formators are attached to the seminarians' hostel. Seminarians are encouraged to be open to their formators without fear of being sent home; and in some of the seminaries, they openly evaluate both themselves and the formators. External rules are implicitly considered an imposition or encroachment on the freedom of the individual. It is believed that in this kind of free atmosphere, seminarians will be themselves and thus be able to take initiative and responsibility in forming themselves.

One can identify some aspects of humanistic theories in this model. First, it subtly harbours the idea that the seminary environment in the institutional model oppresses the seminarian, and therefore, aims at liberating him from it[14]. Secondly, it wants to remove signs of imposition from the seminary environment and interactions so that the seminarian can live in freedom and so be the subject of his actions. In being the originator and regulator of his choices and actions without external interference, it is expected that he will live a self-determined life as a priest rather than merely conform to the ideals of the institution[15].

The language and structure of this model suggest a tendency to trust the authenticity of the individual so that sometimes only timid attempts are made to crosscheck his varied intuitions. It is believed that with his good will, the individual seminarian can make use of his freedom to appropriate the objective ideals of priestly vocation. All he needs is to be accompanied in his growth-process and he will be the kind of priest he *chooses* to be but not necessarily the kind he *should* be. Most of the time the criterion for assessing how far the seminarian had entered into the process of formation is the extent of his openness to the formators and to his fellow seminarians, an openness which the seminarians themselves have learned so well to manipulate.

Historically, the various forms of the progressive model emerged as a reaction against the institutional model that had obtained in the Church from the Council of Trent until the Second Vatican Council. Thus, it attempts to relax the formal juridical structures and create a more relaxed and unconditional one that will permit self-expression. More and more the priestly and religious vocations came to be seen in purely psychological and sociological terms, with only a passing reference to their spiritual dimension[16].

The adverse effect of the various forms of this model is verifiable in industrialized Europe and America where confusion about the values of Christian faith and the emotional needs of the individual is strongly felt. Not only have many vocations been lost, quite a good number of those who come into a vocation, especially religious congregations, are often driven into them by the emotional need of security such that identification with the community is very strong[17]. Obviously, as long as the vocational environment gratifies the need of the individual in formation, the person remains in it[18] and the question of living an effective Christian life in his own person and before the world may be neglected, or even forgotten.

The progressive model, with its permissive tendency, can favour the psychologically immature vocationers by gratifying their dissonant needs, and inadvertently frustrate the mature ones by making them doubt their consonant needs.

What Difference does it make?

Is there any difference in the outcomes of the two models? At this moment, some priests are questioning the relevance of the spiritual year seminaries since there does not seem to be a real difference in the life of the newly ordained priests who had passed through the program and those who did not. There are no empirical data available to support or disagree with this impression. However, based on the findings of the present research, it can be suggested that there does not seem to be much difference in the outcome. The reason basically lies in the fact that the anthropological starting-points of both models of formation have limitations that affect the lives of seminarians and priests.

The institutional model of formation presupposes that more and more information or knowledge within a well-structured environment will make a good priest out of a seminarian; and this often consists in the conformity of his mind to the ideals of the priesthood. The direct object of formation becomes the intellect. Thus the model tends to exalt the rational-thinking man and neglects his subjective experiences which are expressed in his psychological history and motivation. Inappropriate behaviours are often interpreted as consequences of ignorance and moral weakness, and the remedy is more knowledge and the reinforcement of spiritual identity of the priest understood mostly in terms of a man separate from others and from the world[19].

Thus, G. Weigel, tracing the crisis-situation of the Catholic priesthood in the United States to the culture of dissent in the seminaries sternly suggests, in terms typical of the institutional-instructional model, that the candidates for the priesthood should be *taught* what the priesthood is all about[20]. He strongly advocates that the man who wants to be a priest should be a mature Christian, a man who demonstrates a love for Christ and for Christ's people, a man who understands "that the priesthood is a call to a more complete emptying of himself so that Christ may work through him..."[21]. He is absolutely correct and in line with the teaching of the Church. He may be wrong in his optimistic assumption that correct information or knowledge about the priesthood and the Christian life would be enough to turn a seminarian into a mature priest. C. McGarry would definitely disagree with him, emphasising that "people are changed and develop living convictions not through instruction but through experience"[22], by which he means the personal experience of Jesus Christ. However, he does not explain how the experience effects the change that brings about living conviction in a seminarian; he implies by his position that we cannot trust mere instruction to deliver the kind of priests the Church needs, people convinced of their Christian and priestly vocation because the human person is not only rationality.

As a reaction, the progressive model begins with the assumption that more freedom in the seminary-environment will produce mature seminarians and priests who are convinced of their vocations because they are free. Yet, it has not been said, either by the priests themselves or by the people, that a significant positive difference has been noticed in the seminarians and new priests formed with this model. As a matter of fact, seminarians trained in this 'free system' appear to be laissez-faire and irresponsible. Many of them seem too self-centered as if the world revolves around them. Things are important which refer to their needs and desires; otherwise, they are not. Hence some priests question the value of the Spiritual Year seminaries, for example.

The subjects of this research come from different houses of formation where these two principal models obtain. But the results show that majority of Igbo Catholic diocesan and religious seminarians are immature in their priestly ideals, meaning that the formation models adopted in training them are effective to a limited degree. This is true despite the fact that the religious seminarians are more mature in their experience of discipleship than their diocesan counterparts.

Why the Situation has remained unchanged

It seems to me that there are two basic reasons why things have remained largely the same in the formation of our priests. First, both models of formation are based on a reductionistic view of the human being: the institutional model has a pessimistic view of human nature, and seeks to enlarge the intellect of those in formation with the hope that, knowing the truths of faith and avoiding the evils of society, they can live good priestly lives. It underestimates the power of the non-rational in man and forgets that man is also feeling, experiencing, relating, and not only thinking. Because of this, it neglects the personality-constellations of the seminarians. When an intelligent seminarian manifests an embarrassing behaviour, often it is attributed to his lack of knowledge, sinful habits, or to bad will. No further exploration is considered necessary. This model usually divides seminarians into those who behave well (who conform better) and those who are disobedient (nonconformists). Yet, some of those believed to have obeyed well in the seminary are disappointing after ordination. The explanation often given is that they hid themselves during the formation years. This seems believable because the number of seminarians is so large. But the fact is that, as C. McGarry observes, "if some of our spiritual formation has not been as effective as we would have hoped, it is usually because the soil of our humanity has not been adequately prepared to receive the transforming word of God. Grace and nature work hand in hand"[23].

On the other hand, the progressive model believes that once freedom is guaranteed in the formation-environment, seminarians can be themselves and make proper use of it to choose the values of the priestly vocation. Inconsistent behaviours from the seminarians and young priests who have passed through this model are attributed to their lack of openness to the formation process; they utilised their freedom to choose not to be open, by means of manipulation and deceit. In actual fact, seminarians can present false stories or feign experiences that, according to this model, are signs of openness. This again appears understandable when the number of seminarians is very large and an important motivation is to avoid expulsion. The formators may not be able to see these deceits because of their trust in the openness and freedom of the seminarians.

This model does not recognise that the human person is a mystery. It underestimates the complex nature of the motivational system of the individual, and naively believes that the conscious questions of the individual, as signs of his openness and freedom, are his real questions and that his conscious motivations are always to be trusted instead of understood and interpreted[24]. Like all theories that have their roots in secular humanism, it overlooks the ambivalences that are present in human freedom, which Lonergan's distinction between essential freedom and effective freedom clearly brings out.

Lonergan notes that human beings, by their nature, are essentially free but not always effectively free[25]. This means that they can grasp possible courses of action by practical insight, reflect on them, make decisions, and execute them. But the range of operation of this dynamic structure of human freedom, which is called effective freedom, can be limited or broad. A man, for instance, may grasp the alternative ways of quitting from smoking, but may not be able to quit. He is essentially free, but the effectiveness of his freedom is limited.

The range of one's effective freedom, according to him, depends on certain factors, such as the external circumstances, the psychoneural state of the person, limitations of intellectual development, and the presence or absence of antecedent willingness[26]. But the key factor in the broadening of one's effective freedom is "to reach a willingness to persuade oneself and to submit to the persuasion of others"[27]. When one has acquired this, it means that he does not merely adopt "an affective attitude that would desire but not perform" but "an effective attitude in which performance matches aspiration"[28]. The smoker will not only desire to quit, but will be able to perform certain concrete actions that lead him to quit smoking.

For Lonergan, to broaden one's affective freedom, the key factor is the achievement of antecedent willingness. He recognizes that human freedom is not the pure state that secular humanistic theories and models based on them would want us believe. Human freedom can be ambivalent because of human limitations. When some people say, "give them freedom to grow", it does not mean that all the seminarians can use it. M. Drennan realistically observes that "a person's level of awareness is the door to change, but does not mean that they will go through it. There are those who can't and those who won't but generally formators are dealing with blindness, not ill-will"[29].

In addition to being reductionistic in their fundamental presuppositions, both the institutional and progressive models do not take the cultural situation of the candidates into consideration. The data of the present study shows that culture is stronger than the current structure of the formation for the Igbo seminarians, religious and diocesan alike. This neglect contributes to the situation remaining unchanged as far as the formation of Igbo religious and diocesan seminarians is concerned.

Having presented and examined the formation models in vogue in the seminaries and houses of formation in Nigeria, we are faced with a more direct question: what shall we do? In the following chapter, which is the last one, we intend to make certain theoretical and practical proposals that will enable the development of formation programs that will help future priests reach a reasonable level of maturity that they need to confront the changing situation of the world today.

VII

Theoretical and Practical Orientation for the Formation of Igbo Priests

The major finding of this research, that a large portion of the Igbo seminarians has ideals that are immature, and the fact that this immaturity has cultural nuances, does not mean that these vocations are not genuine; it rather indicates an ambiguous situation which is typical of all human conditions. At the more existential level, the finding testifies to the presence of ambivalence in the human heart and the enduring nature of cultural values. The ineffectiveness of certain formation methods seem to be rooted in the neglect of these factors. Thus, I am proposing in this study a new orientation to the current formation situation of our seminarians that will incorporate these factors. First, I shall outline the theoretical foundation of such formation; secondly, I shall draw out the levels of its practical application; and thirdly, I shall state certain concrete issues that require serious attention if such formation should be realized.

Theoretical Starting-Points

Human Condition and the Problem of Mixed Motivation

Every human situation contains some ambiguities. If there were pure states or conditions so that things and persons were exactly as they present themselves, there would be fewer problems in human relationships and in human societies. Then there would be no need for scientific investigations of the deeper roots of certain situations because they would be clear.

Ambiguity means that a particular situation does not have one meaning; it may have two or more meanings, and these meanings may be located at different levels. Thus, a particular situation may have a specific meaning in its theoretical definition, but may have different meanings to different individuals. An individual may have the motivation to adhere to the meaning given to the situation by definition, and, at the same time, he seeks to actualise, in his own way, the particular meaning the situation has for him. Thus, his motivation becomes mixed. The more general tendency is that the meaning in definition, the objective meaning, can be transformed by the individual's personal meaning.

The ambiguity of human situations has its source in the ambiguity of the human heart. This is clearly brought out by T.F. O'Dea in his analysis of the relationship of organised religion and society. He observes that the institutionalisation of religion generates five dilemmas from which derive the internal strains and functional problems of religious bodies. The first of these five dilemmas is the dilemma of mixed motivation[1]. In the period when the founder of an organised religious body was alive or in the immediate charismatic period after his death, there was a closer relationship between the leader and his disciples characterised by single-mindedness toward the goals and values taught by the founder. As time passes and the religion becomes more organised or institutionalised, important changes take place which have certain consequences.

Institutionalisation is about stability. Stability is ensured through specific statuses and roles which are defined in terms of functions with certain rights and obligations. Thus "there arises a structure of offices which involve a stratified set of rewards in terms of prestige, life opportunities, and material compensations"[2]. The structure developed in these terms is able to elicit "a wide range of individual motives and of focusing diverse motivations behind the goals of the organisation as specified in prescribed role behaviour"[3]. The functional significance of this process is that it maintains the stability of the institution through the interested motivations of individuals. But there is the shadow side of it:

Mobilization of a variety of motives in support of the goals and values of the organisation can, and often does, result in the subtle transformation of the goals and values themselves. When a professional clergy emerges in the Church, there comes into existence a body of men for whom the clerical life offers not simply "religious" satisfactions of the earlier charismatic period, but also prestige and respectability, power and influence, in both church and society, and satisfactions derived from the use of personal talents in teaching, leadership, etc[4].

The dilemma becomes that of following the goals and values taught by the founder or the satisfaction of personal desires of individuals reinforced by the dynamics of institutional stability. The basic goal of the religious organisation is to follow the values and goals of the founder. It follows then that if a large portion of the persons who direct the affairs of the religious organisation are in the main motivated by these incentives of power, prestige, social influence and other personal ambitions, it is expected that there will result a more massive transformation of and deviation from the goals and values of the religion. This, according to T.F. O'Dea, was what happened in the history of the Christian Church.

The higher clergy in Christian history became important functionaries and dignitaries in society, with all the rewards and benefits accruing to people in such positions. The higher clergy, in terms of both church office and of non-ecclesiastical governmental functions, became part of the ruling and dominant classes in society, and their interests fused with those of such classes. These new interests of the clergy often deviated from the goals and values of the church. The church was transformed in a subtle way. It became secularized; the clergy became "worldly"[5].

It is also a historical fact that not all the members of the clergy really deviated from the values of the Christian vocation. Otherwise, Christian history would not have such great Christian witnesses like Francis of Assisi, St. Dominic, St. Ignatius of Loyola,

Blessed Cyprian Iwene Tansi, and the missionaries who were ready to give their lives to the spread of the gospel even in most dangerous lands. Their lives were a demonstration of convinced adhesion to the goals and values of the Christian Church. The pertinent question would then be: why are some Christian vocationers more driven into vocation by the motives of prestige, financial benefits, power and influence, and others principally by the values of the Christian vocation? The psychological researches done on groups and on Christian vocationers could provide basis for the response to this question.

D. Katz and R.L. Kahn observe that "each individual responds to the organisation in terms of his or her perceptions of it, a subjective or psychological 'organisation' that may differ in various ways from the actual organisation"[6]. Their statement puts no one in doubt as to the existence of misperception of an organisation's or a group's objectives by individuals. The research of N.A. Lieberman and colleagues on encounter groups demonstrate what could lie at the heart of this perception. The major finding of their research is that the values the person brought to the encounter group and his conceptions of others, his interpersonal schema, are the two powerful predictors of subsequent outcome in participating in the group[7].

In their own research on Christian vocationers, L.M. Rulla, J. Ridick and F. Imoda note that "persons may have psychological 'blind spots' or scotomas, and a way of seeing things that is partial and distorted. This makes it more difficult to have an objective orientation to, and interpretation of, reality, ..."[8]. The data of their research showed that 60-80% of the population of the Christian vocationers, guided by their own perceptions, were actually seeking their own interests in the vocation than the values and goals of the Christian vocation[9]. The research located the fundamental problem in the immaturity of the second dimension, such that "an assessment of maturity or immaturity on the second dimension is a sufficiently reliable index of the person's disposition or lack of disposition to internalising self-transcendent ideals"[10]. Second dimension is the dimension of non-pathological immaturity[11], due to the influence of the subconscious needs.

What happens is that the central subconscious needs of the persons becloud the challenge of the values, which are then subtly transformed to gratify the needs of the individual[12]. The practical effect is evident in incongruous lifestyles, the "worldliness" of some Christian vocationers. While those who are mature to a high degree in the second dimension attend to the challenges posed by the values of the vocation and in so doing transcend their personal interests.

Although O'Dea is inclined to blame the process of institutionalising the Christian Church for the subtle transformation of the Christian values[13], it should be understood that ultimately the issue goes back to the ambiguity of the human heart. For, as B.J.F. Lonergan affirms, it is the inauthenticity of individuals that generates the inauthenticity of traditions[14]. The work of institutionalisation is the work of individuals. And institutionalisation or organisation is inevitable in the normal development of any group of persons including religious groups.

The dilemma is therefore real if it is recognised that the organisation of the Christian Church and the possibility of deforming the values of the Gospel by the interested motivations of individuals are also real. The way out of the dilemma cannot be *either* deinstitutionalising the Church *or* excluding individuals who, by their very nature as human beings, have subconscious needs. Either way is impossible because what is involved is inevitable: organisation of the Church and the fact that human beings have psychological needs.

A tacit search for the resolution of this dilemma can be observed in the strategies of different formation-models: those ones that tend to be progressive, that are in sympathy with the freedom of the individual as against the authority (institution), seem to expect the resolution of the dilemma through deinstitutionalisation of the church. The weak presence of the authority in the formation-environment suggests a de-emphasis of structure and of organisation, which is implicitly blamed for producing unholy Christian vocationers. Individuals should be trusted to know what the goals and values of the Christian Church are and freely live them.

On the other hand, models that emphasise structure and institutionalisation of the formation-environment seem to be suspicious of the unpredictable motivations of the individuals. Seminarians should therefore be controlled; hence the tendency to more rigid structures. It is presumed that if the individuals can be helped to understand the values and goals of Christian vocation, control their passions, and conform to the structural objectives of the seminary, for instance, they will turn out to be good and holy priests. Then, the dilemma would have been resolved.

Historical events and scientific research testify that neither of these two methods of resolving the dilemma succeeds effectively. If the goals and the values of the Christian Church are there to be followed and lived, and the Christian vocationer with his subconscious needs can transform those values in serving his interests despite his goodwill[15], it seems reasonable that the resolution of the dilemma does not lie in abolishing the values of the Christian vocation, but in enabling the Christian vocationer to become aware of how his motivations threaten the values he had consciously desired to live and to redirect his psychodynamics towards the values of the Gospel. In order for the individual to be helped in this manner, it is important to know the configuration of his motivational system, his expectations about his vocation, and his psychodynamics. *The knowledge and the redirection of the individual's psychodynamics towards Jesus Christ, the personification of Christian values, should be the primary objectives of the formation process.* Without the interior freedom which comes from this, it will be difficult for anyone to come to give a fuller "yes" to the Lord Jesus as Christians and as priests[16].

Though the dilemma of mixed motivations will never go away, it can be managed better. The strong place occupied by achievement and symbols of social status in Igbo culture makes the dilemma real and in need of careful attention. In order to manage it well, formators need to know the candidates they are forming. They should also help the candidates to know themselves, their significant values, important needs, relevant conflicts, and the manner in which these are configured in their lives.

Culture and Person: Paradox of Growth in Christian Vocation

An Igbo proverb states that *onye ma na ya na ndị mụọ na-eri nri, na-eji ogologo ngaji* [he who knows he is eating with the spirits should do so with a long spoon]. If a person does not know that he or she is eating with the spirits and uses the usual spoon, he or she will surely be in danger. Another proverb states that *ụsụ sị na ya ma ka ya dị wee were abalị na-efe* [the bat says it is aware of its ugliness and that is why it prefers to fly in the night].

These two proverbs emphasise the need *to be aware* of the situation (the first proverb) and of one's limitations (the second proverb). With such awareness, the situation and the limitations can be better handled; this is the main point of the fundamental paradox of vocational growth. This means that the knowledge of the culture of the candidates, its values and shadows, and of the gifts and limits of the candidates themselves, is of tremendous help to both formators and candidates.

There are two structures of the self: the ideal self (constituted by the values of the Christian vocation and tending towards self-transcendence) and the actual self (constituted by both the manifest and latent aspects of the self and tending to be egocentric). Between these two structures of the self, there is a dialectical tension, which is present in every Christian. The fundamental paradox is this: the more this dialectic is *conscious* and *accepted*, the more it can be handled; but the more it is unconscious, the more it is difficult to handle[17].

The problem of the dialectic concerns primarily those aspects of the personality, such as a person's desires, needs and attitudes, that are in disagreement with being a Christian or a priest[18]. Christians are called to make gifts of themselves to God and to others. But this is often obstructed by these desires of the person especially if they are subconscious. Subconscious desires or needs always seek to be satisfied, so that, the person, believing him or herself to be serving God and others, is in reality serving him or herself.

Here enters the importance of basic paradox: when a need is conscious, it is possible to renounce it consciously even if it entails some pain and suffering; but if a need is subconscious, there will always be a hidden search to satisfy it; thus, the person grows more and more egocentric since that which is important for him or her, prevails over what is truly important in itself[19].

In the present research, the fundamental paradox can be understood to have two aspects, one more general, and the other personal. The general one, has to do with the recognition of the way this dialectical tension manifests among Igbo seminarians. This entails the knowledge of those desires, aspirations, and attitudes that are prominent among them as people from a single culture. The personal one concerns how these desires, aspirations, needs and attitudes are configured in and expressed by each Igbo seminarian. In knowing those aspects of himself that are in opposition with the priestly vocation he wants to live, a seminarian will be able to choose how to handle them.

What this means is that the struggle to live the Christian vocation takes different forms in different cultures. From the results of the present research, the struggle of Igbo seminarians and priests is mostly related to the need to exhibit visible signs of success and achievement as indices of self-assertion in the community one belongs. The struggle consists first, in being aware that in the priestly life and ministry, the real fruit of their work is the spiritual growth of the people they serve; and this is largely invisible and intangible. The Fathers of the Special Assembly for Africa of the Synod of Bishops emphasise that in the circumstances in which the people of Africa live today, evangelization "stands for many of those essential values which our Continent very much lacks: hope, peace, joy, harmony, love and unity"[20]. These values are basically experienced but are not often visible or tangible. Yet, these remain the ground work necessary for the establishment of lasting order in society.

Secondly, the struggle involves the management of one's

independence and the need for others (dependence). The growth needed is toward interdependence, which entails the recognition of one's abilities and limitations and those of others. This tension is lived by the Igbos as a group and because it largely eludes our consciousness, often it degenerates into the tendency to fragmentation both within ourselves and with others.

The way the basic dialectics manifests among the Igbos as a group and as individuals should not only be known, but also *accepted*. This acceptance is, first of all, an acceptance of one's culture and oneself. Secondly, this is important because since grace builds on nature, it is necessary that this nature, expressed in the giftedness and weaknesses of cultures and individuals, be open to the grace of God. But how can this openness happen without the acceptance of one's weaknesses and gifts?

This also means that seminarians should not expect that formation will make them free of all problems and tensions, but should lead them to know themselves and trust in the help of God. St. Paul tried to free his life from difficulties and weaknesses, but God let him know that His grace was enough for him. Then he knew he would accept his weaknesses so that the grace of God would be his strength[21]. The purpose of formation, or of psychology applied to formation, is not to produce nice little Pharisees who feel perfect. Psychology in particular, if well applied, does not take the place of grace; it makes the need for grace more clearly felt.

African-Igbo Cultural Consciousness: A Systemic Interpretation

It is also important to be aware of the cultural milieu of the African people from which the candidates come. The communitarian life of Africans makes provision for an understanding of priestly formation for a Church that is a Family.

In African religion and tradition, it is believed that the universe consists of visible and invisible beings whose life forces are constantly in interaction, with the human person at the center[22]. This means that "all life forces, that is, all creation, are intended to serve and enhance the life force of the human person and society"[23]. Human life is enhanced when the harmony among these life forces is maintained. This demands the observance of specific moral and religious norms and mores.

The African principally sees himself or herself as belonging to a network of relationships whose outcome is the community, a community that embraces the visible and the invisible world. Nyamiti emphasises that for the African, "man is regarded as intimately related to other fellow-men and beings; and the universe is conceived as a sort of organic whole composed of supra-sensible or mystical correlations or participants"[24]. He is conscious of his culture as a system of interrelated segments, the world of man and the world of spirits, that are harmoniously coordinated through the relationships of persons, living and dead. To be human "is to belong to the community, and to do so involves participating in the beliefs, ceremonies, rituals and festivals of that community. A person cannot detach himself from the religion of his group, for to do so is to be severed from his roots, his foundation, his context of security, his kinships and the entire group of those who make him aware of his own existence"[25]. For this reason, "one form of existence, when considered isolatedly without relation to other forms or beings, is seen to be incomplete and unauthentic"[26].

The communitarian consciousness of the African people includes the whole universe, the visible and the invisible, and harmony is maintained by their relationships. Thus, the systemic understanding of reality, which is recent in the west[27], has long been at home in Africa. The fundamental characteristic of a system is that it has a specific structure or organisation which is made up of certain relationships among its parts. The result of these relationships cannot be reduced to a single part but to the functioning of the whole[28]. Thus "what makes a group what it is, is not just its membership, but the mutual *relations* of the members"[29]. It is therefore important to know *the system* and where the members stand in the *relations*. In a family system, for instance, "it is the fatherly attitude of a man that elicits a filial attitude from the child; in turn, this filial attitude strengthens and intensifies the father's identity and behaviour as father"[30]. The father knows his *relations* in the *family system*.

Africans "have a profound religious sense, a sense of the sacred"[31], and they live "in an intensely religious universe"[32]. And this is why priests occupy a significant place in African cultures, and certain kinds of conduct are required from them:

> Certain standards of social, moral and ethical behaviour are expected of priests, though this is by no means uniform. On the whole, they are men and women of respectable character: trustworthy, devout, obedient to the traditions of their office and to God or to divinities that they serve, friendly, kind, 'educated' in matters of their profession, and religious[33].

These moral and religious qualities are expected of the priest in African Traditional Religion because he is entrusted with the work of building a bridge between God and the people, between the visible and the invisible worlds: "The priest is the chief intermediary: he stands between God, or divinity, and men. Just as the king is the political symbol of God's presence, so the priest is the religious symbol of God among His people"[34]. The distinction between the political and the religious is not to be taken too strictly because both functions operate together to achieve harmony in the community and in the cosmos. The king does not live for himself nor does the priest; they live in and for the community. When priests live good and holy lives in service of God and of the community, people respect them. Nwagwu is therefore right when she observes that "the respect and honour heaped on religious [and priests in Nigeria] borders on that given to the priests and priestesses or 'oracles' of our African traditional religion"[35].

This is a fundamental structure of African religion and cultures, and it permeates all aspects of life. And just as the personality of each person mediates his or her contact with the environment, so is the contact between cultures mediated by their various structures because each culture is a system[36]. In African-Igbo society, the Catholic priest is taken as a religious symbol and his celibate life remains a remarkable aspect of his identity and efficacy, so that the bishops of Onitsha and Owerri ecclesiastical province in their document, *The Igbo Catholic Priest at the Threshold of the Third Millennium*, emphasise that "in the eyes of people and whether we like it or not, celibacy is the test of integrity for the Catholic Priesthood"[37]. It is because the priest is a religious symbol that he wields influence in society: he can denounce evil openly and take risks in defending the truth and the life of the people against malignant forces, visible and invisible.

A system is regulated by its wholeness. When this is lost and different parts act independently, the ability of the system to regulate itself is shaken and in some instances, it disappears[38]. This is disorganisation. It is what happens, for instance, to the individual in psychosis where the originally unifying function of consciousness has broken down and cognition, memory, and emotions act independently of each other. It also happens in cases of severe borderline personality organisation in which the central regulatory system is too shaky to bind anxiety and channel emotions that the individual resorts to the use of primitive defences[39]. In social systems, chaotic situation is experienced when the segments of the society act independently of others. For instance, when the leadership class in Nigeria can no longer ensure the security of the people, and those entrusted with making and enforcing laws are corrupt and neglect their duties, life becomes precarious for the ordinary Nigerians: unemployment increases, criminality rises, artificial scarcity of gasoline emerges, and business opportunists raise the prices.

In knowing and living his authentic identity in *relation* with other segments of the African-Igbo culture and Church, the priest does his part in maintaining the social, political and ecclesial life of the people. From this systemic perspective, the model of the Church-as-Family, chosen by the Fathers of the Special Assembly for Africa of the Synod of Bishops, as a model for the Church in Africa, has a lot of meaning: it "emphasizes care for others, solidarity, warmth in human relationships, acceptance, dialogue and trust"[40]. This model of the Church brings out the African understanding of family as implying "the complementarity of the role of the members of the family. Each member of the family knows his or her role"[41]. Thus, within the Church as the *Family of God*, the priest is seen as a spiritual father[42] who, as a father, seeks the good of the people and should be ready to take any risk to protect them rather than exploit them. Inability to live according to the standards required by his position *in relation* to other segments of the ecclesial and social community, endangers the life of the people and his own life too.

An Integrated-Systemic Approach to Personal Formation

The implications of the findings of this research call for a kind of formation that will focus on the individual in his relation to the community; a kind of formation that helps make his priestly vocation his own. This means that this formation has to consider the culture of the candidates, as well as the systemic view of the world of the Africans. Put together, this will entail first, the knowledge of the place of the priest in the social and ecclesial lives of the Igbo people in the context of the social and ecclesial lives of the African-Igbo. This makes the future priest aware of the legitimate claims the society and the Church make on him. Secondly, in order to help a seminarian to appropriate his true identity as a priest in the family of the Church, it is necessary that the formators should know him well, his desires and aspirations, as well as the meaning he attributes to the priesthood. This is necessary because "what the 'reality' is, that affects the existence of social institutions, states, economies, and so on, depends not only on what the case is, but on what its members, or its leadership, *believe* that is"[43]. Thus, formation of the Igbo priest should be both integrated and systemic. This approach considers both the individual and his relations with different segments within the Church and society. What it means in the concrete shall now be presented in the following subsections.

Broader Community-Ecclesial Consciousness

Despite the perturbations brought to Africans by colonialism, the encounter with the dualistic philosophy of the west, and the more recent values of modernity that are leading to the "de-traditionalisation" of societies[44], Africans remain principally community-oriented people[45]. The involvement of the people in the training of their priests brings out this clearly and shows how they perceive the Catholic priest.

In Igboland, the people believe that priests belong to the whole community of the people of God and are spiritual fathers to everyone. For this reason, their training is not left to their individual families, but to all the people. First, right from the minor seminary, parishes take turns to contribute food and money on a particular day of the week, usually Saturday, to feed the seminarians; something that does not happen in other secondary schools. Secondly, during the holidays, the seminarians are sent to different parishes for their apostolic work. In these places, they are well cared-for by the parishioners and at the end of their stay, collections are organised on their behalf to help them through their training. Thirdly, at their ordination, all the parishioners make heavy contributions and donations as a whole community of the Church to provide for the new priest, not only those things he directly needs for his priestly work, but also other things that will make him feel comfortable, like a refrigerator, a television set, electric fans, music or video sets. In addition to all this, the people offer him also some cash for his keep and, in most cases, a car. There are also the prayers and many nights of vigils the lay faithful keep for their seminarians and priests. This treatment continues even after the ordination, and no other class of people in Igboland receives it.

These gestures of the Igbo people reflect their belief about the priests: they belong to God and to the whole community, not just to their families, friends, or ethnic groups. This is an essential reason why the people respect them a lot. It follows therefore that when the priesthood is taken as a private venture or as a place to fulfil one's personal desires either to enrich one's nuclear family or to climb the social ladder, the priest not only obstructs the mission of the Church, but he also endangers the systemic relationship he lives with the whole people. It is unfortunate when the seminarian or the new priest loses consciousness of the different communities that brought him to where he is. Instead, those gestures of the people may even be taken as entitlements. It is the case now that since some priests are becoming obviously rich persons and sometimes unavailable elites, the people begin to begrudge the contributions they make to maintain them.

All this goes to show the importance of educating the seminarians to have a broader sense of community and of the Church-as-Family and guiding them to draw out the implications it might have for them as future priests. The starting-point must be the presentation of these gestures of the people and challenging them to find out their connection with the systemic worldview and social life of African-Igbo people. This would provide an opportunity for the seminarians to evaluate the attitudes appropriate to priests and their effects on the social, political, and religious lives of the people.

Knowing the Candidates and their Culture

In *Pastores Dabo Vobis*, John Paul II asks the formators "to foster and verify the suitability of candidates in regard to their spiritual, human and intellectual endowments, above all in regard to their spirit of prayer, their deep assimilation of the doctrines of the faith, their capacity for true fraternity and the charism of celibacy"[46]. The Pope is asking the formators two things: first, *to verify* the original capacity of the candidates, whatever they come into the seminary with, and secondly, *to foster* in them suitable qualities for the priestly vocation. The second presupposes the first. To be able to foster suitable qualities in the candidates for the priesthood, it is important to know who the candidates are: their spiritual and moral values, their humanity, their needs, and their intellectual endowments[47]. With this knowledge, the formators will be able to know how and where to help them as unique individuals.

In order to know the candidates, there is need to assess them at three levels: that of faith, psychological development, and of clinical status. Where screening of the candidates for the priesthood takes place, it often stops at the second and third levels, because it is presumed that all those coming into priestly vocation "are moved by motives which are inherently spiritual and altruistic"[48]. The research of L.M. Rulla and colleagues confirmed that most people coming into the priestly or religious life were moved by those values that are Christian and self-transcendent[49]. However, evidence is increasing that persons who seek to be priests and religious today may not be sure of the moral and religious values of these vocations as at the time L.M. Rulla and his colleagues carried out their research. In the research which she concluded in 2000, O'Dwyer found out that the Christian values people proclaim seem to have declined among those in priestly and religious vocations[50]. The result of the present research is another example.

With the presumption of good moral and religious values in the candidates, assessments are usually concerned with verifying the presence or absence of psychopathology or criminal records, using self-reports. Once a candidate is cleared of these, it may be presumed he can proceed with formation.

But this is the least challenge in knowing and helping candidates to the priesthood or the religious life. The greater difficulty is that of knowing the developmental deficits of each candidate and how these may obstruct their assimilation of the values of Jesus Christ. *It is the task of ascertaining whether a candidate has a reasonable possibility of growing in formation.* This requires a detailed knowledge of family history, interpersonal history, faith development, and general psychological health and resources. An in-depth or structured interview would be able to give a picture of a candidate in these areas.

To obtain a complete picture of a candidate, it is necessary to know first, his religious and moral values and how he learned them. This level also ascertains the validity of his conscious intentions for wanting to become a priest. The candidate should be able to give adequate reasons for the choices he wishes to make[51]. He should be able to show, for instance, why it is a good thing to give up marrying despite the ideals of Igbo culture. The psychological reason is that every renunciation must find a satisfactory reason, a justification; otherwise, the person can get frustrated[52]. It will be good also to know why, in addition to giving up marrying, he would want to give up becoming a popular and titled Igbo man with demonstrable signs of achievement as business, money, houses and expensive cars. Does he think, for instance, he would be happy as a priest if he did not go overseas, or make lots of money, or get high academic degrees? In whichever way he responds, it is necessary to know his reasons.

But since the major problems of priests and religious persons are not necessarily those of ignorance or not knowing the right things[53], there is the need to assess the psychological development of the candidate. This should be able to show the dynamic pattern of emotional or affective attitudes already formed in him and the central needs which can block his response to the call of Jesus Christ in priestly vocation. This is the area where the subconscious is very influential. The needs of the person which have strong root in the subconscious can prevent the pursuit of the values of the priestly vocation by confining the person to pursue more or less his personal inclinations, however discrepant they might be to his chosen project of life[54]. The difficulty manifests as embarrassing behaviours, incongruity in lifestyle, a discrepancy between the values proclaimed and the concrete life of the person. It is also necessary to assess the strength of his achievement need, traces of antisocial characteristics[55], and whether his sense of self can be sustained by being a priest or by those symbols of achievement which usually lead to incongruity in lifestyle and ministry among the Igbos.

The third level of assessment of candidates should focus on identifying persons who are not psychologically healthy. It is concerned with "ruling out significant psychopathology, personality disorders, crippling developmental deficits, and neurotic tendencies; any psychological qualities antithetical to healthy, normal personal relationships; or attitudes that might provoke avoidant reactions to others"[56]. In many instances, it is not too difficult to detect clearly pathological conditions as, for example, when persons show signs of delusion or hallucination. However, in some circumstances, "considerable difficulty exists in piercing through a cloud of disinformation or engaging behaviour behind which self-serving pathology lies concealed"[57]. That is why it is appropriate to use both objective and projective instruments in psychological testing so as to have a more complete psychological profile of an individual. In assessing Igbo candidates, it is also important to know the specific ways some psychopathology may manifest itself in African-Igbo culture[58].

The knowledge of the candidates is only to prepare the formators to give them the kind of attention each of them needs; it provides the formators the information about the humanity of each candidate. Helping the candidates involves the redirection of their psychodynamics toward the values of the priestly vocation: a strengthening of their moral and religious values and tilling the soil of their humanity to enable them assimilate those values[59]. This happens first through presenting the values of the priestly vocation to them and engaging them in vocational growth process.

This integrated method of forming the candidates has been empirically tested in India. After two years of novitiate, out of the 65 subjects studied, 72% showed a positive change in growth in the reinforcement of their moral and religious values. Understanding their inner motivations and being helped with their integration, they grew in the capacity "to renounce their selfish goals, to renounce their own 'goods' and to grow in abandonment to God's providential care"[60]. About 6 of the remaining 18 subjects did not show either significant advancement, or regression. Only 12 subjects did not appear to profit from this method[61].

Concerning the redirection of the psychodynamics in the personality of the subjects, a large number of these Indian subjects showed a statistically significant improvement in the integration of their needs, defences, conflicts and emotions, that ranged between 80-89%[62]. And when these different aspects were assessed together under the *Total Index of Dynamic Orientation*, out of the 65 subjects, 61 (94%) showed an overall change in their psychodynamics.

This meant that the subjects had responded to the vocational growth sessions, by becoming more conscious of what had been previously their subconscious needs, defences, emotions and conflicts and at the same time, had moved qualitatively in being able to integrate them at a maturer level of personality development. The results also indicated that a minority, i.e. 4 (6%) subjects, had not changed or grown as a result of the process[63].

C. McGarry noted that the kind of formation needed in present day Africa must help the candidate to see and experience Jesus Christ as to what the human person *should become* (the ideal self), and be enabled to *commit all his energies* to become like Christ – emphasizing the redirection and re-channelling of the psychodynamics. Christ as the ideal is the root of the Christian vocation; but this ideal must interact with the dynamics of the individual seminarian. It is through this interaction by means of the relationship established with the person of Jesus Christ[64] and the continuous skilful intervention of the formator, that change takes place in the candidate.

Formators Should Know Themselves

In the formation of future priests, as observed by John Paul II, "it is evident that much of the effectiveness of the training offered depends on the maturity and strength of those entrusted with formation, both from the human and from the Gospel points of view"[65]. Citing a proposition of the Synod Fathers, he enjoins formators to "witness to a truly evangelical lifestyle and total dedication to the Lord"[66]. Already, the Second Vatican Council in the Decree on the Training of Priests, *Optatam Totius*, had exhorted formators to be "keenly aware of the extent to which their mental outlook and conduct affect the formation of their students"[67].

Discrepancy between what the formators say and how they live is most of the time an effect not only of what they know to be right or wrong, but most likely from those aspects of their personalities that they may not be fully aware of[68]. As. G.D. Coleman observes, such lack of awareness could lead to unhealthy relationship among the formators themselves and the crossing of boundaries between them and the seminarians. For instance, there are times in which formators are divided among themselves, oftentimes, by their political interests, and at other times, by their areas of origin. This attitude is very dangerous to the seminary formation because seminarians could easily be trapped into the camps. In occasions like this, the objective of the seminary and formation itself is largely put aside, and seminarians, especially those who are more interested in getting to ordination than in being a true priest, could exploit the opportunity to advance their personal interests. In some instances also, formators can subconsciously seek emotional support from the seminarians[69] or the central needs of the seminarians can collude with their own and the seminary environment may be turned into a place of mutual need-gratification.[70]. For instance, a formator who has a strong need to be praised finds a seminarian with the need to ingratiate an authority in order to evade responsible growth. The stage is set for mutual manipulation and the relationship between them is turned into a game.

All this indicates that academic competence is not enough to qualify a person to be a formator: he should also possess a reasonable degree of human and spiritual maturity, show stability in his vocation, and is capable of working with others[71]. The work of formation is a difficult task, and demands from the formators not only mastery of the courses they teach; it also makes demands on their style of life, thinking, relationships, and attitudes.

It is therefore necessary that those who form candidates to the priesthood should know themselves, their values, relevant needs, and conflicts, and how these usually find expression. They should be able to transmit the values of the priestly vocation to the candidates not only in words but also by their lives. In practical terms, this means that the criteria for selecting those who work in the seminary should go beyond academic intelligence and orthodoxy, to include these personality variables that cause more havoc to the seminary environment and the seminarians.

Practical Issues that Need Attention

If the model of formation suggested in this work is to be concretely realized, certain practical issues have to be addressed by the leaders of the Church in Igboland. This section examines four practical aspects which demand urgent attention if personal formation is to be practicable in the formation houses and seminaries in Igboland. These four aspects are, first, the number of seminarians; secondly, the need for more formators with preparation; thirdly, the existential presentation of the priesthood; fourthly, coordination between the seminaries.

The Number of Seminarians: Quantity or Quality?

The bishops of the Catholic Church in Igboland and the formators in the seminaries will admit that there is a serious problem with the very large number of seminarians. Efforts at decongestion have been made by building more major seminaries. But when a new one is constructed it is soon overpopulated with seminarians. The table below shows the number of seminarians in each of the major seminaries in the Onitsha and Owerri ecclesiastical provinces during the academic year of 2005/2006.

Table 4

The Number of Major Seminarians[72]

Name of the Seminary	Number of Major Seminarians
Bigard Memorial Seminary, Enugu	636
Seat of Wisdom Seminary, Owerri	629
Pope John Paul II Major Seminary, Okpuno	289
Blessed Iwene Tansi Major Seminary, Onitsha	256

These figures present formidable challenges to the formators who may not be more than twenty-five in a particular seminary. Table 5 shows the number of formators in each of the major seminaries in Onitsha and Owerri ecclesiastical provinces in the academic year, 2005/2006.

Table 5

Number of Formators in the Seminaries

Name of the Seminary	Number of Formators	Spiritual Directors
Bigard Memorial Seminary, Enugu	18	4
Seat of Wisdom Seminary, Owerri	22	4
Pope John Paul II Seminary, Okpuno	9	3
Blessed Iwene Tansi Seminary, Onitsha	11	3

Table 6

Ratio of Seminarians to Each Formator

Name of the Seminary	Number of Seminarians to the formators
Bigard Memorial Seminary, Enugu	35
Seat of Wisdom Seminary, Owerri	28.5
Pope John Paul II Seminary, Okpuno	32
Blessed Iwene Tansi Seminary, Onitsha	23

Table 7

Ratio of Seminarians to each Spiritual Director

Name of the Seminary	Number of seminarians to Spiritual Directors
Bigard Memorial Seminary, Enugu	159
Seat of Wisdom Seminary, Owerri	157
Pope John Paul II Seminary, Okpuno	93
Blessed Iwene Tansi Seminary, Onitsha	85

These figures may appear small in relation to each formator, but it is not that easy to know each seminarian well or give the kind of attention he might need[73]. Each of the formator teaches at least two courses and some are also engaged in diocesan assignments. While the ratio of the seminarians to formators in external forum appears to be relatively small, it is not really small if we consider the enormous attention each person in formation would need. Secondly, some formators see their work as mainly teaching and living their lives as they want it. It is possible that if a formator devotes himself to knowing personally these number of seminarians, he might be able to do so reasonably. This would, however, demand a serious change in the lifestyle of some of them.

The attention seminarians need should not be limited to their outward conduct or presence at community exercises. Personal knowledge of a person should be more in-depth, reaching to the attitudes and tendencies of that person. Unless the formators in the external forum are ready to meet with the seminarians under their care many times during the year in order to know them personally, it may be difficult for them to give a fair and balanced account of the inclinations of the seminarian and the developmental achievements made during the year. But the large number of seminarians and the lifestyle of some formators would make this objective difficult to realize.

On the other hand, it is absolutely impossible for the spiritual directors to handle these numbers and accompany them thoroughly; it is simply inhuman to try to do so. The overwhelming nature of the situation contributes to making the major seminary less and less a house of formation and more and more an institute of higher learning where a good number of those who are sent to form the seminarians see themselves as lecturers rather than as formators; and one cannot blame them much for that is the most feasible option.

Since the number of seminarians is large, and the formators are few, efforts are directed, naturally, at keeping the seminarians under control rather than knowing their situations and attending to them. Thus, emphasis is laid on observing the rules and regulations of the seminary, such as waking up on time, going to prayers with others, doing one's functions, participating in manual labour and keeping the rule of silence. The rest of the time is devoted to academic lectures and personal studies. Sometimes, seminarians have the impression that going for spiritual direction is only a part of the seminary rules and regulations. The reason is that, in an effort to maintain control of the situation, spiritual matters could be presented, without intending it, in the language of obligation than of persuasion about their meaning.

The proposals made in this chapter may not be realisable unless something is done about the large number of seminarians and small number of formators and spiritual directors. The Church and the formators owe it to the seminarians to give them the attention they need for their vocational development, so that they do not turn back in the future and blame the seminary for their difficulties. Quality formation should not be sacrificed for the sake of large number. This is common sense. During his visit to Nigeria in 1982, Pope John Paul II rejoiced that "God has blessed Nigeria with many junior and senior seminarians", but noted that "the high number of your seminarians must never be used as a reason for accepting a lower quality of performance"[74]. In his intervention during the 8th Synod of Bishops, A.K. Obiefuna, then the bishop of Awka diocese, summarized the problems of the large number of seminarians in Nigeria; these include an insufficient number of formators, lack of space, lack of personal formation to maturity and a deeper spiritual life[75]. Schineller, who works in Abuja, Nigeria, observes that because of the large number of seminaries, students do not receive the personal care and guidance they need; training is concentrated on academics; spiritual formation is very weak, often monastic rather than active/apostolic; pastoral formation often is presented as a means of testing the seminarians rather than as formation. Izu Onyeocha observes that "with increased numbers, there is diminished care, less of family and more of crowd, less of personal responsibility and more of crowd mentality. Not only does the quality of care for the individual diminish, the quality of the individuals also diminishes"[76]. Consequently, "there is insufficient modelling or training in a more collegial or collaborative model of education or ministry and, thus, after ordination the young priests themselves take on the authoritarian model in exercising leadership"[77]. It is not a surprise then that some people feel that "in the African seminaries, we are training clerics rather than priests. The cleric is one who falls back upon his privileged position and office. The priest is one who gives his life in service to God's people"[78]. It is being proposed here, that it ought to be part of the selection process for a diocese to state the number of candidates it can accept in a year, depending on the resources it has. This will help to give individual formation to that number.

In choosing the number of candidates a diocese can accept, the following guidelines are suggested: first, that the candidates be properly evaluated according to the suggestions already given above on the knowledge of the candidates. This evaluation should focus on the motivations of the candidates and the possibility of their growth in formation. Secondly, that the candidates be interviewed by at least three priests experienced in formation. This is already being done in some spiritual year seminaries. In-depth psychological evaluation is still absent in the selection of candidates for the diocesan priesthood in Igboland. Thirdly, the interview of the candidates should focus on the whole person and not be confined to the academic. In addition to these suggestions, each diocese and each seminary should know the resources it has and the estimated number of candidates it can handle; this can also contribute in making decisions, especially if the number is still large.

Often it is argued among priests that, since priestly vocation is a divine call, no one has the right to refuse anyone who feels called to it, as if the desire to be a medical doctor immediately qualifies a person to be one. Therefore as many as knock on the door of the formation-houses should be accepted. For this reason, both priests and lay people often get angry with the formators or the bishop when an applicant is not accepted or a seminarian is advised to withdraw from the seminary or is expelled. [This is different from those situations in which a seminarian is sent home maliciously]. Some also argue that as many candidates as present themselves should be ordained priests because "this is our time", so that when shortage of candidates hits Africa as it is already happening in Europe and North America, we shall have an abundance of priests to sustain the Church. Others still maintain that in comparison with some parts of the world, the Church in Igboland does not have enough priests because the ratio of priests to the lay faithful is still very small[79]. A fourth argument is also put forward namely, that the priests serve the universal Church. This means that if we fix our eyes on the universal Church, we can easily see that the number is not as great as we tend to think.

These arguments emphasise the importance of taking advantage of the abundance of vocations in Igboland by ordaining many candidates. But they seem to neglect the concrete issue of the difficult circumstances surrounding the formation of priests, and the size and socio-economic conditions of the dioceses. None of these arguments addresses the question of the quality of the candidates being ordained, for example. Just as poor families with many children live in a vicious circle of poverty, disease, and illiteracy, so does the Church and society suffer from the many priests who did not receive individual formation because they were so many in the seminary.

Though the Church desires to have many priests, the specific limitations imposed by the circumstances need to be acknowledged and respected. If Canon Law stipulates that priests should be appropriately remunerated, this implies that each bishop should ordain the number of priests he can maintain[80]; this, even though that priesthood is a divine call. As the Church desires good, convinced and dedicated priests, the quality of the priests, rather than their quantity, takes precedence[81]. In the present condition of the major seminaries in Igboland, it is practically impossible to give to seminarians the kind of formation they truly deserve in order to meet the challenges of today's world. A conscious choice must then be made between having a large number of seminarians and a smaller number that the formators can handle. We can as well learn from Jesus himself: he chose only few men with passion for God and for humanity, rather than thousands who could be tepid and reluctant to stake all they were and had for God and for the world.

Number and Preparation of Formators

This point can be made briefly because some aspects of it have been discussed. In order to give individual formation to the seminarians, it is also necessary to increase the number of formators and the level of their preparation. To increase the number of formators and give them better preparation will not be easy. Yet, the "economics" of the situation are clear enough: if a given formator can help his seminarians so that one good priest is formed (who might otherwise have left, or become a trouble-maker within the priesthood) then the formator has in a real sense replaced himself. And a formator who is dedicated and well-prepared might hope to do much more than that.

What is often baffling is that despite the large number of seminarians and the large number of priests ordained every year in the dioceses in Igboland, the number of formators in the seminaries is few. Majority of them are experts in different areas of philosophy and theology, but very few specifically are prepared for formation. This is a big lack in our seminaries. The seminary needs lecturers in philosophy, theology, social and human sciences, but it also needs personnel who are trained in the dynamics of formation.

Existential Presentation of the Priesthood

This point has been discussed in the section dealing with the basic paradox of growth in Christian vocation; we shall touch it only briefly here.

The way the priesthood is presented existentially, and not only in the dogmatic sense, but also by the example and words of the seminary-staff, is also important. The priesthood should not be presented as a prestigious career, nor as a state in which one is "already perfect", but as the gift of self to God and His people, to be lived out amid all the weaknesses and temptations to which all priests are subject, with the help of God and the a *spirit of constant prayer.*

Coordination among the Seminaries

Spiritual Year seminaries have been established in almost all the dioceses in Nigeria to give to seminarians deeper spiritual and human formation which the major seminaries may not provide adequately. But unfortunately, there are two principal difficulties to realising the goal of these spiritual year seminaries: first, there is no coordination of programs among the spiritual year seminaries that supply seminarians to particular major seminaries. The consequence is that these seminarians learn different things and when they get into the same major seminary, there is no basis to continue from where they had stopped. Secondly, there is no coordination between the spiritual year and the major seminaries so as to ensure continuity or consistency. Sometimes what the seminarians learned in the spiritual year may clash with the personal beliefs or values of some of the formators in the major seminaries. In these circumstances, the seminarian suffers because he is not helped to build on the experiences he had in previous stages of his formation.

If each diocese had her spiritual year and major seminary, the situation would be different. But since we have regional or provincial major seminaries, coordination is necessary between different spiritual year seminaries, and between spiritual year and major seminaries. More concretely, all the spiritual year seminaries in a region or province should be aware of the programs they provide to their seminarians, and as far as possible, there should be congruence. Secondly, the formators in the major seminaries should also know what goes on in the spiritual year seminaries and structure the programs in the major seminaries in such a way as to make the seminarians experience continuity between the two stages of their formation.

Final Remarks

This book is born out of the desire I have to see that we, as the Church in Igboland, utilize well this springtime of the many vocations to the priesthood. The future of the Catholic priesthood in Igboland depends on the kind of formation given to the seminarians of today. The pattern that emerged from the findings of this research matches what many, including the Igbos, think of the Igbo people and their culture, and the difficulties they might have in their vocations.

What has become clearer is that the current way of forming Igbo candidates to the priesthood is not sufficient; there is need to consider this pattern which defines Igbo people and the ambiguity it creates for the Igbo Christians, priests and lay alike. *This means that the formation of Igbo priests will have to focus on some strategic points, like their strong need for achievement and success, the ambiguity of their sense of responsibility and autonomy, and their focus on external sources of self-esteem.* It should also harness their gifts such as their strong work habits, dedication, adventurous spirit, and their concern for justice and the family. All this should be presented to the seminarians against the background of the objective meaning of the priesthood and the basic paradox underlying the growth in one's vocation.

The task of formation is to help the candidates give their *personal response* to the God who calls them, as both Igbo persons and as Catholic Christians. This entails that the candidates should know what the priesthood is, and be helped to acquire authentic priestly identity through the internalization of the values of the priesthood. Adequate preparation of Igbo priests today requires that candidates have a clear and deeper understanding of the priesthood and their cultural values that help or obstruct their living as authentic Igbo and authentic Catholic priests. It is also necessary for their formators to know how these cultural and Christian values are configured in each of them, so as to give each person the kind of attention he needs and deserves. The present research work is an attempt to draw out the relevant variables that constitute the ideal of priestly life and how Igbo seminarians, religious and diocesan, relate to them in order to see the extent they have been able to integrate the priestly ideals into their own lives. It is an indirect research on the effectiveness of formation in their lives as future priests.

This research work provides an empirical documentation of the differences in the self-ideals of religious and diocesan priests and seminarians. Secondly, it offers some useful information concerning the quality of the many vocations to the priesthood in Igboland, which can challenge or support our impressions and presuppositions about these vocations. Thirdly, it provides some insight about the effectiveness of formation methods used in training Igbo Catholic diocesan and religious seminarians and the nature and extent of the influences of the Igbo socio-cultural context. The empirical evidence may help to develop appropriate formation-models that will be capable of delineating the problems of Igbo young men training for the diocesan priesthood and address them adequately for the future of the Catholic priesthood in Igboland. Thus, fourthly, this research may prove to be an empirical support for the need to inculturate formation in the Church in Igboland and other parts of Africa. It is only with good and effective formation that we, as a church, will be able to reduce the havoc that immature priests could wreck in themselves and in the Church. If due attention is not given to the selection and formation of future Igbo priests beyond their intellectual formation, the Church in Igboland may as well prepare herself for the onslaught of anti-clericalism which is already brewing in many parishes. It is a challenge that has to be faced because we trust that the grace of God is always with us.

Limitation of the Study

This study on the future of the Catholic priesthood in Igboland does not pretend to be exhaustive or perfect. One outstanding limitation it has is the fact that it is based on a single instrument. Moreover, the instrument is still very young, and has not generated many replicated researches that will give it more incremental validity. This means that the conclusions of this study are within these limitations, and they stand to be confirmed or unconfirmed in subsequent studies.

Notes

Introduction
[1] J. Tomko (1994). Situazione della Chiesa in Africa e in Madagascar: Alcuni aspetti e osservazioni, *L'Osservatore Romano*, 16 April, 6.

[2] John Paul II (1995). Post-Syodal Apostolic Exhortation, *Ecclesia in Africa*, 14th September, nn. 33-34. Henceforth *EA*

[3] Pontificia Opera Vocazioni (2002). Dati Statistici sui sacerdoti, i religiosi, le religiose e i seminarisiti nel mondo, *L'Osservatore Romano*, 21 April, vii-viii.

[4] John Paul II (1994). Homily "La Chiesa d'Africa, nata grazie all'opera dei Missionari, ora si prepara ad essere essa stessa missionaria verso di noi", *L'Osservatore Romano*, 18-19 April, 4.

[5] *EA*, 53..

[6] J. Tomko, Ibid., 8.

[7] *EA*, 77.

[8] Benedict XVI (2006). Address to the Bishops of Ghana, April 24, in http://www.zenit.org

Chapter I
[1] Second Vatican Council (1965). Pastoral Constitution on the Church in the Modern World, *Gaudium et Spes*, 7 December, in *The Basic Sixteen Documents of the Vatican II Council* ed. A. Flannery, Dublin, Ireland Dominican Publications, n. 4. Henceforth, *GS*.

[2] Organizational dynamics is specifically concerned about how an organization views the environment and the kind of response it gives to the signs of the time. The template for reading the signs of the times and interpreting them is its identity and mission. Cf. S.C. Schneider & P. Shrivastava (1988). Basic Assumptions Themes in Organizations, *Human Relations*, 41, 497.

[3] Bernard Lonergan (1973) had noted that inattention to a particular situation – which manifests itself in neglect of certain facts, oversight of insight, superficial analysis of a situation – always leads to faulty judgements which usually bring about greater unauthenticity in the individual, retrogression in group functioning and decline in society. See his *Method in Theology*, Toronto, 55.

[4] Given at Onitsha on the 6th of August, 1999. The document was signed by the Archbishop Emeritus of Onitsha Archdiocese, Most Rev. A.K.

Obiefuna and the incumbent Archbishop of Owerri archdiocese, Most. Rev. A.J.V. Obinna.

[5] *The Igbo Catholic Priest at the Threshold of the Third Millennium,* the Preface, Henceforth, *ICP*.

[6] *ICP*, 6. Emphasis is mine.

[7] *EA* 31, 32,33.

[8] *ICP*, 2

[9] *ICP*, 3.

[10] *ICP*, 4. In his homily that marked the end of the First Awka Diocesan Synod with a votive mass of the patron saint of the Cathedral, St. Patrick, the Local Ordinary, S.A. Okafor recalled also to the priests and lay faithful alike the tremendous heritage of faith left to us by the missionaries. He used almost the same words as contained in *The Igbo Catholic Priest at the Threshold of the Third Millennium.* Cf. his homily, "Put out into the Deep", in *Synod Acta*, Appendix II, 89.

[11] *ICP*, 5.

[12] *ICP*, 20.

[13] *EA*, 1.

[14] *ICP*, 29.

[15] *ICP*, 45-50.

[16] *ICP*, 51.

[17] *ICP*, 52, 53.

[18] *ICP*, 54, 55.

[19] *ICP*, 56, 57.

[20] *ICP*, 58-65.

[21] *ICP*, 59.

[22] *ICP*, 60-65.

[23] *ICP*, 7.

[24] John Paul II (1982). Address to the Priests and Seminarians at Bigard Memorial Seminary, Enugu, 13th February, 3.

[25] *ICP*, 26.

[26] *Awka Diocesan Liturgical Diary/Directory, 2006,* 76, 97.

[27] F.U.Okafor (1998). Priests, Politics and the Law in Contemporary Nigerian Society, in *The Catholic Clergy Under Nigerian Law,* ed. C.C. Nwez & C.O. Ugwu, Enugu, 112-113. He mentioned in particular, *Redeeming Nigeria through Massist Ideology,* written by Geo Ben Ezeani; *National Consciousness in Nigeria,* written by Israel Okoye; *Squandermania Mentality: Reflection on Nigerian Culture,* written by late professor Barnabas Okolo, along with other works.

[28] Some of his works include: *Nigeria: Search for Peace and Social Justice* (1987), *The Days of the Jackals* (1999), *Christians, Politics and the Nigerian*

Dilemma (1999), *After the Madness Called Election 2003* (2003), *The Dawn of Democratic Tyranny* (2003), and a host of other works.

[29] J.Ezeilo (1998). Women's Human Rights, Catholicism: Challenges of Evangelisation at the Dawn of 21st Century, in *The Catholic Clergy Under Nigerian Law*, 87-88. She mentions in particular the challenging contributions of Frs. John Patrick Ngoyi of Ijebu-Ode diocese, Mattew Kukah formally of the Catholic Secretariat Lagos, and Obiora Ike of the Catholic Institute of Justice, Peace and Development, Enugu.

[30] Some good researches have been done on this and the conclusion is the same. Cf. L. Eaton & J. Louw (2000). Culture and Self in South Africa: Individualism-Collectivism Predictions, *Journal of Social Psychology* 140/2, 213-216; B. Mesquita (2001). Emotions in Collectivist and Individualist Contexts, *Journal of Personality and Social Psychology*, 80/1, 68-73.

[31] The film was produced by Alex Okeke and Ugo Emmanuel of Emmalex Associates Limited.

[32] *Fides* Newspaper, January 1999, 14.

[33] Building on the teaching of the Second Vatican Council that evangelisation must aim at the whole man, "body and soul, heart and conscience, mind and will", (*GS*, 3), Elochukwu Uzukwu writes in the Nigerian context that the Christian proclamation must promote fundamental human rights, and liberate people who are living subhuman lives. Cf. E.E. Uzukwu (1991). Evangelisation in Context: Human Promotion and Liberation, *West African Journal of Ecclesial Studies*, 3, 27-28.

[34] *ICP*, 24.

[35] Source: *Annuario Pontificio*, 1985, Città del Vaticano, 13-662.

[36] Source: *Annuario Pontificio*, 1992, Città del Vaticano, 13-715.

[37] Source: *Annuario Pontificio*, 1999, Città del Vaticano, 11-747.

[38] *Annuario Pontificio*, 2006, Città del Vaticano, 15.

[39] *Annuario Pontificio*, 2006, Città del Vaticano, 15-18.

[40] Catholic Diocese of Ahiara, Mbaise, *Diary and Directory of Pastoral Events 2006*, Nguru, Mbaise, Ndulo & Generation Printers, 2006, 7.

[41] *Awka Diocesan Liturgical Diary/Directry, 2006*, Nimo, Rex Charles & Patrick, 86-97.

[42] *Annuario Pontificio*, 2006, Città del Vaticano, 68.

[43] *Annuario Pontificio*, 2006, Città del Vaticano, 235.

[44] Catholic Diocese of Nnewi, *2006 Liturgical Diary & Directory*, Nnewi, Catholic Communications, 20-23.

[45] Catholic Diocese of Nsukka, *Diary & Directory 2006*, Enugu, CIDJAP Press, XIX – XXIII.

[46] Diocese of Okigwe, *Official Directory and Diary, 2006*, 6-12.

47 Archdiocese of Onitsha, *Liturgical Diary & Directory, 2006*, Enugu, Snapp Press, 93-103.
48 Orlu Diocese, *2006 Diary and Calendar of Pastoral Events*, the Silver Jubilee Edition, 17-23.
49 Catholic Archdiocese of Owerri, *2006 Directory and Liturgical Diary*, Assumpta Press, 41-46.
50 *Annuario Pontificio*, 2006, Città del Vaticano, 773.
51 *ICP*, 24.
52 "Priests of dioceses which are blessed with greater abundance of vocations should be prepared to offer themselves willingly – with the permission or encouragement of their own ordinary – for ministry in countries or missions or tasks that are hampered by shortage of clergy". Cf. Second Vatican Council (1965). Decree on the Ministry and Life of Priests, *Presbyterorum Ordinis*, 7 December, n.10. Henceforth, *PO*.
53 "No particular Church, not even the poorest, can ever be dispensed from the obligation of sharing its personnel as well as its spiritual and temporal resources with other particular churches and with the universal church....". Special Assembly for Africa of the Synod of Bishops, *Lineamenta*, 42.
54 Cf. for example the Catholic Diocese of Awka, *2002 Liturgical Diary and Directory*; Catholic Diocese of Enugu, *Diocesan Directory and Diary, 2001*.
55 *Awka Diocesan Liturgical Diary/Directory, 2006*, 76-78.
56 Catholic Diocese of Ahiara, Mbaise, *Diary and Directory of Pastoral Events 2006*, 7.
57 S.A. Okafor, Inaugural Address Given at the Opening of the Awka Diocesan Synod, in *Synod Acta*, Appendix I, 75.
58 D.B. Cozzens (2000). *The Changing Face of the Priesthood*, Collegeville, Minnesota, The Liturgical Press, 132-133.
59 Ibid.,133
60 J. Aniagwu, on his reaction to George Ehusani's Paper (2000). *Challenges for the Church in the 21st Century: A Memorandum to Leaders of the Nigerian Church*, Lagos, Publication of Catholic Secretariat, 18. Henceforth, *Memorandum*.
61 Ibid.
62 Ibid., 20.
63 B.S. Aniko (1986). *The Pastoral Care of Priestly Formation in Nigeria*, Unpublished Doctoral Dissertation, Pontificia Universitas Lateranensis, Rome, 30.
64 I.R.A. Ozigbo (1985). *Igbo Catholicism*, Onitsha, 40.
65 Ibid.
66 Ibid., 40-41.
67 J. Aniagwu (2000), Memorandum, 20.

---

[68] D.R. Hoge, R.H. Potvin & K.M. Ferry (1984). *Research on Men's Vocations to the Priesthood and the Religious Life*, Washington, D.C. United States Catholic Conference, 63-68. Most recent research on the matter confirms that these same factors are still affecting priestly vocations in the United States. See D.R. Hoge (2002). *The First Five years of the Priesthood*, Collegevilee, Minessota, The Liturgical Press and D.R. Hoge & J.E. Wenger (2002). Changing Commitments and Attitudes of Catholic Priests, 1970-2001, *Seminary Journal*, 8/2, 55-68.

[69] J.S. Okwor (1997). *The Priesthood from an Igbo Perspective*, Nsukka, Nigeria, 49-50.

[70] A. Godin (1983). *The Psychology of Religious Vocations*, Lanham, 65.

[71] F.A. Arinze (2002). Vocations: Facing the Future Filled with Hope, *Encounter*, 5, 11.

[72] Ibid.

[73] John Paul II (1992). Post-Synodal Apostolic Exhortation, *Pastores Dabo Vobis*, 25 March, 8. Henceforth, *PDV*.

[74] A. Ekwunife (1992). The Image of the Priest in Contemporary Africa: The Nigerian Experience, Third Missiological Symposium on the Clergy in Nigeria Today, SIST, Attakwu Enugu, 4.

[75] Ibid., 6.

[76] Ibid., 6-7, citing A.B. Fafunwa.

[77] Ibid., 7.

[78] Ibid., 8.

[79] Ibid.

[80] I.R.A. Ozigbo (1985), 54.

[81] Ibid.

[82] Ibid.

[83] F.A. Arinze, (1983). *Answering God's Call*, London, 23.

[84] A.K. Obiefuna (1993). Presenting *Pastores Dabo Vobis* to the Nigerian Priests and Seminarians, Symposium on Priestly Formation in the Spirit of *Pastores Dabo Vobis* of John Paul II, Imezi-Owa, Enugu, 6. Henceforth, *Symposium*. See also O.Ike (1993). The Priest in the Modern World: Inadequacies in the Priestly Formation in the Context of Nigeria, in *Symposium*, 13.

[85] D.R. Hoge, R.H. Potvin & K.M. Ferry, (1984), 41.

[86] "In the past, the priesthood at least in the United States enjoyed an enormous prestige in the Catholic community. Many of its best and brightest chose the priesthood as a vocation. For others it was a step up, a way ahead, and they responded with generosity. But today the priesthood no longer commands the same respect". T.P. Rausch (1992). *Priesthood Today*, New York, Paulist Press, 44.

[87] C.I. Eke (1985). Priestly and Religious Vocations, in C.A. Obi (Ed.), *A Hundred Years of the Catholic Church in Eastern Nigeria 1885-1985*, Onitsha, 329.

[88] C.A. Obi (1985). The Development of Priestly Vocation in Igboland and the Genesis of the Bigard Seminary, in C.A. Obi (Ed.), *A Hundred Years of the Catholic Church in Eastern Nigeria 1885-1985*, 17-19.

[89] Cf. *EA*, 50.

[90] See the story of C.G. Valles (1986) *The Art of Choosing*, India, 26-37.

[91] *ICP*, 29.

[92] *ICP*, 42.

[93] This inclusive language could be noticed from the beginning of the document when the bishops say, "humility, however, demands that we take cognisance of lapses that occur in our ranks", *ICP*, 8. This statement implies that the approach of this document in terms of the assessment of priestly behaviour and lifestyle is consciously chosen by the bishops.

[94] Paragraph 40

[95] Cf. *ICP*, 31, 35 and 55.

[96] A.K. Obiefuna (1993). A Talk to the Priests of Awka Diocese on Postings Day, September 1st, 3.

[97] *ICP*, 40.

[98] T.O. Anyanwu (1988). *Spiritual Formation for Seminarians in the Nigerian Situation*. S.T.D. Dissertation, Pontifical University of St. Thomas Aquinas, Rome, 33.

[99] D.D. Dodo (1992). The Priest in Nigeria, A Layman's Perspective, the Third Missiological Symposium, SIST, Attakwu-Enugu, 10.

[100] G. Ujomu (1992). The Priest in Nigeria, A Layman's Perspective, the Third Missiological Symposium, Attakwu-Enugu, 10.

[101] M.H. Kuka (2000). *Memorandum*, 45.

[102] A. Njoku (2000). *Memorandum*, 65.

[103] B. Okolo (1993). Priestly Formation and the Challenges of Christianity: Nigerian Situation Revisited, in *Symposium*, 14.

[104] Catholic Bishops Conference of Nigeria (1987). *A Priest Forever*, Bodija, Ibadan, 14-15.

[105] *ICP*, 31.

[106] *ICP*, 31.

[107] *ICP*, 40.

[108] A.O.C. Anigbo (1989). Priests and Money: The Quest for a New Finance Policy for the Diocese. In U. Igboaja & O. Ike (Ed.), *The Challenges of a Young Church*, Rnugu, 52.

[109] G. Ujomu (1992), 9.

[110] D.D. Dodo (1992), 10-11.

[111] *ICP*, 40.

[112] T.O. Anyanwu (1988), 34.

[113] A. Ekwunife (1993), 11.

[114] Ibid.

[115] Ibid.,12

[116] That is why George Ehusani was so angry for the honorary traditional titles conferred on some 340 Nigerians by the President Olusegun Obasanjo because there was no reason to honour such people who were responsible for the traumatic condition of the country. "Traditional titles used to be a symbol of deserved recognition, a stamp of authority, an acknowledgement of moral leadership, a testimony to sterling qualities, and a proof of honour, achievement and service in the community. But how deserving are those who trade in chieftaincy titles in Nigeria today?" G. Ehusani (2001). National Awards and Chieftaincy Title: An Anomaly. In *The Guardian Online, http://ngrguardiannews.com,* Sunday, March 11, 2.

[117] C.B. Okolo (1993), 13.

[118] *ICP*, 40.

[119] *ICP*, 40.

[120] *Vanguard,* Thursday, August 20 1992, 1 & 17 cited by A. Ekwunife, 14.

[121] E.E. Uzukwu (1996). *A Listening Church*, Maryknoll, New York, Orbis Books, 99-100.

[122] A.K. Obiefuna (1993), 3.

[123] The rise of anti-clericalism in Nigeria is largely attributed to this materialistic spirit in many priests. Priests are beaten up or killed; rectories are broken into and some sacred objects are even desecrated. As an example, on 3 January, 2002 a group of people assaulted Fr. Francis G. Akpedo and desecrated the Church. *Leader* newspaper, April 21, 2002, 1. On this issue, Cf. also G. Ochiagha, Lenten Pastoral 1994, *An Echo From the Past: Anti-Clericalism Around the Corner,* 24; G. Odigbo (2000), *Memorandum,* 32-33; J. Aniagwu (2000), *Memorandum,* 22. H.U. Obia (1994). Anti-Clericalism: An Offshoot of Secularism, *The Torch,* 106, 16.

[124] S.A. Okafor (2004). Priests as Light for People", 2004 New Year Message to Awka Diocesan Presbyterium, January 7, n. 2.1.

[125] Catholic Secretariat of Nigeria (1999). Church in Nigeria: Family of God on Mission, *Lineamenta,* 68.

[126] *ICP*, 36.

[127] *ICP*, 36.

[128] Catholic Secretariat of Nigeria, *Lineamenta,* 68.

[129] G. Ujomu (1992), 9.

[130] Ibid.

[131] Ibid.

[132] P.N. Chinyelu (1999). *Priesthood,* Enugu 29.

[133] D.D. Dodo (1992), 9.

[134] Ibid.

[135] Ibid.

[136] This is a typical example of what P.L. Berger calls a clash between the normative and the cognitive presuppositions of the individual. In this case, celibate priesthood as the normative may well be accepted by the seminarian or priest, but the cognitive translation of it by the individual excludes chastity. He cites an example of a fellow white draftee to the military in 1950s who accepted, at the normative level, that racism was odious, a myth that legitimised the oppressive system present in the southern part of the United States in those years. Berger asked his friend why he was not morally troubled by the state of affairs and his friend responded: "I do very well under this system, and I see no reason why I should feel or do anything that is against my own interests". P.L. Berger (1969, 1990). *A Rumour of Angels*s. New York, Anchor Books, 151. It happens also that some people argue in favour of celibate priesthood because it offers them the freedom to have as many girls as possible, and not because of serious spiritual yearning.

[137] I.R.A. Ozigbo (1985), 55.

[138] D.D. Dodo (1992), 9-10.

[139] Cf. his commentary on the film on *Fides* newspaper, January 1999, 14.

[140] C.J. Uzor (1999). *Living Between Two Worlds*, Appendix D, C3, 537.

[141] CBCN (2006). *Called to Love*, Lagos: A Publication of the Catholic Secretariat of Nigeria, 39.

[142] *ICP*, 41.

[143] *ICP*, 41.

[144] *ICP*, 42. The phrase *"amoris officium"* was used by St. Augustine in describing the priestly ministry. John Paul II used it as an operative phrase in describing pastoral charity as the center of the priestly ministry. Cf. *PDV*, 23 & 24. The document quoted from the *Directory on the Ministry and Life of Priests*, published by the Congregation for the Clergy, 16.

[145] *ICP*, 42.

[146] *ICP*, 42.

[147] Catholic Secretariat of Nigeria, *Lineamenta*, 71.

[148] Reported by E.E. Uzukwu (1996), 121.

[149] B. Itsueli (2000), *Memorandum*, 25.

[150] Catholic Secretariat of Nigeria, *Lineamenta*, 71.

[151] *ICP*, 38.

[152] *ICP*, 38.

[153] *ICP*, 38.

[154] G. Ochiagha (1994), *An Echo from the Past*, 26.

155 G. Ujomu (1992), 7.
156 *ICP*, 32.
157 *ICP*, 32.
158 T.O. Anyawnu (1988), 40.

Chapter II
1 *ICP*, 8.
2 *ICP*, 21.
3 *ICP*, 20.
4 *ICP*, 31.
5 *ICP*, 31.
6 *ICP*, 22.
7 A.S. Reber (1985). *The Penguin Dictionary of Psychology*, New York, Penguin Publications.
8 Psychologists of different theoretical perspectives describe this frame of reference in different ways. For example, there are some who refer to this frame of reference as dispositions of individuals to act in certain ways. This is a perspective generally held by psychologists with psychodynamic bent. The working of this frame of reference, this psychological disposition, is played out in the intrapsychic dynamics of the individual as he relates with *alterity*. Cognitive psychologists see it in terms of mental constructs which persons use to navigate their worlds. These mental constructs function by the principle of consonance-dissonance in interaction with the environment. Social psychologists prefer to speak in terms of «social schemas» as some kind of cognitive patterns used by people to process information that comes up in relating with the world. For more details on this cf. S.R. Maddi (1996). *Personality Theories: A Comparative Analysis*, California Brooks/Cole Publishing Company; A.S.R. Manstead & M. Hewstone (Eds.) *The Blackwell Encyclopaedia of Social Psychology*, on the entry "Schemas/Schemata".
9 Sociologists hold that the development of "frames of reference" in societies is unavoidable since societies must impose some order in the apparent chaos that threatens human beings. This search for order leads to the development of worldviews, and hence, provides individuals in particular societies a bearing or a compass with which to view the world. For a brief but insightful description of this sociological process cf. P.L. Berger (1967). *The Sacred Canopy*, NY, 1-25. In this regard also, Clifford Geertz sees culture primarily in terms of its program of ordering the behaviour of individuals through its traditions, habits and customs. It is what he calls the "control mechanism" view of culture. Cf. C. Geertz (1973, 2000). *The Interpretation of Cultures*, New York, 44-51. In other

words, through its traditions, habits, customs, usages as interpretative schemes, a culture orders the behaviour of an individual by offering him a model of life to be followed. On this important theme, see also G. Bateson's (1972). Culture Contact and Schismogenesis, in G. Bateson, *Steps to an Ecology of Mind*, Chicago, University of Chicago Press, especially 65-68.

[10] A. Ekwunife (1993). The Services of African Traditional Religion to Humanity: the Nigerian Experience, *Bigard Theological Studies* 12/2-13/1, 9-10. See also E. Lszlo (1996). *The Systems View of the World*, Cresskill NJ, Hampton Press, Inc., 12-13

[11] A. Ekwunife (1993), 10.

[12] A. Shorter (1998). *Celibacy and African Culture*. Nairobi, St. Pauls, 9.

[13] P.L. Berger (1967), 20-21.

[14] *ICP*, 20.

[15] L.N. Mbefo (1991). Igbos and the Culture of Excellence, *The Torch*, 97, 29.

[16] P.N. Chinyelu (1999), 27-28.

[17] T.O. Anyanwu (1988), 41.

[18] *ICP*, 32.

[19] L.N. Mbefo (1989). *Towards a Mature African Christianity*, Enugu, 30.

[20] C.J. Uzor (2003), 37.

[21] V. Ekezuike, (1994). The Religious Dilemma of African Conscience. *The Torch*, 106, 32.

[22] C.B. Okolo (1993), 51.

[23] C.J. Uzor (1999), 38.

[24] I.R.A. Ozigbo (1985), 69

[25] Ibid., 62.

[26] A. Ekwunife (1993), 12.

[27] C.J. Uzor, (2003), 399.

[28] Ibid., 401.

[29] Ibid.

[30] Ibid., Appendix A1, 503. In connection to these directions, see also L.M. Rulla, J. Ridick & F. Imoda (1988). *Entering and Leaving Vocation*. Rome, Gregorian University Press. Appendix B-1, 325, henceforth, *ELV*; B.M. Kiely (1987). *Psychology and Moral Theology*. Rome, Gregorian University Press, 81.

[31] C.J. Uzor (2003), 412 – 413.

[32] For BMS seminarians the relationship PB-SI results in, r = 0.018, $P = 0.800$; for those from SWS, r = 0.113, $P = 0.1$ Cf. Ibid., Appendix A3, 525 - 526.

[33] For BMS seminarians, r = 0.016, $P = 0.79$, and for those from SWS, r = 0.05, $P = 0.36$. Cf. Ibid., Appendix A3, 526.

34 Cf. D.R. Hoge (2002), 5. The written testimonies of three priests who left the priesthood in Italy, for example, indicate their persistent difficulty in trying to live the value of celibate chastity in the context of popular Italian culture. Cf. *Vita Pastorale* (2001), 1, 127-138.

35 The editorial of *America*, of November 11, 2002, titled, "Ordaining Gay Men" takes up the arguments against admitting homosexual men in the priesthood one by one. At the end, the author appeals to everyone to see that "the ministry of gay priests has represented a significant contribution to the Catholic Church. Preventing the ordination of gay men would deprive the church of many productive, hard-working and dedicated ministers and would, moreover, ignore the promptings of the Holy Spirit, who has called these men to holy orders". While the Church's position rests on matters of principle, the editorial deals with issues of profit and loss, typical of the American pragmatic culture. At least, the struggle of this writer and many others in America today, shows that this tension between native cultural values and Christian message is always there. When the tension is not understood as clash of principles or values, confusion can cloud the understanding of concrete situations, as can be seen in an article written by G.D. Coleman in which he writes: "During the process of seminary formation, formators must assist a seminarian to be ego-syntonic, rather than ego-dystonic, about his sexual orientation". In the next paragraph, he says: "It is additionally important to assist a seminarian to carefully critique his ego-syntonic sense of his orientation: e.g. formators should rightfully become 'alarmed' if a seminarian is 'in sync' with a sexual orientation that is directed toward children (the fixated pedophile) and does not see anything wrong or dysfunctional in this regard". G.D. Coleman (2002). Human Sexuality and Priestly Formation. *Seminary Journal*, 8/1, 18. The question of sexual orientation and sexual disorder at the level of principle is set aside. It becomes a problem only when it is a fixated state, like in the paedophile.

36 See D.R. Hoge (2002), 23-31; D.R. Hoge & J.E. Wenger (2002), 66, Table 8.

37 For a summary-exposition of the situation, see R.F. Leavitt (2002). The Formation of Priests for a New Century: Theological and Spiritual Challenges. *Seminary Journal*, 8/2, 15-16.

38 "Priests ordained in the 1960s and 1970s were more 'post-Vatican' in ecclesiology than their predecessors ordained earlier, but in the 1980s the attitudes of young priests shifted back again. There is a bulge of post-Vatican ecclesiology slowly passing through the priesthood. In the future when the men holding these views are gone, the prevailing

ecclesiological attitudes will again be similar to those held by priests ordained prior to the 1960s". D.R. Hoge & J.E. Wenger (2002), 68.

[39] A. Shorter, 10.

[40] M. Rokeach (1979). Some Unresolved Issues in Theories of Beliefs, Attitudes, and Values. In *Nebraska Symposium on Motivation*, Lincoln NE, 297.

[41] G.K. Chesterton (1959) rightly observes: "Every act of will is an act of self-limitation. To desire action is to desire limitation. In that sense every act is an act of self-sacrifice. When you choose anything, you reject everything else.... Every act is an irrevocable selection and exclusion. Just as when you marry one woman you give up all the others, so when you take one course of action you give up all the other courses". *Orthodoxy*. New York, Image Books, 39-40.

[42] L.M. Rulla (1971). *Depth Psychology and Vocation*. Rome, Gregorian University Press, 108. Henceforth, *DPV*

[43] Ibid.

[44] See J.J. Gill (2002). The Study's Implications Related to Health. In D.R. Hoge (2002), 119-120.

[45] C.J. Uzor, (1999), 414.

[46] E.E. Uzukwu (1996),120.

[47] A. Ekwunife (1992), 6.

[48] Ibid., 10.

[49] Ibid.

[50] A.T. Ukwuoma (2000). *Being a Priest in a Changing Society*. Kearney, NE, Mater Dei Publishers, 30.

[51] In the reaction to the paper presented by A. Ekwunife on "The Image of the Priest", R.C. Arazu (1992) remarks that the priests could exercise such unlimited power over the masses because the people themselves are not aware of their rights. "Right when not claimed", he states "is not respected, and because the masses of the people do not know their rights and cannot, therefore, claim them, the full-power conscious priest does not usually respect a lot of human and un-claimed rights". See his, Reaction, in *The Third Missiological Symposium on the Clergy in Nigeria Today*, SIST, Attakwu-Enugu, 1992, 2.

[52] S.A. Okafor (1998). *Stewards of the Mysteries of God*. Message of the Local Ordinary to the Plenary Fathers Meeting of the Awka Diocesan Presbyterium, September 2, 6-7.

[53] A. Ekwunife (1992), 12.

[54] CBCN (1996). *Guidelines for the Healing Ministry in the Catholic Church in Nigeria*. Lagos, Catholic Secreteriat Publication.

[55] E.E. Uzukwu (1996), 123. C.J. Uzor (1999, 340), observes in this regard: "Many priests and their seminarian apprentices exploit the fundamental

religious penchant of the people and their unbroken traditional affinity to the 'world-in-between' to stack their pockets full of money. Instead of leading their 'flock' to green pasture, they have turned into predators, having prepared them prior to that with sufficient doses of negative and intimidating theological soporifics".

56 E.E. Ekwunife (1992), 13.

57 Ibid., 14.

58 D.D. Dodo (1992), 1.

59 C. McGarry (1989). Ministry in the Church, *African Christian Studies*, 5/2, 65; cf. also E.E. Uzukwu (1996), 120.

60 Second Vatican Council (1964). Dogmatic Constitution on the Church, *Lumen Gentium*, 21 November. In A. Flannery, (Ed.), *The Basic Sixteen Documents of the Vatican Council II*, nn.10-12. Henceforth, *LG*.

61 D.D. Dodo (1992), 2.

62 This is one of the reasons advanced for the exodus from the priesthood that shook the Catholic Church in Europe and North America at the close of Second Vatican Council. The new ecclesiology recovered the centrality of the people of God and in so doing it upturned the "edifice of the holy" represented by the priesthood and the consecrated life. This led to some confusion regarding priestly identity. For more details concerning this development, Cf. D. Power (1999). Evolution of the Priesthood. In K.S. Smith (Ed.) *Priesthood in the Modern World*. Franklin, Wisconsin: Sheed & Ward, 30; M.E. Hussey (1999). The Priesthood after the Council: The Theological Reflections. In K.S. Smith (Ed.), 22.

63 S.A. Okafor (1992). Opening Speech at the Third Missiological Symposium, SIST, Attakwu-Enugu, 2.

64 A.T. Ukwuoma (2000), 89.

65 P.L. Berger & T. Luckmann (1966). *The Social Construction of Reality*. New York: Anchor Books, 61.

66 Ibid.

67 Ibid., 67.

68 This is graphically shown in these words of David G. Myers (1999): "Whether we equate beauty with slimness or shapeliness depends on when and where we live. Whether we define social justice as equality (all receive the same) or as equity (those who produce more receive more) depends on whether Marxism or capitalism shapes our ideology. Whether we tend to be expressive or reserved, casual or formal, hinges partly on whether we have spent our lives in an African, a European, or an Asian culture". See his *Social Psychology*. Boston: McGraw-Hill College, 174. Ayisi gives another example: "The English kiss loved ones: a man may kiss a lady on the cheek as a symbol of affection or on the lips with deep passion if they are lovers. The continental European do

something quite different – men kiss their fellow men on both cheeks. The Ghanaian who has never lived in either of these cultures would consider men kissing their fellow men as ridiculous and feeble, although chiefs may embrace distinguished guests as a sign of cordiality and welcome". E.O. Ayisi (1992). *An Introduction to the Study of African Culture*. Nairobi, Kampala, 2-3.

[69] H.S. Sullivan (1970). *The Psychiatric Interview*. NY, London: W.W. Norton & Company, 26-27.

[70] L. Sperry (2001). Approaches to Transformation. *Human Development*, 22, 18.

[71] Heb. 5.1.

[72] *PDV*, 5. Emphasis is mine.

[73] *PDV*, 5. Emphasis is mine.

[74] P. L. Berger (1976). *Pyramids of Sacrifice*. New York: Anchor Books, thesis no. 21, xiii; 21-25.

[75] "Individuals may, on occasion, reject their culture's shared beliefs and construct instead another system that operates with different values". Cf. J. Nuttin (1984). *Théorie de la motivation humaine: du besoin au projet d'action*, Eng. Trans. *Motivation, Planning, And Action*, by R.P. Lorion & J.E. Dumas, Leuven: Leuven University Press, 28.

[76] G.A. Arbuckle, "Cross-Cultural Pastoral Intimacy", 18-19.

[77] This is what Watzlawick aptly describes as "nostalgic misery" which is one of the most successful ways of getting one's desired unhappiness. Cf. P. Watzlawick (1983). *The Situation is Hopeless, But not Serious*. New York, London: W.W. Norton & Company, 25-27.

[78] There is a difficulty with the selection of the population in this study. Nigeria is a country with more than 250 tribes and cultures and languages. The research is carried out in the specific area of Igboland, namely, the Owerri ecclesiastical province. It is important to note from the very beginning that the research does not cover the whole of Nigeria, but is basically a research on Igbo priests.

[79] J.B.C. Okorie (1995). *Social Interest, Lifestyle, Stress and Job Satisfaction of Nigerian Catholic Priests*. Unpublished Doctoral Dissertation, University of San Francisco, 11.

[80] C.S. Hall & G. Lindzey (1978). *Theories of Personality*. 3rd Ed. New York: John Wiley, 164.

[81] Ibid., 165.

[82] Ibid., 164.

[83] R.S. Lazarus (1966). *Psychological Stress and the Coping Process*, New York: McGraw-Hill.

[84] J.B.C. Okorie (1995), 11.

[85] Ibid., 15-16.

[86] Ibid., 68-79.
[87] Ibid., Appendix H, 160-161.
[88] Ibid., 78.
[89] Ibid., 81.
[90] Ibid., 90.
[91] Driven behaviour ($F = 2.21$, $P < 0.03$) and Hostility ($F = 2.03$, $P < 0.05$).
[92] $R^2 = 1.63$, $t = 2.49$, $P < 0.02$, Ibid., table 8, 94.
[93] Ibid., 111.
[94] Ibid., 113.
[95] $F = 2.09$, $P < .04$, Ibid., Table 7, 93.
[96] Ibid., 113.
[97] Ibid., 115.
[98] Ibid.
[99] Okorie himself did not sort out these stressors in the order of their frequencies in the two sections of the in-depth interview. It is a weakness in his data classification. If he had classified these stressors according to their presence and frequency in the two sections of the in-depth interview, it would be easier to make more valid statements. His statement that "almost 100% of the priests interviewed said that work overload, culture conflicts, and their own families are the factors which cause the most stress in their lives" Ibid., 118, seems to be based more on a personal hunch than on the data of the in-depth interview. The statement can apply only to the workload but not to the other two stressors.
[100] C.S. Hall & G. Lindzey (1978), 163.
[101] T.M. Gannon (1971). Priest/Minister: Profession or Non-Profession? *Review of Religious Research*, 12, 70-74. Okorie himself had earlier recognised that the Catholic priesthood "is not just a job, but a way of life". But he could not see that this distinction makes a world of difference. And so he did not consider it necessary to choose a theoretical framework that incorporates it.
[102] Ibid., 116.
[103] A.T. Ukwuoma (2000), 25.
[104] Ibid., 26.
[105] Ibid., 29-33.
[106] Ibid., 35. He refers to the work of J.B.C. Okorie. But Okorie did not actually prove the hypothesis of his thesis. He only observed this phenomenon among the Nigerian-Igbo priests.
[107] Ibid.
[108] Ibid., 40. A detailed highlight of each of the stressors is treated in this first domain is to be found in 40-70.
[109] Ibid.,70-86.

---

110 Ibid., 71.

111 Ibid., 74.

112 Ibid., 77.

113 Ibid., 78.

114 Ibid., 80.

115 Ibid.,86-92.

116 Ibid., 93-98.

117 Ibid., 93. It has to be noted that it is not yet clear if there is anything like "Nigerian culture" in the true sense of the word. Ukwuoma, like Okorie, tends to think of a single "Nigerian culture". But the terminology he used indicate that the research was carried out mainly among the Igbo people. The *omenala* is an Igbo expression; the *"Nshiko* syndrome" [crab syndrome] derives from an Igbo proverb; the *Ikwu n'ibe* syndrome [relatives] is an Igbo phrase; "*umu fada*" [the children of the priests] is another Igbo expression. Though he may use these concepts to express his point, it seems they reflect the background of the subjects of his research.

118 Ibid., 99-112.

119 Ibid., 134.

120 R. Ardrey (1970). *The Social Contract: A Personal Enquiry into the Evolutionary Sources of Order and Disorder*. New York, 286-287.

121 Cited by N. Cameron & J.F. Rychlak (1985). *Personality Development and Psychopathology*. Boston: Houghton Mifflin Company, 521.

122 Cited in USCC (1982). *The Priest and Stress*. Washington, D.C., 3-4.

123 A.K. Obiefuna (1993)., 6.

124 U.C. Nwosu (1992). The Image of Indigenous Clergy, *African Christian Studies*, 8/4, 52.

125 C.B. Okolo (1993), 9.

126 E.E. Uzukwu (1996), 99-100; I.M. Onyeocha (2001). Truly African and Truly Religious. The Challenge of a True Religious Identity in the African Church, *Claretianum*, 41, 229.

127 A.K. Obiefuna (1993), 6.

128 F. Nwatu (1997). A Paradigm Shift in Clergy Formation. A Sine Qua Non for Inculturation in Africa, *The Asia Journal of Theology*, 11/1, 104.

129 E.E. Uzukwu (1996), 102.

130 G. Odigbo (2000), *Memorandum*, 32-33.

131 Ibid., 32.

132 F. Nwatu (1993). Africa and the Return of Priestcraft, *AFER*, 35/4, 243.

133 Ibid., 245.

134 A priest had an experience of another priest who was getting drunk in a bar very close to a higher institution of learning. When he gently told the priest that it would be better to drink like that at home than in the

public place, the priest flared up and warned him not to add more to the burdens he was already carrying, that is, the burden of celibacy and lack of children.

[135] I. Nwafor (1996). *Redeemed by the Lamb. A Reflection on Priesthood.* Enugu: Snapp Press, 10.

[136] The historical preoccupation with self-evident truths led to the building of systems of thought and a gradual forgetfulness of the human subject until Kierkegaard and the existentialists revolted. Cf. the analysis of Bernard Lonergan (1974) in his lecture on "The Subject", in *The Second Collection*. Toronto, 69-86.

[137] F. Imoda (1998). *Lo Sviluppo Umano.* Eng. Trans. *Human Development,* by E. Dryer, Leuven, Belgium, 107.

[138] U.C. Nwosu (1992) 59.

[139] C.J. Uzor (2003), 342.

[140] Cf. C. McGarry (1999). Formation of the Agents of Evangelisation for the Realities of Africa Today: Its Urgency and Importance, *AMECEA Documentation Service*, 16, 309.

[141] A.K. Obiefuna (1993), 7.

[142] Writing about the formation houses in the Church in Igboland, Onyejekwe writes: "Many of our formation houses are still filled with the atmosphere of fear and tension coupled with the threat of immediate or deferred expulsion as a result of personal conflict or relaxation in the observance of the regulations, even when no serious transgression is involved. How often one hears the awful statement: 'if he does not go, I go', coercing the authorities of an institute into personal whims.... The formator is more of a police than a brother/sister, making sure that every regulation is kept to the least, even when situation demands a simple relaxation". M.C. Onyejekwe (2000). Christian Consecrated Life: The Igbo-African Situation, *Claretianum*, 40, 184-185. See also I. Nwafor (1996), 11; O. Ike (1998). *Freedom is more than a Word. Toward a Theology of Empowerment.* Enugu, 70-79.

[143] The United Nations Development Programme reported that in Nigeria, 70.2% of the population live below the poverty line, that is, below US$1 a day. Cf. UNDP, Human Development Report 2001, in *hhttp://www.undp.org/hdr2001*. What this means is further clarified in the report of IFAD: "Those below the World Bank dollar-a-day poverty line typically spend at least 70-80% of all income on food, most of it basic staples, and are at risk of consuming too few calories for health and efficiency". *Rural Poverty Report 2001*, 19. This means that 70.2% of Nigerian population are under the threat of food-deprivation and spend most of what they have on food. It is in this condition of poverty that Nwatu invites everyone to think "about a young priest who owns a

mansion and lives like a lord in a rural area made up of poor peasants whose lives are a day-to-day struggle for survival, majority of whom are not able to as much as give their families at most one balanced meal every day. If the priest does not react with sensitivity to their plight, it is simply because he is a stranger to it". F. Nwatu (1993), 249.

144 T.P. Rausch (1992), 82

145 Ibid.

146 Ibid.

147 Ibid., 91. See also M. Otene (1983). *To be with Christ, Chaste, Poor and Obedient*. Nairobi, St. Paul Publication, 16.

148 Ibid., 89.

149 Ibid., 88.

150 T.P. Rausch (2000). Priesthood in the Context of Apostolic Religious Life. In D.J. Georgen & A. Garrido (Eds.), *The Theology of Priesthood*. Collegeville, Minnesota: The Liturgical Press, 106-107.

151 I.M. Onyeocha (2001), 211.

152 M.C. Onyejekwe (2000). *Rites of Initiation in Africa: The Igbo Experience*. An Excerpt of a Doctoral Dissertation, Faculty of Theology, Universidad Pontificia de Salamanca, Spain, 61. A story was told concerning a group of young boys who applied to a clerical religious congregation. They were about 23 in number. The vocations director gathered all of them together for the interview. In one of the sessions, he asked them to break into small groups and discuss any question that worried them and report back to the general group. When they all came back to the general group, the common question asked to the vocations director was whether they should submit the car that would be given to them at their ordination to the congregation. The vocations director said yes but told them not to worry about that because if they needed a car for their ministries, it would be provided them. At the end of the interview, 17 left and 6 persons continued.

153 Ibid., 74.

154 M.J.A. Anochie (1994). *The Igbo Woman and Consecrated Life*. Onitsha, 64.

155 I.M. Onyeocha (20010, 222.

156 This impression goes back to the earliest periods of missionary presence in Igboland. Chika Uzor recounts that in those early days, the secular or diocesan priest was a mere auxiliary to the religious priest. This "bias" against the diocesan priests also was behind the reluctance of the missionaries to appoint secular priests to the Episcopal seats; instead, they chose native religious priests. Cf. C.J. Uzor (1999), 292-293 especially footnote no. 139.

157 I remember the story told by a priest colleague about how a parent was angry towards his son for wanting to become a religious seminarian. The parent asked the priest, "Isn't it stupid for my son to do that since religious priests do not bring anything to their families?" There are religious brothers who have been consistently pressured by their relatives to get into the diocesan priesthood. Some are even insulted for remaining religious brothers who, according to their families, are simply "wasting" themselves as servants of the priests.

158 G. Aschenbrenner (1997). Diocesan Seminary Formation, *Human Development*, 18, 34.

159 S.J. Rossetti (1999). Understanding Diocesan Priesthood, *Human Development*, 20/1, 35. See also E. Untener (1997). Using the Wrong Measure. In D.B. Cozzens (Ed.), *The Spirituality of the Diocesan Priesthood*, Collegeville, Minnesota, The Liturgical Press, 21.

Chapter III

1 F. Imoda (1998), 78-79.

2 J. Nuttin (1985). *Future Time Perspective and Motivation*. Leuven: Leuven University Press & Lawrence Erlbaum Associates, 12. This interrelatedness between the past, the present and the future is summed up in the following statement of Lewin: "The life-space of an individual, far from being limited to what he considers the present situation, includes the future, the present, and also the past. Actions, emotions and certainly the morale of an individual at any instant depend upon his total time perspective". K. Lewin (1948). *Resolving Social Conflicts. Selected Papers on Group Dynamics*, New York, 104. Imoda adds: "If each one's present is like a summary of his entire past, embracing of course both conscious and unconscious memories, it is equally the expectation of what is yet to come. For as future, it does not strictly exist, except somehow in the present", F. Imoda (1998), 80-81.

3 Ibid., 36.

4 Ibid., 32.

5 Ibid., 32-33.

6 R. Zavalloni (1959). *Educazione e Personalità*, Milano, 62-63.

7 W. Lens(1986). Future Time Perspective: A Cognitive-Motivational Concept. In D.R. Brown & J. Veroff (Eds.), *Frontiers of Motivational Psychology*, Berlin, Heidelberg, Springer-Verlag, 175, 180.

8 J. Batten (1981). *Expectations and Possibilities*. Santa Monica, California, 9.

9 Ibid.

10 C.J. Uzor, (1999), 76.

[11] "Take away a person's hope and you have taken away the person's reason for living. You have taken away the person's basic motivation to play, work, love, care, share, and build". J. Batten (1981), 9.

[12] B.M. Dolphin (1990). *The Values of the Gospel. Personal Maturity and Thematic Perception*. Unpublished Doctoral Dissertation in Psychology, Pontifical Gregorian University, Rome, 36, footnote 29.

[13] T. Merton (1958). *Thoughts in Solitude*. Great Britain:Burns & Oates, Ch. XII. B. Schwartz (2001) gives a typical example with students. "Are the objectives of the student game to prepare for a career that will be financially rewarding? Are they to prepare for a career that will be intellectually rewarding? Are they to prepare for a career that will serve the public? In any of these cases, a good student will map out a program that provides appropriate training and then work hard to develop the skills necessary for success in that career. Possibly, the objectives of the student game have nothing to do with careers but instead involve becoming knowledgeable, sensitive, compassionate, committed, ethical person who will be an informed and responsible citizen. The good student at this game will look very different from the good student at the other games". See his Self-Determination: The Tyranny of Freedom, *American Psychologist*, 55/1, 80. One can notice the connection between how each student looks to his future and the different impacts their visions have on their concrete plans and actions in the present.

[14] J. Nuttin (1984), 40.

[15] R.M. Gula (1989). *Reason Informed by Faith. Foundations of Catholic Morality*. New York, Mahwah, 79. The ideal of the priesthood, according to Agostino Favale (1990), must assume the position of the fundamental option of priests "that should involve and direct all the other choices of their life,...". See his Identità Teologica del Presbitero, *Lateranum*, 56, 477. [Translation supplied] The priestly ideal, as the fundamental option of the priest, not only gives direction and meaning to the actions of the priest in the present, it also *integrates* those actions.

[16] L.M. Rulla (1986). *Anthropology of Christian Vocation*, Vol. 1, Rome, Gregorian University Press, 168. Henceforth, *ACV,I*. See also, N.T. Feather (1982). Human Values and the Prediction of Action. An Expectancy-Valance Analysis. In N.T. Feather (Ed.), *Expectations and Actions. Expectancy-Value Models in Psychology*, Hillside, NJ, Lawrence Erlbaum Associates, 277.

[17] K.M. Sheldon & T. Kasser (1995). Coherence and Congruence. Two Aspects of Personality Integration, *Journal of Personality and Social Psychology*, 68, 531.

[18] Ibid., 531-532.

[19] N.T. Feather (1982), 154.

[20] Ibid.

[21] Ibid., 155.

[22] The particular types of expectations usually studied by psychologists reveal that their main concern is this structural link between future expectation and the present behaviour or action. Examples of kinds of expectation generally studied include, "outcome expectations", "efficacy expectations", "generalized expectancies", and so on. Cf. N.T. Feather (1982). Expectancy-Value Approaches: Present Status and Future Directions. In N.T. Feather, (Ed.), *Expectations and Actions*, 406-410. None of these kinds of expectations is concerned with investigating the *nature* of the goal that the person expects to achieve. The distinction made by R. Janoff-Bulman and P. Brickman (1982) between low and high expectations and their pathologies deals with the question of goals and their relationship to the expectations people have concerning them. Their analysis basically relates to the issue of attainability and nonattainability of a particular goal and the importance of learning when to quit. The approach is very pragmatic and prescinds from consideration of the objective nature of any goal in question. See their article, Expectations and What People Learn from Failure. In N.T. Feather (Ed.), *Expectations and Actions*, 207-237.

[23] K.M. Sheldon & T. Kasser (1995), 531.

[24] Ibid., 541.

[25] They used such scales as General Causality Orientation Scale, Self-Actualization Scale, Psychological Vitality Scale, Positive/Negative Affect Scale, Interpersonal Reactivity Index, the Scale of Openness to Experience and Rosenberg's Self-esteem Inventory.

[26] Ibid., 532.

[27] Ibid.

[28] K.M. Sheldon & A.J. Elliot (1999). Goal Striving, Need Satisfaction, and Longitudinal Well-Being: The Self-Concordance Model, *Journal of Personality and Social Psychology*, 76, 495. (Emphasis is mine).

[29] D.S. Browning (1987). *Religious Thought and the Modern Psychologies*. Philadelphia: Fortress Press, 3-14.

[30] B. Kiely (1990). Can There Be a Christian Psychology?, *Studies*, 79, 151.

[31] P. Fraisse (1963). *The Psychology of Time*. Wesport, CT, 151.

[32] W. Lens (1986), 180.

[33] *ELV*, 121.

[34] Ibid., 122.

[35] Ibid., 120.

[36] Ibid., 128. Appendix A, Table 7.1.

[37] Ibid., 137.

[38] L.M. Rulla, J. Ridick & F. Imoda (1989). *Anthropology of Christian Vocation*, Vol. II, Rome: Gregorian University Press, 167. Cf. also Figure 11B, 162. Henceforth, *ACV,II*.

[39] C. O'Dwyer (2000). *Imagining One's Future: A Projective Approach to Christian Maturity*. Rome Gregorian University Press, 159-160.

[40] Ibid., 46.

[41] Cf. J.B.C. Okorie (1995); C.J. Uzor (1999, 2003).

[42] G.D. Coleman & R.L. Freed (2000). Assessing Seminary Candidates, *Human Development*, 21/2, 18.

[43] D. L. Kelley (1999). *Measurement Made Accessible*. London: Sage Publications, 81; Cf. also E. Aronow, M. Reznikoff, & K.L. Moreland (1995). The Rorschach: Projective Technique or Psychometric Test?, *Journal of Personality Assessment*, 64/2, 213-228.

[44] G.D. Coleman & R.L. Freed (2000), 18.

[45] B.M. Dolphin (1991), 89.

[46] P. Moessinger (2000). *Irrationalité individuelle et ordre social*, Eng. Tr. *The Paradox of Social Order. Linking Psychology and Sociology*, by S. Scher & F. Worrall, New York, 46.

[47] D. Rapaport, M.M. Gill & R. Schafer (1968). *Diagnostic Psychological Testing*. Connecticut: International Universities Press, Inc., 224.

[48] Ibid. 225; J.E. Exner (2003). *The Rorschach. A Comprehensive System*, 4th ed. Hoboken, NJ: John Wiley & Sons, 20.

[49] H.D. Murray (1971). *Thematic Apperception Test: Manual*, USA, 1.

[50] B.M. Kiely (1987), 89.

[51] J.E. Exner (2004), 9. (Italics in the text)

[52] B.M. Dolphin (1991), 94.

[53] G.D.Coleman & R.L. Freed (2000), 18.

[54] L.K. Frank (1939). Projective Methods for the Study of Personality, *Journal of Personality Assessment*, 36, 403-408.

[55] *ACV,II*, 85-88.

[56] C. O'Dwyer (2000), Tables, 3.7, 3.8, 3.9.

[57] Cf. *ACV,II*, 124-127, Appendix B-4.1 and B-4.2, 423-424; *ELV*, 24-27, Appendix B-1 and B-2, 325-350.

[58] A. Macintyre (1984). *After Virtue*, 2nd ed. Notre Dame, Indiana: University of Notre Dame Press, 206, 221.

[59] C. O'Dwyer (2000), 69-75.

[60] The story of each person originates and develops from the community or the social context in which one grows and lives. A proper understanding of any story demands the knowledge and understanding of the social context in which the storyteller lives. Cf. A. Macintyre (1984), 206-221. If narratives always take place within a social context, then it implies that a projective technique in narrative form, like the

"story of the imagined future", is appropriate to the situation of being both an Igbo and a Christian.

[61] C. O'Dwyer (2000), 103.

[62] For the distinguishing characteristics, see Ibid.

[63] B.M. Dolphin (1991), 212-217.

[64] C. O'Dwyer (2000), 130-131.

[65] J.B. Chassan (1967). *Research Design in Clinical Psychology and Psychiatry.* New York, 34-38.

[66] D.W. Fiske (1971). *Measuring the Concepts of Personality.* Chicago, 24; See also *ACV,*II, 83.

[67] *ACV,*II, 85.

[68] All of the discarded protocols are either about the past histories of the writer or they are about the formation in the seminary, but not about the writer's future.

[69] B.M. Dolphin (1991), 280-284.

[70] M.P. Garvin (1999). *Stories of Commitment: Women's Interpretation of the Consecrated Life ad the Values of the Gospel.* Published Extract of Doctoral Dissertation in Psychology, Pontifical Gregorian University, Rome, 56-57.

[71] C. O'Dwyer (2000), 162-166.

[72] Ibid., 147.

[73] Ibid., 148-149.

[74] Ibid., 149.

[75] Ibid., 150-151.

[76] Ibid., 152.

[77] Ibid., 155.

[78] Ibid., 158.

[79] Ibid., 157.

[80] Power ($t = 2.0.64$, $P = 0.041$) and Security ($t = 2.023$, $P = 0.045$).

[81] Ibid., 114-115.

[82] Power ($t = 2.313$, $P = 0.022$), Security ($t = 4.639$, $P = 0.00002$); and Harm Avoidance ($t = 2.074$, $P = 0.039$).

[83] Chastity ($t = 2.583$, $P = 0.011$), Responsibility ($t = 2.013$, $P = 0.046$).

[84] Power ($X^2 = 5.009$, $P < 0.05$), Security ($X^2 = 23.869$, $P < 0.0001$), and Harm Avoidance ($X^2 = 8.349$, $P < 0.01$)

[85] Total no. of variables present ($t = 2.413$, $P = 0.017$), and no. of experience-variables present ($t = 3.110$, $P = 0.002$).

[86] for the Igbo religious seminarians, $t = 2.522$, $P = 0.013$; for the Igbo diocesan seminarians, $t = 2.832$, $P = 0.005$; and for the entire Igbo group, $t = 3.432$, $P = 0.001$.

87 FGI is basically an index that distinguishes the deviant immature from the non-deviant immature. Persons who are deviant immature are those who show signs of psychopathology. Cf. Ibid., 139, 156-157.

88 for the Igbo religious seminarians, $X^2 = 11.20$ and $P< 0.001$; for the Igbo diocesan seminarians, $X^2 = 9.55$ and $P< 0.01$, and for the entire Igbo group, $\chi^2 = 11.03$ and $P< 0.001$.

89 Ibid., 175.

90 Ibid., 213.

91 Synod of Bishops 1990, *Instrumentum Laboris*, 28.

92 Bishop D.S. Tsinda-Hata of Kenge, Zaire observed that the formation of priests should be considered at three levels of challenges: the formation of the formators, the development and formation of seminarians, and the inculturation and the formation in the seminary. Concerning the challenge of inculturating formation of priests he notes: "The concern is how to form future priests who are not only good at celebrating the Eucharist and teaching the catechism with the accent, colours and rhythm of Zaire; it is to form priests who can evangelize profoundly the whole person, the people of Zaire and our culture ...". Cited in G. Caprile (1991). *Il Sinodo dei vescovi: ottava assemblea generale ordinaria*: Rome, 120. S. Wewitavidanelage, Bishop of Galle, Sri Lanka notes that the lay people often find a way of the gospel in their life especially expressed in their religiosity. But for the priest, "whose formation affects his manner of living, his vision of the world, his theology, his method of reflection and his manner of expression, he seems to be culturally alienated. But he can avoid this if he is given personal, cultural and spiritual formation through the dialectical process of continuous dialogue between the gospel and the culture in which he lives and works". Cited in Ibid., 145. The Fathers of African Synod also affirm that "today more than ever there is need to form our future priests to the true cultural values of their country, to a sense of honesty, responsibility, and integrity". *Proposition*, 18. Cited in African Faith and Justice Network (1996). *The African Synod, Documents, Reflections, Perspectives*. Maryknoll, New York: Orbis Books, 93.

93 T. Costello (2002). *Forming a Priestly Identity*. Roma: Editrice Pontificia Università Gregoriana, 113-114.

Chapter IV

1 C.J. Uzor, (1999), 187.

2 Cf. F. A. Oborji (1998). *Trends in African Theology Since Vatican II. A Missiological Orientation*. Romae, 17; M.M. Green (1964). *Igbo Village Affairs*. London, 121-129; C.J. Uzor, (1999), 173-176; V.C. Uchendu (1965). *The Igbo of Southeast Nigeria*. USA: Harcourt Brace Jovanovich College

Publishers 44; E.G. Ekwuru (1999). *The Pangs of an African Culture in Travail.* Owerri, 20-21; E. Amadi (1982). *Ethics in Nigerian Culture.* Ibadan, 97.

[3] C.J. Uzor, (2003), 228-230.

[4] T.U. Nwala (1985). *Igbo Philosophy.* Lagos, 233. See also M.C. Onyejekwe (2000), 200.

[5] C.J. Uzor, (2003), 235.

[6] E. Isichei (1976). *A History of the Igbo People.* London, 121.

[7] M.C. Onyejekwe (2000), 58. Onyejekwe cites this aphorism in the context of the Igbo people's attitude to poverty, concluding that "poverty is a vice and not a virtue, not a blessing but a curse, a misfortune". Ibid., 58. But he seems to be unaware that this attitude to poverty is rooted in the general psychological principles of the Igbo people which leans to autonomy and independence. The *I na-enye m nri*? is a statement made in reference to an *other*, implying that the Igbo man must affirm his autonomy before an-*other*, and he needs that other to do so.

[8] C.J. Uzor,(2003), 235.

[9] Ibid., 249 - 250.

[10] S. Leith-Ross (1939). *African Women: A Study of the Ibo of Nigeria.* New York, 356-357.

[11] C. Achebe (1988). The Igbo World and Its Art. In his *Hopes and Impediments. Selected Essays.* New York, Anchor Books, 63.

[12] Ibid., 64.

[13] Ibid.

[14] Ibid.

[15] L.N. Mbefo (1996). *Coping with Nigerian's Two-fold Heritage.* Onitsha, 95.

[16] P.L. Berger (1990), 26.

[17] The contact with the Europeans "brought about an unbridled and excessive lust for Western form of material goods and welfare. Wealth became might. Impatience in the acquisition of material wealth advanced to the status of a common experience among the people. Many people are all out to make quick money. In this bid they are ready to walk over corpses to achieve their goal". C.J. Uzor, (2003), 334. Cf. also N.I. Ndiokwere (1998). *Search for Greener Pastures. Igbo and African Experience,* USA, 27.

[18] C.J. Uzor, (2003), 333.

[19] Ibid., 332.

[20] E.G. Ekwuru (1999), 123.

[21] G. Bateson (1972, 2000), Morale and National Character. In his *Steps to an Ecology of Mind,* 100.

[22] This kind of attitude is very close to superstition because what impresses both the listener and the speaker is mystification and

incomprehension and not really the brilliance of the content or the ability of the speaker to communicate it. Cf. P.Watzlawick (1976). *How Real is Real?* New York: Vintage Books, 48-51.

[23] E.G. Ekwuru (1999), 137-143.

[24] See O. Wambu (2003). The Igbo Agenda and the 2003 Elections, *World Igbo Times*, 3/1, 16.

[25] J.N. Uwalaka (2003). *The Struggle for an Inclusive Nigeria. Igbos: To Be or not To Be?* Enugu: Snaap Press, 75

[26] C.C. Agu (1989). *Secularisation in Igboland. Socio-religious Change and its Challenges to the Church among the Igbo.* Frankfurt, 217.

[27] C.J. Uzor, (2003), 236.

[28] See J. Uwalaka (2003), especially Section I, which, according to the plan of the book, explains the unhealthy attitudes of Igbos in Section II.

[29] See H.R. Manturana & F.J. Varela (1998). *The Tree of Knowledge: the Biological Roots of Human Understanding*, Rev. ed. Boston & London: Shambhala; D. Myers (1999).

[30] C. Ikeazor (2003). Crisis of the Igbo Nation, *Wold Igbo Times*, 2/2, 15.

[31] N.I. Ndiokwere (1998), 27.

[32] E.G. Ekwuru (1999), 129-130. This is also the reason why President Obasanjo succeeded in using Igbos against themselves in the National Assembly of 1999-2003 such that in two years the nation had three senate presidents, and all of them were Igbos. See the commentary of J. Uwalaka (2003), 72-73

[33] J. Uwalaka (2003), 71-72.

[34] I.R.A. Ozigbo (1985), 40-41.

[35] G.E.M. Adibe (1992). *The Crisis of Faith and Morality of the Igbo Christians of Nigeria.* Onitsha, 114.

[36] V.C. Uchendu (1965), 20.

[37] Ibid.

[38] It was not possible to examine the international group in the same way, their original stories no longer being available.

[39] G. Bateson (1972, 2000), 65.

[40] Ibid., 90.

[41] B.J.F. Lonergan (1957, 1992). *Insight: A Study of Human Understanding.* Toronto: University of Toronto Press, 141-144.

[42] Ibid., 235.

[43] Ibid., 144.

[44] For a complete description of this need, Cf. *ACV,I*, 465.

[45] For the religious seminarians: -0.333±0.914, and for the diocesan seminarians: -0.160±0.717

[46] Mbiti observes: "The deep sense of kinship, with all it implies, has been one of the strongest forces in traditional African life. Kinship is

reckoned through blood and betrothal (engagement and marriage). It is kinship which controls social relationships between people in a given community …. Indeed, this sense of kinship binds together the entire life of the 'tribe', and is even extended to cover animals, plants, and non-living objects through the 'totemic' system". J.S. Mbiti (1969, 1999). *African Religions and Philosophy*. UK-Nairobi, 104.

47 C.J. Uzor, (2003), 234.

48 J.B.C. Okorie (1995), table 8, 94.

49 Ibid., 115.

50 Ibid. Table 7, 93.

51 Ibid. Table 7, 93 and 113

52 M.R. Leary, - *al*. (1995). Self-Esteem as an Interpersonal Monitor: The Sociometer Hypothesis, *Journal of Personality and Social Psychology*, 65/3, 519.

53 Ibid., 519.

54 Ibid., 520.

55 Ibid.

56 W.D. Mcintosh, L.L. Martin & J.B. Jones III (2001). Goal Orientations and the Search for Confirmatory Affect, *The Journal of Psychology*, 135/1, 5-6.

57 Ibid., 7.

58 Ibid., 8.

59 Ibid., 9.

60 J.S. Mbiti (1969, 1999), 3.

61 J.Schimel, J. Arendt, T. Pyszczynski & J. Greenberg (2001). Being Accepted for Who We Are: Evidence that Social Validation of the Intrinsic Self Reduces General Defensiveness, *Journal of Personality and Social Psychology*, 80/1, 36-37.

62 There are strong positive correlations on SI-II in the two schools on eight out of the ten scales of his survey. More negative correlation was found on scale (2) *Family Ties* and scale (5) *Traditional belief.* Cf. C.J. Uzor, (2003), 524-526.

63 Ibid. 412.

64 Some of the items are (i) "Paying no attention to omens, e.g., a vulture perching on one's housetop, or the song of a screech owl believed to announce an impending death incidence, or the cry of an owl in the night" (ii) "Believing that nothing evil happens without either a supernatural being or somebody being behind it" (iii) "Being on your guard when you see a charm" (iv) "Carrying a good luck charm" (v) "Finding nothing wrong in going to a fortune teller or a *dibia* for advice on something important". Cf. Ibid. Appendix A2, (2003), 511-518.

[65] For BMS seminarians the relationship PB-SI results in, r = 0.018, P < 0.800; for those from SWS, r = 0.113, P< 0.1; on SI-II, for BMS seminarians, r = 0.016, P< 0.79, and for those from SWS, r = 0.050, P< 0.36. Cf. Ibid. Appendix A3, (2003), 526.

[66] Y. Hong – al., "Multicultural Minds", 709.

[67] Cited in C. McGarry (1995). The Implications of the Synod Discussions for the Church in Africa, *AFER*, 37, 15-16.

[68] In a field research, Adibe asked Igbo Christians what difficulties they encountered in keeping the first commandment. He summarised their responses in the following statement: "At crisis moments, when he expects a quick answer to his prayers and the solution is not immediate, relatives and friends drag one into traditional religious practices". G.E.M. Adibe (1992), 100.

[69] Magesa contends that the values of African Traditional Religon persist in the mind of the African Christians alongside Christian teachings so that one could say that "Christianity in Africa today may be said to have two different forms of thought-system and faith expressions – one official and one popular. Official Christianity is the faith expression that is promulgated in the seminaries and other centers of training, as well as in sermons and homilies by various pastoral agents. The vast majority of the Christian faithful, however, appropriate the teaching of the official Church according to their own circumstances and needs using the dominant symbol sytem of African Religon". L. Magesa. 20. He goes on to note that though professors and ministers of government and highly placed people in society publicly profess their Christianity with zeal, they usually visit diviners and mediums in secret when they are in crisis. This expression of Christian faith through the symbols of African Religion is what he calls popular Christianity; and it is widespread in Africa.

[70] P.L. Berger (1976, 1999, 32.

[71] G.E. Vaillant (1993). *The Wisdom of the Ego*. London: Harvard University Press, 240.

[72] This dialectic between the Christian values and cultures is present everywhere. The difference lies in the contents through which the dialectic is expressed.

[73] P.E. Aligwekwe (1991). *The Continuity of Traditional Values in African Society: The Igbo of Nigeria*. Owerri, 54-64.

[74] This is the condition of Mgbafọ in Tony Ubesie's novel *Ụkpana Okpoko Buuru*. Mgbafọ has everything; her husband is rich. All her six children died. She did all she could, and spent all the money they had to see if she could save any of those children, but they died. Ubesie writes that a rich man without children is a waste because if he dies, others will take over

his riches. When she had lost all hope, she conceived the seventh child who was a girl. She named her *Kasiemobi* [Console my heart].
75 M.C. Onyejekwe (2000), 199.

76 P. E. Aligwekwe (1991), traces the Igbo traditional lineage according to five different 'fathers' namely, I) the *umunna* of the father – the paternal patrilineage; ii) the *umunna* of the mother – the maternal patrilineage; iii) the *umunna* of the mother of the father – the patrilineage of the father's mother; iv) the *umunna* of the mother of the mother – the patrilineage of the mother's mother; v) the *umunna* of the spouse – the patrilineage of the spouse. Cf. see p. 54.

77 N.I. Ndiokwere (1998), 47.
78 Cf. the dramatic story of Dr. X in Ibid., 47-48.
79 Ibid., 63.
80 P.E. Aligwekwe (1991), 64.
81 M.C. Onyejekwe (2000), 199.
82 J.S. Mbiti (1969, 1999), 108.
83 Ibid., 108-109.
84 E. Ilogu (1974). *Christianity and Igbo Culture*. New York, London, Enugu, 25.
85 "The maintenance of social and cosmological balance in the world becomes, therefore, a dominant and pervasive theme in African-Igbo life. They achieve this balance, for instance, through divination, sacrifice, appeal to the countervailing powers of their ancestors (who are their invisible father-figures) against the powers of the malignant, and nonancestral spirits, and, socially, through constant realignment in their social groupings". V.C. Uchendu (1965), 13.
86 See P.E. Aligwekwe (1991), Chapter 9 on the five levels of social dignity in Igbo traditional society and their characteristics.
87 L.N.Mbefo (1996), 84.
88 I.R.A. Ozigbo (1985), 60.
89 ST. Augustine, *The City of God*, Bk. V, 13.
90 Ibid. Bk. V, 14.
91 P.E. Aligwekwe (1991), 130.
92 M.A. Onwuejegwu, cited in Ibid., 129.
93 L.N. Mbefo (1996), 94-95.
94 Ibid., 95.
95 Ibid.
96 V.C. Uchendu (1965), 16.
97 C.J. Uzor, (2003), 216.

98 In the terminology of the system theorists, incongruous lifestyles of the Igbo priests, like exaggerated opulence and highhandedness, would constitute a "runway" in the Igbo social system. And like all runway systems, it contains the seeds of its self-correction in the form of criminal attacks on rectories, verbal attacks on and the loss of respect for the priest. The presence of a runway and the dynamics of self-corrective mechanism indicate that the structural network of a system is becoming dysfunctional. But most importantly, it indicates what that network was. It was that Igbo culture had eventually opened itself to the Catholic celibate priesthood and had adjusted its structures to it by providing it with spiritual and social relevance. The abuse or abandonment of that component of the cultural and social system in forms of incongruous lifestyles becomes a perturbation of the system as a whole resulting in disrespect and/or attack on priests, which are efforts to maintain the structural synthesis of the system. For more details on this, see G. Bateson (2002). *Mind and Nature*. Cresskill, NJ, Hampton Press, Inc., 98; H.R. Maturana & F.J. Varela (1998), 95-99. Igbo people rejected the Catholic celibate priesthood initially, just like any other society would object to the customs of a foreign culture at the beginning. However, with the passage of time through the structural coupling between Igbo society and the Christian message, it came to accept the Catholic celibate priesthood because sexual continence already had a place in Igbo system of values. Even if there was nothing like permanent celibacy among the Igbos before the coming of Christianity as some authors argue (See T. U. Nwala (1985), 233; C.J. Uzor (1999) 186), the presence of intermittent sexual abstinence was always connected with the service of divinity. Cf. J.S. Mbiti (1969, 1999), 189. The acceptance of Catholic celibate priesthood by the Igbo culture should be seen to have its seed in this intermittent abstinence from sexual intercourse during spiritual activities. When this adjustment had been made, the priests, like every other group in Igbo society, was given a place following the dynamics of patterned allocation of places and power in any social system. Cf. T.F. O'Dea (1966). *The Sociology of Religion*. New Jersey, 72-73.

99 W.H. Shannon (1997). Priestly Spirituality: 'Speaking Out *For the Inside*". In D.B. Cozzens (Ed.), *The Spirituality of the Diocesan Priest*. Collegeville, Minnesota: The Liturgical Press, 91.

100 B.M. Kiely (1987), 100-101.

101 Ibid., 101.

102 This is the problem of the priest Carl in D.R. Hoge (2002), 71-77.

103 B.M. Kiely (1997). Maturità del ragionamento Morale e Maturità nella vocazione cristiana. In L.M. Rulla (Ed.), *Antropologia della Vocazione Cristiana III: Aspetti Interpersonali*, Bologna, 22.

[104] B.J.F. Lonergan (1973), 104.

[105] Ibid., 49-50.

[106] Ibid., 50.

[107] *ACV*,I, 43.

[108] C. O'Dwyer (2000), 213.

[109] *ACV*,I, 158.

[110] B.J.F. Lonergan (1957, 1992), 646.

[111] G. Aschenbrenner (1998). Presumption for Perseverance and Permanence – A Rudder for Direction and Balance in Priestly Formation, *Seminary Journal*, 4/1, 20.

[112] Ibid, 22.

[113] *ACV*,I, P.48.

[114] This idea comes from P.L. Berger's discussion of alienated consciousness in the society as a consequence of socialization. Cf. P.L. Berger (1967), especially Ch. 4.

[115] *ACV*,I, 316.

[116] *ACV*, II, 160.

[117] E.C. Kennedy & V.J. Heckler (1972). *The Catholic Priests in the United States. Psychological Investigations.* Washington, D.C., 91. These persons are defensively consistent in their lives: their subconscious inconsistency is masked by an apparent consistency. Cf. *ACV*,I, 221-225.

[118] *ACV*,II, 160.

[119] H.R. Maturana & F.J. Varela (1998), 96.

[120] Ibid.

Chapter V

[1] R. Rohr (2002). Beyond Crime and Punishment, *Sojourners*, July-August, 29. See also D.R. Hoge (2002), 83-68.

[2] E.C. Kennedy & V.J. Heckler (1972), 89.

[3] B.M. Kiely (1987), 92.

[4] Ibid., 93.

[5] I Corinthians, 13.3. This quotation is from *Christian Community Bible*, Catholic Pastoral Edition.

[6] B.J.F. Lonergan (1973), 105-109.

[7] *The Catechism of the Catholic Church*, Libreria Editrice Vaticana, 1994, n. 1996. Henceforth, *CCC*.

[8] *PO*, 14.

[9] *PO*, 14.

[10] *OT*, 8.

[11] Synod of Bishops (1990), *Lineamenta*, 25; *Instrumentum Laboris*, 30.

[12] Ibid. *Lineamenta*, 26.

[13] Ibid. *Instrumentum Laboris*, 22. Italics are in the text.

[14] Ibid. *Instrumentum Laboris*, 23. Italics are mine.

[15] Ibid. *Instrumentum Laboris*, 30. Italics are in the text.

[16] Cf. G. Caprile (1991), 264.

[17] Ibid., 266.

[18] Ibid., 232.

[19] *PDV*, 19 & 20.

[20] *PDV*, 25. In the letter he addressed to priests on Holy Thursday 1990, Pope John Paul II reminded the priests of the "*mystery of that friendship* to which Christ the Lord called us in the Upper Room", and then invited them to rediscover and deepen it. John Paul II, Letter to the Priests of the Church Holy Thursday 1990, 2. In his address to the priests and seminarians of Bigard Memorial Seminary Enugu, the Pope told them that the first and most important thing "in the seminary must be friendship with Christ centred on the Eucharist and nurtured especially by prayer and meditation on the word of God". John Paul II (1982), 6.

[21] *PDV*, 23.

[22] *PDV*, 25.

[23] *PDV*, 34.

[24] Second Vatican Council (1965). Decree on the Up-to-Date Renewal of Religious Life, *Perfectae Caritatis*, 28 October, 12.

[25] J. Bernardin (1990). Celibacy and Spirituality, *Origins* 20/19, 301.

[26] Congregation for the Clergy (2002). *The Priest, Pastor and Leader of the Parish Community*, 4 August, n. 29.

[27] G. Greshake (1982). *Priestersein*. Eng. Tr. *The Meaning of Christian Priesthood*, by P. MacSeumais, Freiburg, Basle, Vienna, 157.

[28] R. Jackson (1983). Burnout Among Catholic Priests, *Dissertations Abstract International*, 44, 1595B, University Microfilms No. 8319168, 223-224.

[29] D.R. Hoge (2002), 94.

[30] S.J. Rossetti (1999). Understanding Diocesan Priesthood, *Human Human Development*, 20/1, 39. See also W.P. Sheridan (1999). Functionalism Undermining Priesthood, *Human Development*, 29/3, 12-16.

[31] This situation of the diocesan priests is clearly brought out in this advice addressed to them: "Diocesan priests on retreat seem constantly to be making resolutions to re-do their schedule, and find time for patterns of spiritual exercises that they have been looking for since they left the seminary. We would do better to take the pattern that is there … and find ways to build into it an attentiveness to God that runs from morning till night". K.E. Untener (1997), 25-26.

[32] J.C. Murray (1967). The Danger of the Vows, *Woodstock Letters* 96, 426.

[33] B. Schwartz (2001). Self-Determination: The Tyranny of Freedom, *American Psychologist*, 55/1, 82.

[34] Cf. T. Lane (1994). The Religious and Diocesan Priest: A Mutual Enrichment. In B. McGregor & T. Norris (Eds.), *The Formational Journey of the Priest. Exploring Pastores Dabo Vobis.* Dublin, 49.

[35] Congregation for the Clergy, *The Priest, Pastor and Leader*, 12.

[36] For the diocesan seminarians in this research, the variable Security is negative: -0.027 ± 0.958.

[37] D. B. Cozzens (1997). Tenders of the Word. In D.B. Cozzens (Ed.), *The Spirituality of the Diocesan Priest.* Collegeville, Minnesota: The Liturgical Press, 55.

[38] D.R. Hoge, Tables 2.7, 2.8.

[39] It is an aspect of the Igbo culture where frame-switching from Christian to cultural values is so strong.

[40] John Paul II, Letter to all the Priests of the Church, Holy Thursday 1995, 4.

[41] Synod of Bishops, Special Assembly for Africa, *Message of the Synod*, 26.

[42] G. Greshake (1982), 113.

[43] Mk. 1.35; Lk. 4.42.

[44] G. Greshake (1982), 158.

[45] John 21.15-19. Nouwen explains these triple questions of Jesus in the context of the priestly life and ministry in the contemporary world and observes that these questions invite the priest to cultivate the discipline of "dwelling in the presence of the One who keeps asking us, 'Do you love me? Do you love me? Do you love me?' It is the discipline of contemplative prayer. Through contemplative prayer we can keep ourselves from being pulled from one urgent issue to another and from becoming strangers to our own and God's heart". H. Nouwen (1989). *In the Name of Jesus. Reflections on Christian Leadership.* London: Darton & Longman & Todd, 28.

[46] A.K. Obiefuna (1993), 2.

Chapter VI

[1] Arbuckle mentions eight models, namely, the Institutional Model, the Contemplative Model, the Ecclesial Model, the Apprenticeship Model, the Blossom Model, the Personalist Model, the Social Justice Model, and the Pilgrimage Model. Cf. G.A. Arbuckle (1996). *From Chaos to Mission. Refounding Religious Life Formation.* London: Geoffery Chapman, 102-110.

[2] Cf. C. McGarry (1999), 309.

[3] J. N'Guessam Sess (1995). Formation of Priests and Religious for a Church that is Family. In C. McGarry (Ed.), *What Happened at the African Synod*, Nairobi: Pauline Publications Africa, 97.

4 Cf. B. Ojil, "Priestly Formation for Today's Realities", 6.

5 J. N'Guessam Sess, 100.

6 B. Ojil, 6

7 C.J. Uzor (1999), Appendix D, C15, 539.

8 T. Costello (2002), 271.

9 Ibid., 270-271.

10 A. Shorter (200). *Religious Obedience in Africa*. Nairobi: Pauline Publications, 13-14.

11 A.N. Aniagolu (1993). Seminary Formation Today: Problems and Prospects. In the *Symposium on Priestly Formation in the Spirit of Pastores Dabo Vobis of John Paul II*, 10. Emphasis is mine.

12 G. A. Arbuckle, *From Chaos to Mission*, 103.

13 Spiritual Year seminaries are a kind of novitiate for the diocesan seminarians before they go into the Major Seminary for their philosophical and theological studies. It is a program that has been adopted in almost all the dioceses in Nigeria. Its establishment seems to have followed the injunction of John Paul II in *Pastores Dabo Vobis*, that there be a "propaedeutic period" during which sufficient human, intellectual and spiritual formation should be given to the candidates before they go to the major seminary. See John Paul II, *PDV*, 62, citing proposition 19 of the Synod.

14 One often hears some of the seminarians training under this model taunting seminarians in regional major seminaries where the institutional model obtains, as people put in a cage, while they themselves have been liberated and left free. Some verbalised these remarks to the present author.

15 Cf. E.L. Deci & R.M. Ryan (1991). A Motivational Approach to Self: Integration in Personality. In R.A. Dienstbier (Ed.), *Perspectives on Motivation: Nebraska Symposium on Motivation, 1990*, Lincoln, London, 238.

16 E. McDonough (1991). Beyond the Liberal Model: Quo Vadis?, *Review for Religious* 50, 172.

17 P. Spillane (1985). Facing the Future: Formation in Apostolic Spirituality, *Review for Religious* 44, 500.

18 *DPV*, 132.

19 T. Costello (2002), 270.

20 G. Weigel (2002). *The Courage to be Catholic. Crisis, Reform, and the Future of the Church*. New York: Basic Books, especially Chapters 3 & 6.

21 Ibid., 153-154.

22 C. McGarry (1999), 309

23 Ibid., 311.

24 F. Imoda (1998), 116.

[25] B.J.F. Lonergan (1957, 1992), 643.

[26] Ibid., 645-646. Antecedent willingness is that state in which a person does not have to be persuaded to act according to what is good.

[27] Ibid., 646-647.

[28] Ibid., 647.

[29] M. Drennan (1994). Special Issues in Formation. In B. Mcgregor & T. Norris (Eds.), *The Formational Journey of the Priest. Exploring Pastores Dabo Vobis*, Dublin, 89.

Chapter VII

[1] The other four dilemmas not immediately concerned with the theme of our discussion include: the symbolic dilemma: objectification versus alienation; the dilemma of administrative order: elaboration and alienation; the dilemma of delimitation: concrete definition versus substitution of the letter for the spirit; and, the dilemma of power: conversion versus coercion. Cf. T.F. O'Dea (1966), 90-97.

[2] Ibid., 91.

[3] Ibid.

[4] Ibid.

[5] Ibid., 91-92.

[6] D. Katz & R.L. Kahn (1978). *The Social Psychology of Organisations*. New York, Wiley 192.

[7] N.A. Lieberman, I.D. Yalom & M.B. Miles (1973). *Encounter Groups*. New York, 331.

[8] *ACV*,II, 73.

[9] Ibid., 157.

[10] Ibid., 158.

[11] *ACV*,I, 180.

[12] "The more an individual suffers from central inconsistencies between the ideal self and the actual self (between values and needs), the more his need will urge him to seek what is subjectively important, rather than self-transcendent values as important in themselves". *ACV*, II, 62.

[13] T.F. O'Dea (1966), 92.

[14] B.J.F. Lonergan (1971). *Method in Theology*. Toronto: University of Toronto Press, 80. Cf. also T.A. Dunne (1985). *Lonergan and Spirituality. Towards a Spiritual Integration*. Chicago: Loyola University Press, 92-100.

[15] Weiser makes a realistic remark: "Although I would like to think that people could have purely mature and uncontaminated reasons for choosing a religious career, I have never seen that happen any more than I have seen a new marriage grounded solely in reality". C. W. Weiser (1994). *Healers. Harmed and Harmful*. Minneapolis: Fortress Press, 8.

[16] M. Drennan (1994), 83.

17 B.M. Kiely (1997). Dialettica di Base: Desiderio, Limite, e Dono di Sé. In Unpublished *Atti: 3° Convegno di Studio, L'Accompagamento*, 24-27 April, 36.

18 Ibid; *ACV*,I, Appendix B, 465-467 for the list of such needs and attitudes.

19 B.M. Kiely (1987), 43.

20 *Relatio ante disceptationem*, 2, cited by John Paul II (1995), *EA*, 40.

21 II Corinthians 12.9

22 L. Magesa, *African Religion*, 54; C.J. Uzor (1999), 223, Figure 5.

23 Ibid., 54.

24 C. Nyamiti (1973). *The Scope of African Theology*. Kampala, 22.

25 J.S. Mbiti (1969, 1999), 2.

26 C. Nyamiti (1973), 22.

27 System thinking in the west began at the beginning of the twentieth century with the breakdown of the mechanistic theories starting from within Newtonian physics which was considered the most successful science. For this history, see E. Laszlo (1996), 2-13.

28 Ibid., 9.

29 Ibid., 29.

30 N. Fogliacco (2001). The Family: An African Metaphor for Trinity and Church. In C. McGarrry (Ed.), *Inculturating the Church in Africa*, Nairobi: Pauline Publications Africa, 130.

31 *EA*, 42.

32 J.S. Mbiti (1969, 1999), 109.

33 Ibid., 189.

34 Ibid., 188.

35 M.G. Nwagwu (1993). Religious Life in Nigeria Today, *AFER 35/4*, 265.

36 H.R. Manturana & F.J. Varela (1998), 180-201.

37 *ICP*, 36.

38 L. von Bartalanffy (1969). *General System Theory*. Rev. ed. New York: George Braziller, 70.

39 O. Kernberg (1976, 1984). *Object-Relations Theory and Clinical Psychoanalysis*. NJ, London, Jason Aronson Inc.,, 64-67; L. von Bartalanffy (1969), 208.

40 *EA*, 63.

41 F.A. Oborji (1998), 204

42 Synod of Bishop, Special Assembly for Africa, *Nuntius*, 25, 26.

43 E. Laszlo (1996), 49.

44 C. McGarry (1999), 308. See also, C. McGarry (2002). The Impact of Globalization on African Culture and Society. In P. Ryan (Ed.), *New Strategies for a New Evangelisation in Africa*. Nairobi: Pauline Publications Africa, 13-18; R. Mion (1994). I 'nuovi giovani', la fede e la vocazione. Un

approccio socio-pedagogico. In E. Dal Covolo & A.M. Triacca (Eds.), *Sacerdoti per la nuova evangelizzazione. Studi sull'Esortazione apostolica Pastores dabo vobis di Giovanni Paolo II*, Roma, 29-38.

[45] From their research on how far traditional values persist in the midst of globalisation, Inglehart and Baker found out that though globalisation and its changes may be obvious, its effects may never be overestimated. "While it is obvious that young people around the world are wearing jeans and listening to U.S. pop music, the persistence of underlying value differences is less apparent". R. Inglehart & W.E. Baker (2000). Modernization, Cultural Change, and the Persistence of Traditional Values, *American Sociological Review* 65, 23. Making reference to the earlier research carried out by Watson on McDonald's Restaurants in East Asia they note that, "the seemingly identical McDonald's restaurants that have spread throughout the world actually have different social meanings and fulfil different social functions in different cultural zones. Although the physical settings are similar, eating in McDonald's restaurant in Japan is a different social experience from eating in one in the United States or in Europe or China". Ibid., 22.

[46] *PDV*, 47.

[47] "The educator should be sufficiently prepared as not to be deceived or to deceive regarding a presumed consistency and maturity of the student. For this, 'common sense' is not enough. An attentive and refined examination from a good knowledge of the human sciences is necessary in order to go beyond appearances and the superficial level of motivations and behaviour, and to help the seminarian to know himself in depth, to accept himself with serenity, and to correct himself and to mature, starting from real not illusory roots, and from the 'heart' of his person". Congregation for Catholic Education (1993). *Dirretive sulla Preparzione degli Educatori nei Seminari*. Roma: Editrice Libreria Vaticana, 57.

[48] P.D. Cristantiello (2002). Celibate Miscallings. Psychological Factors and Vocational Choice, *Seminary Journal 8/2*, 32.

[49] *ACV*, II, 126.

[50] C. O'Dwyer (2000), 167-169. The suggestion of Costello is worth noting: that "a research design constructed in the present cultural-ecclesial context would probably formulate a less optimistic assumption regarding the presence of vocational values. T. Costello (2002), 239.

[51] *ACV*,I, 371.

[52] F. Imoda (1998), 131.

[53] M. Drennan (1994), 97.

[54] *ACV*,I, 381.

55 The reason for this is because the cultural demand to achieve can drive some Igbo people to manipulative activities in order to get what they want. Uzor describes the situation well: "[The Igbo's] conviction of being at the centre of his universe and of being the ultimate recipient of the benevolent activities of all Life-Forces often leads him to an unbridled desire for success and for material well-being. The fact that he is sometimes ready 'to walk over corpses' to satisfy this need and also within the quickest possible time indicates how strong, alive and influential the experiences of the oral stage of his infancy still are". C.J. Uzor (2003), 234. Uchendu notes that the Igbo strongly believes that the world should be manipulated to his advantage: "If you ask the Igbo why he believes that the world should be manipulated, he will reply 'The world is a marketplace and it is subject to bargain'. In his view, neither the world of man alone nor the world of spirits is a permanent home. The two worlds together constitute a home. Each world is peopled with 'interested' individuals and groups and much buying and selling go on in each. People go to the marketplace for different reasons, but the common motivation is the desire to make a profit". V.C. Uchendu (1965), 15. In the present Nigerian situation, the Igbo is looked at as someone who will not always have scruples when it comes to enriching himself. This remains one of the practical reasons why the Igbo, as a group, finds it difficult to maintain a common political front in the country.

56 G.D. Coleman & R.L.Freed (2000), 16.

57 P.D. Cristantiello (2002). The Self Seeker: Seminary Applicant Characteristics Requiring Caution, *Seminary Journal* 8/2, 26.

58 Cf. American Psychiatric Association, *Diagnostic and Statistical Manual of Mental Disorders DSM-IV*, Washington, D.C., Appendix I.

59 L. Cian (1994). La pastorale e il discernimento delle vocazioni. In E. Dal Covolo & A.M. Triacca (Eds.), *Sacerdoti per la nuova evangelizzazione* . Roma, especially section 4, 65-68.

60 M.E. D'Almeida (1994). *Initial Formation*. Published Extract of Doctoral Dissertation in Psychology, Pontifical Gregorian University, Rome, 69.

61 Ibid., 68.

62 See Ibid., 74-78 for detailed results.

63 Ibid., 79.

64 P.K. Lynn (1999). Jesus as Object: Christian Conversion as Interpreted through the Perspective of Fairbairn's Object Relations Theory, *Journal of Psychology and Theology* 27, 303.

65 *PDV*, 66.

66 Proposition 19, *PDV*, 66.

67 *OT*, 5.

68 *ACV*,I, 371.

---

[69] G.D. Coleman (2002), 21.

[70] *ACV*,I, 384-385.

[71] *PDV*, 66.

[72] Source: the seminary calenders:

[73] P. Schineller (1998, 2001). Reports on Priestly Formation from the Various Regions of the World: Africa, *Seminary Journal*, 4/3, 64; The Architecture of Seminaries, *Seminary Journal* 7/1, 45.

[74] John Paul II (1982), 6.

[75] Cited by G. Caprile (1991), 178-179.

[76] I.M. Onyeocha (2001), 226.

[77] P. Schineller (1998), 64-65.

[78] Ibid., 65.

[79] See S.A. Okafor (2006). *Facing the Future with Hope*. A speech given at the Priests' New Year Get-together, January 4, 5-7.

[80] *CIC*, Canon 281 § 1-2. This canon does not contradict the intention of canon 271 which makes room for a better distribution of priests in the universal Church.

[81] In his encyclical on the Eucharist, John Paul II exhorts, that the need for priests should not make us yield "to the temptation to seek solutions which lower the moral and formative standards demanded of candidates for the priesthood". John Paul II (2003). Encyclical, *Ecclesia De Eucharistia*, 17 April, n.32.

Bibliography

Alday, J.M. *La Vocazione Consacrata*, Roma 1994.

Allport, G.W. "Attitudes", in *Handbook of Social Psychology*, ed. C. Murchison, Worcester, Massachusetts 1935, 794-884.

Azevedo, M. *Os Religiosos, vocação e missão. Um enfoque exigente e actual*, English trans., *Vocation for Mission: The Challenges of Religious Life Today*, tr. J.W. Diercksmeier, New York, Mahwah 1988.

von Balthasar, *Kennt uns Jesus – Kennen wir ihm?* Eng. Trans. *Does Jesus Know Us? Do We Know Him?* Tr. G. Harrison, San Francesco, 1983.

von Bartalanffy,

Bernardin, J. "Celibacy and Spirituality", *Origins* 20/19 (1990) 300-302.

Buechelein, D.M. "The Sacramental Identity of the Ministerial Priesthood: '*In Persona Christi*'" in *Priests for a New Millennium*, USCC, Washington 2000, 37-52.

Cachia, N. *The Image of the Good Shepherd as a Source of the Spirituality of the Ministerial Priesthood*, S.T.D. Dissertation, Pontifical Gregorian University, Roma 1997.

Campbell, R.J. *Psychiatric Dictionary*, New York 1996[7].

Caprile, G. "Il celibato sacerdotale al Sinodo dei vescovi 1990", *Civiltà Cattolica*, 143/4 (1992) 488-501.

Carroll, J.W. "The Professional Model of Ministry – Is It Worth Saving?", *Theological Education* 21 (1985) 7-48.

Coletti, D. "Il Seminario Maggiore", *Seminarium* 32 (1992) 561-574.

Congregation for Evangelization of Peoples, *Pastoral Guide for the Diocesan Priests*, Vatican City 1989.

Congregation for the Clergy, *The Priest, Pastor and Leader of the Parish Community*, 4 August, 2002.

Congregation for Catholic Education, *A Guide to Formation in Priestly Celibacy*, Vatican City 1974.

Congregation for the Doctrine of the Faith, *Inter Insigniores*, Declaration on the Admission of Women to the Ministerial Priesthood, 15 October, 1976.

Costello, T.J. *Forming a Priestly Identity: Anthropology of Priestly Formation in the Documents of the VIII Synod of Bishops and the Apostolic*

Exhortation Pastores dabo vobis, Doctoral Dissertation in Psychology, Pontifical Gregorian University, Roma 2002.

_____ "The Use of Psychology as an Aid to Priestly Formation", *Seminarium* 32 (1992) 629-636.

Daly, C.B., Preface to *FJP*, Dublin 1994.

Danneels, G. "The Priest: Sign of the Eternal in a Culture of Consumerism", in *FJP*, Dublin 1994.

Dolphin, B., "Human Formation, the Basis of Priestly Formation", in *FJP* Dublin 1994.

Drennan, M. "The Word of God: The Radical Source of Christian Formation", in *FJP*, Dublin 1994.

D'Souza, A., *Leadership: A Trilogy on Leadership and Effective Management*, Nairobi Kenya 1994.

Dulles, A. *The Priestly Office: A Theological Reflection*, New York, Mahwah 1997.

Dunne, T.A. *Lonergan and Spirituality*, Chicago 1985.

Easwaran, K. *Original Goodness: On the Beatitudes*, California 1989, 1996.

Favale, A. "Identità Teologica del Presbitero", *Lateranum*, 56 (1990) 441-483.

Flynn, H. "Celibacy: A Way to Love", *Origins* 20/19 (1990) 302-304.

Fowler, *The Stages of Faith Development*,

Frankl, V. *Man's Search for Meaning*,

Gallagher, C. A. & Vandenberg, T.L., *The Celibacy Myth: Loving for Life*, New York 1989.

Gannon, T.M. "Priest/Minister: Profession or Non-Profession?", *Review of Religious Research* 12 (1971) 66-79.

Gerardi, R., "La 'caritas pastoralis' nella formazione e nella vita del pensiero", *Lateranum*, 56 (1990) 553-567.

Grabner-Haider, A. *Letters to a Young Priest from a Laaicised Priest*, California 1989.

Gula, R.M. *Reason Informed by Faith: Foundations of Catholic Morality*, New York, Mahwah 1989.

_____ *Ethics in Pastoral Ministry*, New York, Mahwah, 1996.

Healy, T. "La Sfida dell'Autotrascendenza: *Antropologia della Vocazione Cristiana, I* e Bernard Lonergan" in, *Antropologia Interdisciplinare e Formazione*, ed. F. Imoda, Bologna 1997, 97-158.

Himes, M.J. & Himes, K.R. "Rights, Economics, and the Trinity", *Commonweal*, (March 14, 1986), 137-141.

Hoban, B. "What are we at?" *The Furrow* 43(1992) 491-496.

John Paul II, Post-Synodal Apostolic Exhortation *Pastores Dabo Vobis* on the Formation of Priests in the Circumstances of the Present Day, 25th March 1992.

_____ Post-Synodal Apostolic Exhortation, *Ecclesia in Africa*, 14 September 1995.

_____ Address to the Plenary Meeting of the Congregation for the Clergy, 23 November 2001

_____ Encyclical Letter, *Ecclesia De Eucharistia*, on the Eucharist in its Relationship to the Church, 17 April 2003.

_____ Letter to All the Priests of the Church, Holy Thursday 1990.

_____ Letter to All the Priests of the Church, Holy Thursday 1995.

Katz, D. "The Functional Approach to the Study of Attitude Change", *Public Opinion Quarterly* 24 (1960) 163-204.

Kiely, B.M. *Psychology and Moral Theology*, Rome 1987.

_____ "Formation in Chastity: the Needs and the Requirements", in *Issues for a Catholic Bioethic*, ed. L. Gormally, London 1999, 134-147.

Kiesling, *Celibacy, Prayer and Friendship: A Making-Sense-Out-of-Life Approach*, New York 1978.

Kloppenberg, B. *The Ecclesiology of Vatican II*, Chicago 1974.

Kohlberg, L.

Laghi, P. "La formazione dei sacerdoti alla luce della *Pastores Dabo Vobis*", *Seminarium* 33 (1993) 124-134.

_____ "*Pastores Dabo Vobis*. Presentazione", *Seminarium* 32 (1992) 505-517.

_____ "The Identity and Ministry of the Priest", in *FJP*, Dublin 1994.

Lane, T. *A Priesthood in Tune*. Theological Reflections on the Ministry, Dublin 1993.

_____ "The Religious and Diocesan Priest: A Mutual Enrichment", in *The Formation Journey of the Priest: Exploring Pastores Dabo Vobis*, Dublin 1994.

Leavitt, R.F. "The Formation of Priests for a New Century: Theological and Spiritual Challenges", *Seminary Journal*, 8/2 (2002) 8-16.

Lonergan, B.J.F. *Method in Theology*, Toronto 1973².

Magni, W. "Giovani e coscienza vocazionale", *Palestra del Clero*, 5-6 (2001) 389-407.

McAreavey, J. "Celibacy. A Gift of Pastoral Charity", in *FJP*, Dublin 1994.

McQuillan, I. "Celibacy and the Faithful", *The Furrow* 43 (1992)

Murray, J.C. "The Danger of the Vows", *Woodstock Letters* 96 (1967) 421-427.

Navone, J. *Self-Giving and Sharing: The Trinity and Human Fulfillment*, Collegeville, Minnesota 1989.

Niederauer, G. "A Ministerial Spirituality: Reflections on Priesthood", in *Priesthood in the Modern World*, ed. K.S. Smith, Franklin, Wisconsin 1999.

Nolan, B.M. "What Difference Does Priestly Ordination Make?", in *New Beginnings in Ministry*, ed. J.M. Murphy, Dublin 1992.

NyGren, D. & Ukeritis, M. "Future of Religious Orders in the United States: Research Executive Summary", *Origins* 22 (September 1992) 258-272.

O'Dwyer, C. *Imagining One's Future*,

Okolo, C.B. "Priestly Formation and the Challenge of Christianity: Nigerian Situation Revisited", in *Symposium*, Enugu, March 1993. (Original copy)

Okorie, J.B.C. *Social Interest, Lifestyle, Stress and Job Satisfaction of Nigerian Catholic Priests*, Unpublished Doctoral Dissertation, University of San Francisco, 1995.

Orr, D., "The Giving of the Priesthood to the Faithful", in *Priesthood: The Hard Questions*, ed. G.P. Gleeson, Newton 1993, 61-77.

Osborne, K.B. *Priesthood: A History of the Ordained Ministry in the Roman Catholic Church*, New York, Mahwah 1988.

Paul VI, Encyclical, *Sacerdotalis Caelibatus*, 24 June 1967.

Power, D. *A Spiritual Theology of the Priesthood*, Edinburgh 1998.

Ranson, D. "Priest: Public, Personal and Private", *The Furrow*, 53/4 (April 2002), 219-227.

Ratzinger, J. *Zur Gemeinschaft gerufen: Kirche heute verstehen*, Eng. trans. *Called to Communion: Understanding the Church Today*, tr. A. Walker, San Francesco 1996[2].

Reber, A.S., *The Penguin Dictionary of Psychology*, New York 1985.

Rice, S. *Shattered Vows: Exodus from the Priesthood*, Belfast 1990.

Riddick, J. *Treasures in Earthen Vessels: The Vows*, New York 1984.

Rohr, R. & Feister, J.B. *Jesus' Plan for a New World*, Bandra, Mumbai, 1997.

Rulla, L.M. *Depth Psychology and Vocation*, Roma 1971.

_____ *Anthropology of the Christian Vocation: Interdisciplinary Bases*, I, Roma 1986.

Rulla, L.M. Ridick, J. & Imoda, F. *Anthropology of the Christian Vocation: Existential Confirmation*, II, Roma 1989.

_____ *Entering and Leaving Vocation: Intrapsychic Dynamics*, Roma 1988.

Rypar, F. "La *Pastores Dabo Vobis* alla luce del pensiero conciliare sul sacerdozio e la formazione sacerdotale", *Seminarium* 32 (1992) 530-549.

Scola, A. *Gesù Destino dell'Uomo. Camino di vita cristiana*, Torino 1999.

Second Vatican Council, *Perfectae Caritatis*, Decree on the Up-to-date Renewal of Religious Life, 28 October 1965.

_____ *Presbyterorum Ordinis*, Decree on the Ministry and Life of Priests, December 7, 1965.

_____ *Optatam Totius*, Decree on Priestly Formation, October 28, 1965.

_____ *Lumen Gentium*, Dogmatic Constitution on the Church, November 21, 1964.

Shorter, A. *Celibacy and African Culture*, Nairobi 1998.

_____ *Religious Poverty in Africa*, Nairobi 1999.

_____, *Religious Obedience in Africa*, Nairobi 2000.

Sperry, L. "Neurotic Personalities in Religious Settings", *Human Development* 12 (1991) 12-17.

Sweetser, T.P. "Parish Leadership versus Parish Management", *Human Development* 13 (1992) 13-15.

Synod of Bishops (1990), *De Sacerdotibus Formandis in Hodiernis Adiunctis. Instrumentum Laboris. Textus latinus-anglicus.* 15 July 1990.

_____, *De Sacerdotivus Formandis in Hodiernis Adiunctis. Lineamenta*, 1 April 1990.

Synod of Bishops (1971), "Documentum ultimus temporibus de sacerdotio ministeriali", English Translation: "The Ministerial Priesthood", in A. Flannery, *Vatican Council*, Vol. II, 672-694.

Synod of Bishops (1994), Special Assembly for Africa, *Lineamenta*, Vatican City 1990.

Ukwuoma, A.T. *Being a Priest in a Changing Society: Psycho-Social Analysis of the Nigerian Experience*, Kearney NE 2000.

Valles, C.G. *The Art of Choosing*, India 1986.

VanOosting, J. "Vocation Education", *America*, 187/1 (July 1-8, 2002), 8-11.

Vanzan, P. "*Pastores dabo vobis*. Chiavi di lettura ecclesiologico-trinitaria, cristologica, e pastorale", *Civiltà Cattolica*, 143/4 (1992) 233-343, 353-361.

Wiegel, G. *The Courage to be Catholic*,

Wilensky, H.L. "The Professionalization of Everyone", *American Journal of Sociology*, 70 (1964) 137-158.

Winters, B. *Priest as Leader: The Process of the Inculturation of a Spiritual-Theological Theme of Priesthood in a United States Context*, S.T.D. Dissertation, Pontifical Gregorian University, Roma 1995.

Wuerl, D.W. *The Catholic Priesthood Today*, Chicago 1976.

Wulf, F., -al. Commentary on the Decree [on the Ministry and Life of Priests], in *Commentary on the Documents of Vatican II*, ed. H. Vormgrimler, New York 1989[2].

www.ingramcontent.com/pod-product-compliance
Lightning Source LLC
Chambersburg PA
CBHW031150270326
41931CB00006B/219